LEVINAS'S EXISTENTIAL ANALYTIC

Northwestern University
Studies in Phenomenology
and
Existential Philosophy

LEVINAS'S EXISTENTIAL ANALYTIC

A Commentary on *Totality and Infinity*

James R. Mensch

Northwestern University Press
Evanston, Illinois

Northwestern University Press
www.nupress.northwestern.edu

Printed in the United States of America

10 9 8 7 6 5 4 3 2 1

ISBN 978-0-8101-3054-8 (paper)
ISBN 978-0-8101-3052-4 (cloth)
ISBN 978-0-8101-6818-3 (e-book)

Library of Congress Cataloging-in-Publication Data

Mensch, James R., author.
    Levinas's existential analytic : a commentary on Totality and infinity /
James Mensch.
        pages cm. — (Northwestern University studies in phenomenology and
        existential philosophy)
    ISBN 978-0-8101-3054-8 (pbk. : alk. paper) — ISBN 978-0-8101-3052-4
(cloth : alk. paper) — ISBN 978-0-8101-6818-3 (ebook)
    1. Lévinas, Emmanuel. Totalité et infini. 2. Whole and parts (Philosophy).
3. Infinite. 4. Phenomenology. I. Title. II. Series: Northwestern University
studies in phenomenology & existential philosophy.
    B2430.L483T466 2014
    111—dc23

                                                                    201403320

For the dead of the ghettos of Terezín and Łodz

Contents

Preface

In a conversation with Philip Nemo, Levinas asserts that Heidegger's *Being and Time* is "one of the finest books in the history of philosophy," comparing it to "Plato's *Phaedrus*, Kant's *Critique of Pure Reason*, Hegel's *Phenomenology of Mind*, and Bergson's *Time and Free Will.*" This commentary on Levinas's *Totality and Infinity* has been written with a conviction that it, too, should be added to this list.

It has also been written to fulfill a need. For students working in the field of Continental philosophy, *Totality and Infinity* has increasingly become required reading. Encountering it, however, students often find themselves at a loss. This is because Levinas's work is profoundly original. Following on a tradition that stretches from Parmenides to Heidegger, its goal is that of understanding the nature of being. In doing so, it rethinks the history of philosophy from a novel perspective. Like Kant's *Critique of Pure Reason* and Aristotle's *Metaphysics*, it struggles to find a language that is adequate to the originality of its insights. The result is a text that is dense and often difficult to read. Novel meanings are attached to familiar terms, and arguments often proceed through a series of references that have to be filled out to understand the import of their conclusions. Hence, the need for a commentary on this text.

The goal of my commentary is quite modest. Its models are Norman Kemp Smith's and H. J. Patton's commentaries on the *Critique of Pure Reason*. Readers seeking a groundbreaking interpretation of Levinas or interpretations that push the bounds in our contemporary understanding of Levinas will have to look elsewhere. Norman Kemp Smith wrote of his *Commentary*, "My sole aim has been to reach, as far as may prove feasible, an unbiased understanding of Kant's great work." My aim is the same with regard to *Totality and Infinity*. It is to guide the reader through this text, laying out its arguments, detailing its referents, and thereby situating it in relation to the history of philosophy. In pursuing these tasks, it has limited its references to the issues that animate contemporary scholarly debates to the endnotes. These may be consulted by readers seeking additional information on, say, feminist interpretations of Levinas or his reception by Heidegger scholars. In all this, I have been guided by the difficulties and questions raised by my students over the years as I taught this text. If I have succeeded in some measure in answering these, I shall have succeeded in reaching my goal, which is the modest one of providing an introduction to Levinas's thought through a reading of this text.

I am grateful to the Social Sciences and Research Council for a multiyear grant that allowed me to pursue the research for this book. My gratitude also extends to the PRVOUK P18 "Phenomenology and Semiotics" program at the Faculty of Humanities, Charles University, which financially supported my project's final stages. Finally, I would also like to express my appreciation for my students, whose interest in Levinas has sustained me over the years.

Acknowledgments

I wish to thank the former director of the Husserl Archives in Louvain, Professor Rudolph Bernet, for granting me permission to quote from Husserl's *Nachlass*. Grateful acknowledgment is due to the Social Sciences and Humanities Research Council of Canada for a multiyear grant supporting the research that made this commentary possible. I am also grateful to PRVOUK P18, the Phenomenology and Semiotics program at Charles University, Prague, for the funding that they provided for the final stages of my research in Paris. Finally, I must thank my wife, Josephine Mensch, for her careful proofreading and helpful suggestions for improving my text. Without her input, it would not have reached its present form.

LEVINAS'S EXISTENTIAL ANALYTIC

Introduction

The Nature of Levinas's Text

By virtue of the originality and depth of its thought, Levinas's master-piece, *Totality and Infinity: An Essay on Exteriority,* is destined to endure as one of the great works of philosophy. My aim in presenting a commentary on it is to help students follow its arguments and grasp the subtle phenomenological analyses that fill it. The need for such a guide comes from its extraordinary difficulty. A number of factors enter into this. There is first of all Levinas's language, which often consists of novel uses for terms such as "desire," the "face," and "infinity." This usage is tied to the fact that Levinas is attempting to present a position that is absolutely novel in the history of philosophy. He aims to reconfigure the philosophical tradition from a different standpoint. Thus, a careful reading of his text requires both a knowledge of this tradition and a grasp of how radically different his approach is. Moreover, while Levinas's text is not long—particularly with regard to the task it sets itself—it is extraordinarily dense. His arguments often proceed via a tissue of allusions that have to be specified to see their force. This density does not exclude a continuous return to the same themes. In a kind of spiraling motion, the divisions of his text revisit previous themes, viewing them in different contexts in order to clarify them. This way of proceeding gives the book its nonsystematic character. Terms, when they initially appear, are frequently opaque. The phenomenological analyses that explicate their meaning often seem to have a provisional character. The same holds for the arguments that employ these terms. In a word, Levinas's procedure is the opposite of the *foundational* model that, since Descartes, has characterized philosophical writing. His premises, rather than being stated in the beginning, often appear late in his work.

A tempting response to this nonsystematic, nonfoundational character is to gather all the instances of his themes and present his position as a systematic whole, one that gives the reader a total view of his position. The result, however, would not be a commentary that leads the student, section by section, through the work. It would be a book about *Totality and Infinity* or, more precisely, about the doctrines it presents. But to proceed paragraph by paragraph, like the medieval commentators, and provide a running commentary is not really possible given the nonsystematic character of Levinas's text. To limit oneself to commenting on the initial presentation of a theme would be to leave the reader in doubt as to its direction and sense. A compromise is, therefore, necessary. As I progress through the text, I shall bring in as much later material as is necessary to grasp the section under consideration, leaving in suspense, as far as possible, the insights of later sections.

In this way, I hope to be faithful to the intent of the text. The peculiar structure of *Totality and Infinity* is not accidental. It is not the result of an inability to write systematically. The vision that guides its structure is that teaching proceeds through conversation. To use a pair of Levinas's terms, a conversation consists in the interplay of the *saying* and the *said*. As long as the conversation continues, what is said is not the last word. There is a *saying*, a new speaking, that adds to it, either by correcting it or showing it in a new light. Thus, as the context shifts, terms are adjusted, questions raised and answered. Nothing that is said exists on its own. It is not defenseless like the words of a printed text. The person who utters it can come to the defense of it. The person hearing it can voice his objections. Levinas's text with its spiraling motion is rather like this. It aims to teach by engaging the reader.

The Radical Character of *Totality and Infinity*

The surplus of the *saying* over the *said*, points, for Levinas, to the surplus of a person with regard to every conceptual framework that might be employed to define him. The person exceeds this framework just as the *saying* exceeds the *said*. There is, to use another of Levinas's terms, a certain *infinity* to the person. He is *non*finite in that he cannot be limited or bounded. There is always an excess, an addition that, like a new *saying*, adds to our conception of him. No total understanding of the person is, therefore, possible. For Levinas, this infinity signifies that we cannot think of persons as individuals of a species. What makes them human, what is essential to them, cannot be expressed in a common notion. They are, in fact, irreducibly individual.

One way to grasp this irreducibility is through the Talmud, a text Levinas studied and lectured on. The assertion that each of us is radically singular occurs during the Talmud's discussion of witnesses' testimony in capital cases.[1] Giving false witness in such instances is deadly since "capital cases are not like monetary cases." In the latter, an error can be corrected by "monetary restitution." But "in capital cases [the person giving false witness] is held responsible for [the accused's] blood and the blood of his descendants until the end of time."[2] It is not just that when we kill a person, we kill her descendants; it is that the person, herself, is irreplaceable. There is no substitute that can make good her loss, since each person is a world unto herself. In the Talmud's words, "For this reason was man created alone, to teach thee that whosoever destroys a single soul of Israel, scripture imputes [guilt] to him as though he had destroyed a complete world; and whosoever preserves a single soul of Israel, scripture ascribes [merit] to him as though he had preserved a complete world."[3] Everyone, in fact, is as unique as Adam was on the first day of creation. Everyone can say that the world was created for his or her sake. As the text continues: "if a man strikes many coins from one mold, they all resemble one another. But the Supreme King of Kings, the Holy One, Blessed be He, fashioned every man in the stamp of the first man, and yet not one of them resembles his fellows. Therefore every single person is obliged to say: the world was created for my sake."[4] Since every person is unique, the "world" of each person, the world that comes to presence in and through this person, is also unique. As such, it is irreplaceable. It cannot be made up by the world of another person for "not one of them resembles his fellows." The loss of the person is, then, the loss of "a complete world." Saving the person is saving a world.

If we accept this, then we have to say with Levinas, "That all men are brothers is not explained by their resemblance, nor by a common cause of which they would be the effect, like metals which refer to the same die that struck them" (*Totality and Infinity*, 214).[5] In fact, if each constitutes a world, no overriding or "total" conception of them is possible. Ontologically speaking, the multiplicity of humans is a "radical multiplicity, distinct from numerical multiplicity" (*TI*, 220). A numerical multiplicity is acquired by counting according to a unit, the unit being that by which each thing is to count as one. If my unit is an apple, then I can count apples. If it is fruit, then I can count fruit—for example, apples and oranges. Levinas's claim is that *there is no unit to count human beings*. There cannot be if each person is radically unique.

To see the fundamental character of this claim, we have to note with the historian Leopold von Ranke that three elements formed Europe and, by extension, Western civilization. They are its classical heritage, the peoples that inundated the ancient Roman Empire, and Judeo-Christianity.[6] As Christopher Dawson observed, the totalitarian movements of the twentieth century were distinguished by their attempts to eliminate the third.[7] There is, in fact, a radical incompatibility between the view of humanity advanced by the Talmud—and, by extension, by Judeo-Christianity—and the totalitarian view. In both its fascist and communist versions, totalitarianism proposed a total understanding of humankind. For the Nazis, this was primarily racial and biological; for the communists, it involved economics and class warfare. In both cases, it involved a conception that claimed to leave nothing out, that embraced all human beings, without exception, in a set of "iron laws," be they racial or economic. In Levinas's mind, such ideologies were distinguished by their denial of the excessive or "infinite" character of human being. Their view of "totality" excluded our "infinity." They left no room for our "exteriority"—that is, for our ability to stand outside of every conceptual framework. What this meant is that they denied the biblical insight regarding the radical singularity and irreplaceability of every human being. *Totality and Infinity: An Essay on Exteriority* is, in fact, an attempt to counter this exclusion. Positively, it is an attempt to restore what Levinas takes to be the foundational element of the West's biblical heritage.

Were the effort to exclude this heritage limited to the ideologies of the last century, Levinas's work would have, at most, a historical significance. It would be limited to showing how totalitarianism had to oppose Judeo-Christianity. The radical nature of Levinas's thought, however, goes beyond this. His claim is that this opposition is inherent in the West's classical heritage. The tension between "Athens" and "Jerusalem" concerns, in his mind, philosophy's concealment of the radical singularity of human being. Thus, the temptation of totalitarianism is an ineradicable part of our heritage. It is implicit in its classical, philosophical self-conception. From the beginning, this involves an effort to gain a total conception of being as such and, hence, of human being. This drive towards totality begins with Parmenides's assertion of the all-embracing unity of being, a unity that by definition excludes exteriority. It continues with philosophers such as Plato and Kant, Spinoza and Hegel. *Totality and Infinity* aims at nothing less than overturning this heritage. Its goal is to "oppose the ancient privilege of unity which is affirmed from Parmenides to Spinoza and Hegel" (*TI*, 102). This involves reconceiving philosophical thought such that multiplicity is prior to unity and difference is prior to identity. Levinas, as we shall see, will rework the traditional philosophical themes of ontology, epistemology, ethics, and language by starting with the premise that human singularity is prior to numerical unity and human otherness is prior to sameness.

Heidegger's Existential Analytic

The particular path Levinas takes to reach these goals is deeply indebted to Martin Heidegger. Levinas first met Heidegger when he went to

Freiburg in 1928 to hear the phenomenologist Edmund Husserl lecture. In Freiburg, as he tells Philippe Nemo, he "discovered" Heidegger's magnum opus, *Being and Time* (*Sein und Zeit*). He relates, "It is one of the finest books in the history of philosophy—I say this after years of reflection." Comparing it to "Plato's *Phaedrus*, Kant's *Critique of Pure Reason*, Hegel's *Phenomenology of Mind*, and Bergson's *Time and Free Will*," he asserts, it is "one of the finest among four or five others." In fact, his "admiration for Heidegger is above all an admiration for *Sein und Zeit*."[8] This admiration is, however, conflicted, given Heidegger's "political engagements." According to Levinas, "Heidegger has never been exculpated in my eyes from his participation in National-Socialism."[9] As he elsewhere writes, "It is difficult to forgive Heidegger."[10]

Put philosophically, the praise for Heidegger concerns the latter's "existential analytic." This is a description of our "existing." By this is meant the ways in which we relate to the world, employing its objects to disclose both it and ourselves. What is attractive about this analysis is how it correlates our sense of being to our interactions with the world. Levinas also finds instructive, though ultimately lacking, Heidegger's analysis of the uniqueness of human being. According to Heidegger, being is, for the most part, disclosed pragmatically. We gain the sense of the objects that we encounter by employing them for our purposes. Wind, for example, shows itself as wind to fill my sails, when I use a sailboat to cross the lake. Similarly, water can reveal itself as something to drink, to wash with, or to douse a fire according to my purpose. All such disclosures, according to Heidegger, are guided by an overall understanding of being. Although such an understanding is historically determined, there are features of it that remain the same. These come from the Dasein, the human being, that discloses being. Dasein discloses being through his purposeful, pragmatic activity. The basis of this activity is his peculiar temporal structure, one where he is led by his conception of the *future* to use the resources the *past* has given him to act in the *present* so as to realize his goals. Thus, the water I have on hand from my *past* activity can at *present* be used to douse a fire if this is the *future* state I wish to realize. For Heidegger, this temporal structure serves "as the horizon for all understanding of being and for any way of interpreting it" (*SZ*, 17).[11] It implicitly determines the sense of being as such.

What about the being of Dasein? Heidegger takes "temporality as the meaning of the being that we call Dasein." Throughout *Being and Time*, he will interpret the "structures of Dasein" as "modes of temporality" (*SZ*, 17). As for Dasein's uniqueness, this stems, first of all, from the fact that each of us must die our own death. This makes us realize that the life we lose in death is as individual as the death that takes it from us.

Its individuality, for Heidegger, is a matter of the choices Dasein makes. Each chosen action defines him as its author. He becomes the person having done it. This "authorship" is not determined in advance by his "nature." He does not have a generic essence with a biologically inherited set of behaviors. His choices are, in fact, up to him. If he is willing to accept this and take responsibility for his life, his choices are "authentic." He, himself, rather than the anonymous crowd, sets the direction of his life. Doing so, he becomes unique as its author. Such uniqueness, it should at once be noted, has no essential content. Dasein's freedom to choose his course in life (and his own being-in-the-world) is such that he can always overturn the choices he has made. His self-determination through his choices is absolute precisely because he has no nature, that is, no inherent limitations (as the animals do) on his behavior. Given this lack of essential content, the uniqueness of an individual Dasein has a certain abstractness. As such, it does not override Heidegger's universal account of human being as a temporal structure. It is, in fact, in terms of this universality, that Heidegger can use it to investigate the meaning of being *as such*.

Levinas's Counter-Analytic

Levinas's alternative to this, in his existential analytic, is to maintain Heidegger's correlation of the sense of being to our Dasein, but to radically pluralize this sense by providing an alternate foundation for our uniqueness. This is given by our organic functioning—more particularly, by its non-substitutability.[12] Thus, the fact that no one can die for another is but one of a host of phenomena, all of which point to the uniqueness of our embodiment. None of our bodily functions can be replaced by someone else's. No one, for example, can eat for us. The fact that someone else has had his dinner does not lessen my need for my own. The same holds for sleeping, breathing, or a host of other functions that are part of our being alive. Our experience of such functioning, which makes up our affective life, thus defines a sphere of privacy and intimacy. The experience of the flesh of a peach as you bite into it, chewing and swallowing it, is fundamentally different than the experience of some public object like a book on a table. The very act of consuming removes the peach from the public realm. It makes it affectively unavailable to all but yourself. This is why the "taste" that relates to our affective life is not disputable. Even with regard to the experience of public objects like a book or a table, embodiment imposes a certain privacy. As embodied, individuals never occupy the same spatial position at the same time. Thus, their experience is never precisely the same. The nonidentity or "alterity" that embodiment imposes on us necessitates language. As distinct, we are forced to use language to communicate our experiences. It is only as translated into linguistic signs that such experiences achieve any commonality. To reverse this, the public presence of the world is that of our discourse. It is only by speaking and comparing our experiences with others that we can have any certainty that what we see is objectively there, that is, present not just for us, but for others as well.

In Levinas's analytic, our ethical consciousness grows out of this embodiment. To have a body is to be subject to its needs and exposed to its vulnerabilities. Embodied, we have to live from the world and what it offers. We can be hungry even though, as Levinas writes, "Dasein in Heidegger is never hungry" (*TI*, 134). Circumstances, such as poverty, famine, and war, can prevent us from meeting our needs. Our embodiment makes us vulnerable to these. The ethical correlate of such vulnerability is the appeal that stems from the other in distress. It is expressed in our obligations to feed the hungry, clothe the naked, shelter the homeless, and so on. Heidegger's analytic, by contrast, never focuses on our embodiment. It thus ignores the needs and vulnerabilities associated with it. Because of this, it misses the ethical aspect of our being in the world: it cannot disclose the world where the biblical command to care for the "widow and the orphan" has preeminence. This failure to disclose the moral dimension of Dasein's existence has consequences for this analytic's grasp of being itself. Its silence on embodiment means that there is nothing in its conception of being that immunizes it from the abuses of totalitarianism. It is liable to the latter's exclusion of exteriority since it has no conception of the radical singularity that is based on our embodiment.[13]

Levinas's response to this failure is an existential analytic that grounds our uniqueness, not on our choices, but on our embodied functioning. As with Heidegger's analytic, the focus is on how our being in the world corresponds to our understanding of being. For Levinas, however, this understanding is based on our embodied being with others. As such, it includes from the beginning the ethical obligations that spring from our needs and vulnerabilities.[14] Indicative of Levinas's intent are the Aristotelian terms he uses to characterize this understanding: "metaphysics" and "first philosophy." Aristotle, in his *Metaphysics*, called his investigations into the meaning of being "first philosophy." Its priority came from the fact that it concerned being as such, being prior to its particular divisions, which were the subject of particular philosophical investigations.[15] For Levinas, however, "morality is not a branch of philosophy, but first philosophy" (*TI*, 304). Our ethical obligations are, as it were, the lens through which the genuine nature of being as such comes into focus in its radical plurality. Given this positioning of ethics as "first philosophy," he employs the term "metaphysics" to designate our ethical apprehension of being. The result is an existential analytic that is at once a philosophical anthropology, an ethics, and an elucidation of being as such.

Since so much of this analytic is conceived as a response to Heidegger's position, I have to extend my preliminary remarks regarding it. Thus, before I begin my commentary, I shall sketch out the basic features of Heidegger's analytic as it appears in *Being and Time*.

1

Heidegger's Existential Analytic

The Temporal Structure of Care

As I indicated in the introduction, Heidegger sees our human existence, our Dasein, as a privileged mode of access to the question of being qua being. By "being" he means the sense or meaning of being. Such meaning comes from us, that is, from our ability to disclose beings, such disclosure being guided by our understanding of being. This means that without us, the question of being loses its context. As Heidegger writes:

> Only so long as Dasein *exists*, which means the factual possibility of an understanding of being, "is there" being [*Sein*]. If Dasein does not exist, then there "is" neither the "independence" [of beings] nor the "in itself" [of beings]. Such things are neither understandable nor not understandable. The innerworldly being is neither disclosable nor can it lie hidden. The one can neither say that beings are nor that they are not. (*SZ*, 212)

None of these alternatives are possible if humans with their ability to disclose are not present. If, in fact, the being of the world has its sense from the way we constitute such sense through our disclosures, then the first question must be about Dasein. In other words, given that "fundamental ontology [the study of being qua being] . . . must be sought in the existential analytic of Dasein" (*SZ*, 13), the question is: What kind of being does Dasein have?[1]

Heidegger's answer involves defining Dasein as "care." In his words, "Dasein, when understood ontologically, is care" (*SZ*, 57). "Care" is a care for our own being since Dasein, according to Heidegger, is the entity for whom its own being is an issue (*SZ*, 12). This means that it has to decide what it will be. In other words, its being is a matter of its choices as it makes its way in the world. Such choices involve its projects, that is, the things it wants to accomplish. Engaging in these, it discloses both the world and itself. Thus "paper" can mean something to write on, something to paint or draw on, combustible material to start a fire with, material for making silhouettes, paper airplanes, and the like. Each use gives a different cast to what comes to mind when we think of "paper." As this example indicates, disclosure is primarily pragmatic. It exhibits things in their instrumental value. They are disclosed insofar as they are useful for our projects. Our interpretations of them, our considering them as something definite, is based on this.[2] In Heidegger's words, interpretation "appresents the what-it-is-for of a thing and so brings out the reference of the 'in-order-to,'" that is, its use in a particular project.[3] As a result, the world becomes articulated. It gains its meaningfulness as an "equipmental totality." This disclosure of the world *is also a self-disclosure.* As persons for whom our being is an issue, our being becomes that of the accomplishers of these projects. Thus, the project of writing a book, if carried out, makes a person an author. Similarly, the builder is the person who has built something.

Since such projects involve the world, so does the selfhood that is disclosed through them. Insofar as it is defined through projects involving objects in the world, Dasein's fundamental ontological mode is, according to Heidegger, being-in-the-world. This being-in-the-world involves our "comportment" (our behavior) towards beings, which is itself based on our understanding of being.[4] What is this understanding? It is, as indicated, our knowing how to make our way in the world. It is our implicitly grasping the context of the relations involved in our tasks or projects. Our understanding of "breakfast," for example, is constitutive of our being-in-the-world of the kitchen in the morning. We "understand" how to go about making breakfast. The objects in the kitchen— the eggs, plates, cereal bowls, spoons, and so on—all have meaning; they are "understood" in their purpose; and we behave or "comport" ourselves towards them accordingly. Heidegger calls the place of such interrelated objects a "*Bezugsbereich.*" This term designates an area of relations that is suited to disclose beings in a particular way. The kitchen is one example of a *Bezugsbereich.* Another is the law court, whose trial proceedings are meant to disclose guilt or innocence. A very different *Bezugsbereich* is provided by the scientific laboratory, which discloses being in its measurable material properties. As such examples indicate, the human world consists of multiple areas of relations. Each has its particular manner of revealing being. Corresponding to each is a particular understanding of how we are to make our way among its objects. Thus, the richer and more multiple our understanding is, the richer is our human world. Its meaningfulness increases along with the complexity of our behavior. So does our sense of who (or what) we are in our being-in-the-world.

All this has a reference to our temporality. In fact, the point of Heidegger's descriptions is to exhibit "temporality as the meaning of the being that we call Dasein." This involves "the repeated interpretation . . . of the structures of Dasein . . . as modes of temporality" (*SZ*, 17). Such structures are those of our being-in-the-world as "care"—that is, as beings who face the choice of what sort of beings we shall become through our projects. Thus, the past is what gives us the resources for our choices. The future appears in our projecting ourselves forward in opting for some goal, while the present occurs in our actualization of this goal. Let me go through these one by one, starting with the future. According to Heidegger, the future appears because, in making a choice, "Dasein has already compared itself in its [present] being with a[n unrealized] possibility of itself" (*SZ*, 191). This means that "Dasein is already ahead of itself in its being. Dasein is always [in considering these possibilities of itself] 'beyond itself' ['*über sich hinaus*']" (*SZ*, 192). Sartre expresses this insight as follows: man, he asserts, is the being "who is what he is not, and who is not what he is."[5] Separated from myself in my being ahead of myself, I am not what I presently am. Given this, I can only "be" what I am not, that is, be as projected toward those goals or possibilities that I actualize through my projects. This being ahead of myself is, according to Heidegger, part of the structure of my being as care. In his words, "The being of Dasein signifies, being ahead of yourself in already being in the world as being there with the entities that one encounters within the world. This being fills in the meaning of the term care" (*SZ*, 192). This complicated terminology should not conceal from us the basic phenomenon that Heidegger is pointing to: Someone is knocking at the door. Hearing this, we are already ahead of ourselves, already projecting ourselves forward to the moment when we answer the door. In our being, we *are* there at the door awaiting ourselves as we walk forward to open it. The insight, in other words, is that we are *in our being* temporally extended. This being ahead of ourselves is the origin of our sense of futurity. It is what allows futurity to appear. When, for example, I walk towards the door, I disclose the future by closing the gap between the self that awaits me and the present. As Heidegger writes, "This . . . letting itself *come towards* itself [*auf sich Zukommen-lassen*] . . . is the original phenomenon of the *future*" (*SZ*, 325).

The original appearing of the past also occurs through the accomplishment of my goals. In describing it, Heidegger returns to the fact that my projects spring from my possibilities. I am "ahead of myself" when I project these possibilities forward as practical goals. Such possibilities are inherent in my given historical situation. Thus, my possibility of winning a marathon depends on my given physical makeup, that is, on a history that includes the facts of my birth and subsequent physical development. It also depends on how much I have *already* trained for the event and on my living in a culture that has developed the tradition of running marathon races.[6] It is this dependence that is at the origin of my sense of pastness. The past is what provides me with the resources for my projects.

Such resources are part of my being-in-the-world. In providing me with my possibilities, the "having been" of this being is what allows me to be ahead of myself, that is, have a future. This dependence does not mean that the past determines the future. According to Heidegger, the line of dependence does not go from past to future, but rather the reverse. In his words, "Dasein 'is' its past in the manner of *its* being, which roughly speaking, occurs from its future. . . . Its own past—and this always implies the past of its 'generation'—does not follow after Dasein, but rather is always in advance of it" (*SZ*, 20). His point is that, while the past gives me the possibilities for my future action, it is only in terms of such action that they can be considered possibilities at all. They are such only as material for my projects. Thus, just as paper appears as writing paper when I use it for this purpose, so its very possibility to serve as such is there for me, that is, discloses itself, only in terms of this way of my being ahead of myself. This means, in Heidegger's words, "Dasein can authentically *be* past only insofar as it is futural. Pastness originates in a certain way from the future" (*SZ*, 326).

Heidegger's account of the present follows the same pattern. It, too, is described in terms of the accomplishment of our projects. Such accomplishment results in the disclosure of the things about us. They show themselves as useful to our projects or as simply there, that is, as not having any immediate use value. In any case, our taking action to accomplish our goals results "in a *making present* [*Gegenwärtigen*] of these entities." The result is the "*present* in the sense of making present" (*SZ*, 326). Taken as a temporal mode, the present is thus part of an ongoing process that involves the past and the future. In accomplishing a goal, I make what the goal involves present. I also transform my past by adding to it. This addition transforms the possibilities it offers me. For example, having opened the door in response to someone knocking, my having been—my past—includes this action. My present discloses the result— the presence of the person standing there before me. As part of my situation, this becomes part of my having been, that is, affects the possibilities that now open up to me.[7]

With this account of the temporal modes, Heidegger completes his description of Dasein as care. "Temporality," he writes, "reveals itself as the sense of authentic care" (*SZ*, 326). This is because our temporal distension makes care possible. It is, in fact, its inner structure:

> Dasein's total being as care signifies: [being] ahead-of-itself in already-being-in (a world) as being-there-with (entities one encounters in the world). . . . The original unity of the structure of care lies in tempo-

rality. The "ahead-of-itself" is grounded in the future. The "already-being-in . . ." exhibits the past. "Being-there-with" is made possible in making present. (*SZ*, 327)

According to Heidegger, these three modes can be considered as temporal "ecstasies"—that is, ways in which we *stand out* from ourselves.[8] In our temporal being we are extended along the lines of our having-been and our being ahead of ourselves. Even in the present, we are not self-present but rather there with the things we disclose. In a striking metaphor, Heidegger compares this three-dimensional structure of our temporal apartness to a clearing—that is, to a point in the woods where the trees part and light enters in. He writes, "The being that bears the title being-there [*Da-sein*] is cleared [*gelichtet*]. . . . What essentially clears this being, i.e., what makes it 'open' and also 'bright' for itself, is what we have defined as care" (*SZ*, 350). Since care is temporally structured, he clarifies this by adding: "ecstatical temporality originally clears the there [*Da*]" (*SZ*, 351). This clearing is our openness to the world. It is our clearing in its midst. The fundamental point here is that our being in the world is rooted in our temporality. The transcendence of the world is a function of this temporality. Its apartness—its extension in space—is founded in the apartness of time. It is, Heidegger argues, through my closing the gap between the present and the future that I "spatialize" my world. For example, I disclose the space between the door and my place in the room through my action of walking towards it to answer someone knocking. Had I no such project, this space would not be "cleared." It would not be disclosed or made "bright" (see *SZ*, §23).

Nothingness and the Call of Conscience

Heidegger is not content to describe our being as *care*. His inquiry drives him to seek the ground of our being as care. In his eyes, it is not sufficient to say that we are "care" because we are the kind of being for whom our being is an issue. We have to ask: why is it an issue? Heidegger's answer is that it is an issue for us because of our radical otherness from everything that we encounter in the world. Dasein is not encountered as a mere thing is; neither is it present as something useful for a project. In Heidegger's terms, then, our being is an issue for us because we are "no-thing," that is, we do not fall under the ontological categories that are descriptive of things.[9] Our absence on the level of these categories gives us the nothingness (the no-thingness) that is at the heart of our projective being. This nothingness is what allows us to "be there" with the possibilities we choose to realize. Thus, for Heidegger, "not only is the projection, as one that has been thrown, determined by the nothingness [*Nichtigkeit*] of the being of its basis [*Grundseins*], but also, as projection, [Dasein] is itself essentially null [*nichtig*] . . . the nothingness meant here belongs to Dasein's being-free for its existential possibilities" (*SZ*, 285).[10] Such nothingness belongs to our freedom to choose among our different possibilities precisely because our Dasein is *not some thing, not some entity with a determinate nature*. If it were, then its nature would limit its choices and, hence, its ability to be ahead of itself.

Heidegger relates this nothingness to the fact that we can die, death being understood as the collapse of the inner temporal distance that is our structure as Dasein. A thing, having no such temporal structure, cannot die. A clearing, a temporal apartness, can, however, close up leaving nothing behind. As a clearing I am both subject to the nothingness of death and in my no-thingness an expression of it. This equation of my inner nothingness with my mortality is the paradoxical heart of Heidegger's description of our temporalization. One way to approach it is through the essential futurity and alterity of death. Its futurity follows from the fact that as long as we are alive, death remains outstanding. Death is the possibility that lies beyond all our other possibilities. When it is accomplished, all the others must vanish. This is because, as Heidegger writes, death undoes "our being in the world as such." Facing death, we confront "the possibility of our not being able to be there" in the world at all (*SZ*, 250). Thus, death is always ahead of us. Were we to eliminate it, we would suppress our being-ahead-of-ourselves. We would collapse the temporal distance that makes us Dasein.[11] We would, in other words, reduce ourselves to the category of a mere thing. A thing can neither die nor be ahead of itself. Our not being a thing, our no-thingness, is, however, the nothingness that is at the basis of our projective being. Thus, the essential futurity of death and the futurity (the ahead-of-ourselves) of our projective being both point back to this nothingness that lies at our basis.

Such nothingness is ourselves in our radical self-alterity. We are, at our basis, other than all the possibilities of selfhood that we can realize through our projects. In the "null basis" of our being as care, we are also distinct from all the particular beings we disclose. Our inner alterity is such that it places us beyond everything worldly that we can imagine or know. The radical alterity of such nothingness thus coincides with the radical alterity of death. The identification of this nothingness with death focuses on the fact that death itself, as *my* annihilation, is other than everything I can know. Its radical alterity is my alterity in my being-ahead-of-myself. The self I am ahead of as I project myself forward to my goal is myself in my no-thingness. What I "leap over" in projecting myself forward is the radical absence that allows me to be temporally distended.

What Heidegger calls the "call of conscience" arises when I face this nothingness. Doing so, I realize that my being is not something given to me beforehand, not something I inherit. It is the result of my action. Heidegger puts this in terms of the self-alterity that is our self-transcendence as we project ourselves forward. "If in the ground of its essence Dasein were not transcending, which now means, if it were not in advance holding itself out into the nothing, then it could never adopt a stance towards beings nor even towards itself" (*The Basic Problems of Phenomenology*, 95). This holding itself out into the nothing is its being ahead of itself. In separating Dasein from itself, the "nothing" allows it to assume responsibility both for the beings it reveals and for itself in its revealing them. The "call of conscience" that arises from this is essentially a call to self-responsibility. In Heidegger's words, the call is "a calling-forth to that potentiality-for-being, which in each case I already am as Dasein." This calling-forth is "a summons to being-guilty [*Schuldigsein*]" (*SZ*, 287). "Guilt" here has the double sense of "debt [*Schuld*]" and of "being responsible for something [*Schuld sein daran*]" (see ibid., 282–85). Both senses appear when I resolutely face the fact that I will die. In facing death, I face the nothing at the heart of my projective being. Responding to this, I realize my responsibility for my being. This realization is that of my *self*-indebtedness. I *owe myself* whatever being I have. Thus, the call of conscience is a call to face one's situation, to recognize the factual possibilities inherent in it. In Heidegger's words, "The call of conscience has the character of Dasein's *appeal* to its ownmost potentiality-to-be-itself [*Selbstseinkönnen*]; and this is done by summoning it to its ownmost being-guilty [*Schuldigsein*]"—that is, its ownmost self-indebtedness (*SZ*, 269). Hearing this summons, I realize that my being is the result of my choices. My being springs from the possibilities I choose to actualize.

It is possible to see temporalization as the process of paying this debt. Endeavoring to pay it, I must *anticipate*, that is, see myself in terms of my future possibilities. For such possibilities to be realizable, this projecting myself forward must be done in terms of my factually given past. I must anticipate while *retaining* the past that gives these possibilities their concrete shape. I must, also, work to actualize such real possibilities, thereby making myself something. But, of course, I can never be some thing. I am essentially null. Thus, I am always in debt to myself. The debt of being, as long as I live, can never be repaid. To satisfy the debt would be to collapse my projective being into the inanimate presence of a mere thing. The result of my attempting to pay it is, thus, my life in its ongoing temporalization. The call of conscience to pay the debt of self-hood is, in other words, what drives this life forward. The sense of our impending death animates this call. Both ahead of us and internal to us, death is identified with the nothingness of our temporal distension—that is, our being ahead of ourselves within ourselves. The link of death to the "nothing" that "is neither an object nor any being at all" comes from the fact that death is "the impossibility of any existence at all" (*SZ*, 262). For Heidegger, our facing this end means acknowledging that our being-in-the-world is our responsibility. It is our facing our self-indebtedness in the face of our nothingness.

I shall have occasion to return to and refine this sketch of Heidegger's analytic during the following commentary on *Totality and Infinity*. For the present, it is sufficient to keep the main point in mind. For Heidegger, the "call of conscience," understood as the basis of our ethical responsibility, is self-directed. The notion of our responsibility to the other—that is, to his or her being-in-the-world—is, at most, peripheral to his concerns.[12] This focus on oneself rather than the other is why Levinas asserts that Heidegger would probably be more afraid of dying than of being a murderer.[13]

2

The Preface

The Question

Like Heidegger in *Being and Time*, Levinas in his initial remarks is concerned with opening up a space for the inquiry he is about to undertake. Does it makes any sense to speak of morality? There is no room for an investigation that takes it on its own terms if we assume from the start that morality is an illusion unmasked by the experience of war. Levinas, accordingly, begins the "Preface" by writing: "Everyone will readily agree that it is of the highest importance to know whether we are not duped by morality. Does not lucidity, the mind's openness upon the true, consist in catching sight of the permanent possibility of war?" (*TI*, 21). The attitude he is confronting is that "war . . . renders morality derisory." War is the ultimate reality. This means that "the trial by force is the test of the real." Heraclites, the pre-Socratic philosopher, asserted that "strife is justice"[1] and "war is the father and king of all."[2] Yet, we do not need such fragments to show that "being reveals itself as war to philosophical thought" (ibid.). Philosophy's tendency to equate being with war comes from war's all-embracing quality. Like Parmenides's concept of being, war allows no exteriority. It draws everything in. As Levinas puts this: "Not only modern war but every war . . . establishes an order from which no one can keep his distance; nothing henceforth is exterior. War does not manifest exteriority and the other as other" (ibid.). This all-embracing character is particularly evident in the "total war" that Goebbels advocated (and all nations more or less practiced) during the Second World War. Those who engaged in it used any and all means to prosecute their war aims. In their bombing raids they did not distinguish civilians from soldiers. The Germans were particularly ruthless in their treatment of the occupied populations. Their totalitarian ideology, like war itself, had an all-embracing character. Its ideal was the inclusion of all life under state control, employing everything involved in such life as means for the ends that the state set.

Morality, by contrast, involves never treating individuals simply as means for our purposes. It implies, as Kant argued, treating them as ends in themselves. They should be respected as autonomous individuals who have an existence exterior to our purposes, persons who regard themselves as the end or goal of their own activities. The question Levinas is raising is whether this regard for others is an illusion. Is it something that cannot stand philosophical inspection? Does not the same hold for peace, as the opposite of war? Does not the striving for peace "live on subjective opinions and illusions"? (*TI*, 24). The space for such questions involves the possibility of a negative response. To open it up is to question the obviousness of a positive answer.

Such obviousness, Levinas claims, comes from the history of Western philosophy. Totalization, the denial of exteriority, and war all spring from the nature of its endeavor. In his words, "The visage of being that shows itself in war is fixed in the concept of totality that dominates Western philosophy" (*TI*, 21). The reason why philosophy only regards the aspect of being that shows itself in war is because its ideal is that of gaining a total knowledge, one that leaves nothing out. The goal of an all-inclusive knowledge is, of course, possible only if being itself is inherently graspable. This implies, as Parmenides wrote, "The same thing exists for thinking and for being,"[3] that is, *to be* is *to be thinkable* or, to reverse this: what cannot be known cannot be. It is simply a pure nothingness. This holds, Levinas writes, "unless philosophical evidence refers from itself to a situation that can no longer be stated in terms of 'totality' . . . Unless the non-knowing with which the philosophical knowing begins coincides not with pure nothingness but only with a nothingness of objects." It holds, in fact, unless "we can proceed from the experience of totality back to a situation where totality breaks up, a situation that conditions the totality itself" (*TI*, 24). What is this nontotalizable situation that conditions philosophical evidence? How can it stand as a condition for totality itself? Levinas claims: "Such a situation is the gleam of exteriority or of transcendence in the face of the Other [*autrui*].[4] The rigorously developed concept of this transcendence is expressed by the term "infinity" (*TI*, 24–25). The claim, here, which we shall have to explore, is that the "situation" that "breaks up" totality is the experience of another person. This experience is something that philosophy presupposes in positing a totality. Yet what it points to stands outside of this totality. The other person transcends the totality and, thereby, exhibits his or her "infinity."

Infinity

The meaning of "infinity" is one that Levinas coins for his own purposes. It does not signify a being, as in an "infinite being," but rather a mode of being. Grammatically, its referent is not a noun, but rather a verb designating an activity of being. The action is that of overflowing. In Levinas's words, "infinity overflows the thought that thinks it. Its very infinition is produced precisely in this overflowing" (*TI*, 25). This means that "the idea of infinity is the mode of being, the infinition, of infinity" (*TI*, 26). Infinition is the action of infinity. It "is produced in the improbable feat whereby a separated being fixed in its identity, the same, the I, nonetheless contains in itself what it can neither contain nor receive solely by virtue of its own identity" (*TI*, 26–27). Here, "subjectivity realizes . . . the astonishing feat of containing more than it is possible for it to contain" (*TI*, 27). Infinity, then, is manifested by the surplus, the excess of the object. As a verb, it designates this exceeding.

The transcendence it expresses is not, as Derrida argues, a total transcendence, a complete nonidentity between the subject and that which transcends it. Were this the case, then what is transcendent would be completely unknown. We could neither know nor be aware of it. If this were Levinas's position, then we would have to say with Derrida, "Levinas . . . deprives himself of the very foundation and possibility of his own language. What authorizes him to say 'infinitely other' if the infinitely other does not appear as such . . . ?"[5] Every transcendent Other would be "totally other" and we would be at a loss to distinguish between them.[6] Infinity, as characterizing transcendence, however, only signifies "the exceeding of limits" (*TI*, 26). It implies both limits and their surpassing. The limits are those of the subject or "I" (the "same"). The surpassing of them is accomplished by the presence of the Other as other. It occurs through the Other who is in me and yet transcends me.

One way of understanding Levinas's meaning is by noting the possible relations intentions have to fulfillments. The givenness of what we intend can exactly match our intentions. It can be other than what we intend—as is the case when we are mistaken. The givenness also can be less. It can, for example, not offer the detail that was part of our intentions. Finally, givenness can exceed our intentions. In showing itself, the object presents us with more than what we intended. To intend the object as having such excessive presence is, paradoxically, to intend it as exceeding our intentions. Such presence has a peculiar quality. It makes us aware that more is being offered than we can formulate in our intentions. The interpretations based on our previous experience are not sufficient to grasp the sense it embodies. We have to adjust our interpretation and return to it again. In such a return, however, we face the same situation. Yet another return is called for. The "object" that continually demands such a return is, of course, not an object, but a person. In speaking with the Other, he is always adding to the *said*. His ability to do so points to his transcendence of the *said*. Such transcendence is not just manifested in conversation; it also shows itself in the Other's behavior. In his actions, the Other gives himself as both like and not like me. He behaves generally as I do, but not in any strictly predictable way. There is always a certain excess in what he shows me. He is not limited to the predictions I make from my own experience. I make such predictions based on my interpretation of the situation. His interpretation, however, need not match my own.[7] To intend the Other as manifesting this quality is, as indicated, to intend the inadequacy of one's intention. The intention directs itself towards a fulfillment that will exceed its content. Given this, we have to say with Levinas that the thought of the Other contains "more than it is possible for it to contain." It contains more that what it is possible for it to "receive solely by virtue of its own identity" (*TI*, 27). Its identity as a thought is given by its content. This is what is possible for thought to contain. But the intention to the Other contains more than this as intending the inadequacy of such content, that is, as directing itself towards a presence that will exceed it.

Infinity and Embodiment

Levinas writes that his work will apprehend subjectivity "as founded in the idea of infinity" (*TI*, 26). One of the ways a person manifests his infinity is in the action he takes to alter his circumstances. Viewed in terms of the thought that merely contemplates the world, there is "an essential violence" in action. This violence involves action's ability "to shatter at every moment the framework of a content that is thought, to cross the barriers of immanence" (*TI*, 27). When we act, we "shatter" the thought that represents what is by creating something new. This means that "what, in action, breaks forth as essential violence is the surplus of being over the thought that claims to contain [being], the marvel of the idea of infinity" (ibid.). Levinas's point is that when we act, we do more than simply regard the world. Action involves more than the adequation of thought with its object. A new situation, a "surplus of being," results from the act. Something is present, something exists, that was not there before. Thus, action surpasses the "thought that claims to contain being" by producing the new. It involves the idea of infinity in the sense of presupposing limits (those given by the thought that claims to contain being) and exceeding these limits. What action produces exceeds thought in the sense that the *existence* or being that our action produces is not just *the thought of existence* or being.

Behind this surplus is both the infinity of subjectivity and the embodiment that allows it to act. Both are involved in "the incarnation of consciousness." Such incarnation, Levinas writes, is "comprehensible only if, over and beyond adequation, the overflowing of the idea by its ideatum, that is, the idea of infinity [as such overflowing] moves consciousness" (*TI*, 27). This "overflowing of the idea by its ideatum"—that is, by the existent of which we have the idea—is the overflowing of the content of the idea by the existence that bears this content. Consciousness, in acting, is moved by something more than its ideas. In acting, it presupposes the surplus of actual existence. As an embodied actor, "consciousness, then, does not consist in equaling being with representation . . . but rather in overflowing [representation] . . . and in accomplishing events whose ultimate signification (contrary to the Heideggerian conception) does not lie in disclosing" (ibid.). The reference, here, is to Heidegger's pragmatic theory of disclosure: I disclose things as material for my projects by acting to achieve my ends. It is also to the fact that my action does not just disclose (as if it only revealed what already was there waiting to be disclosed). It actually creates the new. It surpasses disclosure by creating what was not yet there to be disclosed before the action. If we ask for the source of such newness, it is subjectivity itself "as founded in the idea of infinity." Incarnate consciousness, as moved by this idea, acts to create the new.

Ethics and Infinity

Levinas claims that "the idea of infinity . . . is the common source of activity and theory" (*TI*, 27). One way to understand this is to note that theory's claim to grasp objective reality is not something that can be established by a single individual. As I said in the "Introduction," it is only by speaking and comparing our experiences with Others that we can have any certainty that what we see is objectively there, that it is present, not just for us, but for Others as well. To grasp such Others, however, we must possess the idea of infinity, that is, the idea of the exceeding by which the Other shows herself as other. If we accept this, then we can say, with Levinas, not just all practice, but also "knowing qua intentionality already presupposes the idea of infinity" (ibid.).

Because this last point is the linchpin of his argument, Levinas will return to it again and again. If we grant it, we cannot say that morality is an illusion, something that the progress of knowledge gradually dispels. Ethics, with its focus on the Other as other, is not something dependent on objective knowledge. It is prior to it. As the "overflowing of objectifying thought," the ethical relation is, in fact, the "forgotten experience by which [such thought] lives" (*TI*, 28). Objectifying thought, the thought that attempts to get the object in itself, the object apart from our partial and biased apprehensions, inherently has a "transcendent intention." As such, it lives from, but forgets ethics in that "the essential of ethics is in its transcendent intention" (*TI*, 29). The goal of *Totality and Infinity* will be to demonstrate this. In Levinas's words, "The break-up of the formal structure of thought . . . into events which this structure dissimulates, but which sustain it . . . constitutes a deduction—necessary and yet non-analytical" (*TI*, 28). There is here an allusion to Immanuel Kant's "transcendental deduction." In his *Critique of Pure Reason*, Kant traces the possibility of objective knowledge back to the categories and, ultimately, back to the unity of our subjectivity. Levinas's deduction will deduce its possibility from the event of the "transcendent intention" that animates ethics.

In another allusion, this time to Aristotle, Levinas writes, "Already *of itself* ethics is an 'optics'" (*TI*, 29). To consider ethics as an optics is to regard it as a mode of perception, like the sensible and intellectual modes of perception. Aristotle thought that, like these modes, ethical insight has its own special "organ." This, he claimed, was our character. Some fundamental principles, he wrote, have to be apprehended, not by perception nor by induction from examples, but rather by "habituation" (*Nicomachean Ethics*, 1098b4). You need the right habits to perceive them. The character made up of such habits is like the lens of the eye. Without it, you cannot focus on the ethical. Thus, you don't ask an alcoholic about how much to drink, a miser about how much to give, a coward or a reckless person about courage, and so on. Their habits incapacitate them from grasping the correct answer. Levinas makes a similar claim about objective knowledge. Without the "optics" provided by ethics, we lose the sense of objectivity.

What we have here is a certain reversal of the relation between activity and cognition. According to Levinas, we cannot say that "activity rests on cognitions that illuminate it," that is, first we have to know, then we can act (*TI*, 29). In a certain sense, ethical action is its own seeing, its own relation to the truth. Heidegger, as we have seen, makes a similar claim about pragmatic activity. We disclose things—we show "how" and "what" they are—when we use them for our purposes. Such disclosure manifests their "truth"—a term whose Greek equivalent, *aletheia*, he takes to signify their un-hiddenness. When we use things, we bring them, in their "what" and "how," out of concealment. For Levinas, however, ethical action is more fundamental. He asserts: "The welcoming of the face and the work of justice—which condition the birth of truth itself—are not interpretable in terms of [Heideggerian] disclosure" (*TI*, 28). They condition such disclosure and, hence, the "truth" that it exhibits. If our actions are unethical, if they are the actions of totalization or of war, then we get the "evidence of war," the evidence that refutes morality. But this "evidence of war has been maintained in an essentially hypocritical civilization," one claiming to be "attached both to the True and the Good," but in fact "antagonistic" to them (*TI*, 24). Such civilization cannot, in fact, account for its knowledge, since such knowledge, in its claims to transcendence, rests on the ethical relation. Its hypocrisy or bad faith involves its hiding this fact from itself.

Prophetic Eschatology

We are now in a position to understand Levinas's rather cryptic remarks regarding "prophetic eschatology." The term "eschatology" comes from the Greek *eschatos*, signifying "last." It generally refers to doctrines of the "last things," concerning the ultimate end of time and the world. So conceived, eschatology seems to provide "information about the future by revealing the finality of being." But for Levinas, "its real import lies elsewhere." Rather than introducing "a teleological system into the totality" or "teaching the orientation of history . . . eschatology institutes a relation with being beyond the totality or beyond history." Its "relationship," he adds, is "with a surplus always exterior to the totality" (*TI*, 22). Levinas uses "the concept of infinity" to convey this surplus. It is needed "to express this transcendence to totality, non-encompassable within a totality" that, nonetheless, is as "primordial as totality" is (*TI*, 23).

As we have seen, the term "infinity" relates to the Other who is in us and yet transcends us. The morality that springs from this relation "consummates the vision of eschatology." Rather than being derived from it, morality provides the evidence for eschatology. The result, Levinas writes, is "a 'vision' without image, bereft of the synoptic and totalizing objectifying virtues of vision, a relation or an intentionality of a wholly different type—which this work seeks to describe" (*TI*, 23). The perpetual peace that faith-based eschatology sees as reigning at the end of days is part of this vision. "But this," Levinas writes, "does not mean that, when affirmed objectively, it is believed by faith instead of being known by knowledge." In fact, such "peace" is neither an object of faith nor of knowledge. Hegel claimed to *know* (as part of his "science of knowledge") such peace would result from the dialectic of history. It would occur when the oppositions that generate history were resolved in a final synthesis.

For Levinas, however, "peace does not take place in the objective history disclosed by war, as the end of that war or as the end of history" (*TI*, 24). It is always present, continually available in the relation to the Other as other. The point is not to philosophically demonstrate eschatological "truths" such as peace, but rather "to proceed from the experience of totality back to a situation where totality breaks up . . . Such a situation is the gleam of exteriority or of transcendence in the face of the Other" (ibid.). It is through the analysis of this situation that Levinas will provide the evidence for his eschatological vision.

3

Metaphysical Desire

Totality and Infinity, I, A

The Irreversible Relation

Levinas's analysis of our relation to the Other begins with a description of metaphysical desire. Following Heidegger, he sees metaphysics as resting on the distinction between this world and the true world.[1] Its "alibi" is that "'the true life is absent.' But we are in the world."[2] "Metaphysics" is, thus, "turned towards the 'elsewhere' and the 'otherwise' and the 'other'" (*TI*, 33). So is the desire termed "metaphysical." It is not a desire for something I can possess. "The other metaphysically desired is not 'other' like the bread I eat, the land in which I dwell, the landscape I contemplate." Such things are part of the totality of the world. I can possess them. In becoming mine, he writes, "their alterity is . . . reabsorbed into my own identity as a thinker or a possessor." By contrast, "the metaphysical desire tends . . . towards something else entirely, towards the absolutely other" (ibid.).

What we confront here is desire in a very special sense. It is not a desire based on need, on being "indigent." It is not "a longing for return" to a previously satisfied state (*TI*, 33). Not being based on need, it is, Levinas writes, "a desire that cannot be satisfied" by the fulfillment of a need (*TI*, 34). Water, for example, satisfies or completes thirst; food does the same thing for hunger, and so on. But metaphysical desire desires "beyond what could complete it." It is a "desire that nourishes itself . . . with its hunger." The closing of the gap between the desire and the desired does not occur. They form a "relationship that is not the disappearance of distance." What we confront is "a desire without satisfaction, which . . . understands the remoteness, the alterity, the exteriority of the other" (ibid.).

This very remoteness makes the relation between the desire and the desired incomprehensible and irreversible. It is incomprehensible because its terms cannot be comprehended under a single concept. Were the relation of the terms based on need, they could be put together in a totality. Hunger and food, for example, can be brought together in the

27

concept of a sentient organic being that must eat to live. Here, however, the formal characteristic of the desired is "to be other"; its alterity "makes up its content." Thus, the desire and the desired "cannot be totalized" since the very content of the desired is that of escaping such totalization (*TI*, 35). For the same reason, the relation between the desiring person ("the same") and the desired ("the other") is not a reversible relation. Rather, "the same goes unto the other differently than the other unto the same." As Levinas explains this, "the reversibility of the relation . . . would couple them the one to the other; they would complete one another in a system visible from the outside. The intended transcendence would thus be reabsorbed into the unity of the system, [thereby] destroying the radical alterity of the other" (*TI*, 35–36). Levinas's insight is that there is no outside perspective available here. If there were, both the same and the other would "be reunited under one gaze, and the absolute distance that separates them would be filled in" (that is, overcome by the grasp of them together). Here, however, "the radical separation between the same and the other means precisely that it is impossible to place oneself outside of the correlation between the same and the other so as to record the correspondence or non-correspondence of this going with this return" (*TI*, 36). The point follows since there is no way to take up both sides of the relation. The alterity of the other is such that I cannot begin from its side. Were the relation reversible, one could look at it from both sides. I could start with the other just as well as starting with "the same" (the I), but this would mean having the other within one's grasp, comprehending it as a starting point—that is, grasping it as an "I" just like myself. The very content of the other, however, denies this possibility.

The "Same"

Given this, we have to say that the relation has only one available starting point—the "I." Levinas calls this starting point "the same." This is because the "I" or ego exists in the flow of its experiences as identifying itself as one and the same experiencer. The ego, then, "is the primal identity, the primordial work of identification." Not that it remains absolutely the same, but rather "it is identical in its very alterations. It represents them to itself and thinks them" (*TI*, 36). Even when it faces itself and "harkens to itself thinking," it overcomes the implicit subject-object split and "merges with itself" (ibid.). The most immediate referent to this position is Husserl's doctrine that the "I" or ego maintains its identity over time through its self-identification.[3] It also harks back to Descartes's assertion that it is one and the same "mind" or ego that engages in all the different acts of thinking, perceiving, willing, remembering, hoping, and so on.[4] A further reference is to Kant's assertion that "the I think must accompany all our representations," that is, that all consciousness points back to an I as the central reference of its representations.[5]

Levinas extends this tradition by emphasizing that the work of the I's self-identification involves the world. The world is not really other than the I. In fact, the I identifies itself by existing in the world "at home" with itself. "It finds in the world a place and a home" (*TI*, 37). In the world, "dwelling is the very mode of maintaining oneself" (ibid.). Thus, I identify myself as the person who has built and dwells in this house, who has carved out this career for himself, and so on. This does not mean that the world doesn't resist my efforts, that I don't have to struggle. It is, in fact, in overcoming this resistance that I make the world my home, that I fashion my concrete presence in the world. The world, here, is like the air that resists the bird's wings in flight and thus allows the bird to fly by pushing against the air. In Levinas's words, "I am at home with myself in the world because it offers itself to me or resists possession" (*TI*, 38). In neither case do I get out of the same. In both cases, "the identification of the same is . . . the concreteness of egotism." In a veiled critique of Heidegger, he adds, "The reversion of the alterity of the world to self-identification must be taken seriously; the moments of this identification—the body, the home, labor, possession, economy . . . are the articulations of this structure [of the same]" (ibid.). None of these factors are explicitly taken account of in Heidegger's existential analytic of the structures of Dasein. To the point that Dasein does not work, own things, or have a home, he lacks concreteness. To remedy this, Levinas will emphasize these in his own analytic.

The Otherness of the Other

If the I or the "same" is the starting point for metaphysical desire, its object is the other person. According to Levinas, "The other person is absolutely other" (*TI*, 39).[6] The use of "absolutely" does not imply that the other person is "totally" other—that is, indistinguishable from innumerable unknown others. The point is that the other maintains his excess. It is "absolutely" impossible to comprehend someone totally. One way to put this is in terms of Kant's distinction between inner and outer sense, that is, between the reflective acts by which the mind turns inward and outer, sensuous perception. As Kant observes, to grasp temporal relations, I cannot rely on outer perception. I cannot see directly the past when I regard the world; neither can I sensuously intuit the future. Outer perception, which grasps only what is now, limits me to spatial relations. To apprehend temporal relations, those involving the past and the future, I must turn inward and consult my memories and anticipations.[7] Now, to apprehend directly the other in himself is to apprehend his present perceptions, his memories and anticipations. It is to immediately grasp the contents of his consciousness. Such a grasp, however, is not given to me by my sensuous, outer perception of the Other. Moreover, were I to have such inner access to him, his consciousness would merge with my own. My inner sense would include both his contents and my own. As a result, he would not be other, but part of myself. Granting this, the very intention to the *other* person as he is in himself cannot, by definition, be fulfilled. A direct grasp is inconsistent with his alterity. Thus, as I mentioned in the last chapter, the intention directed to the other person intends its own surpassing. I intend the Other as other than me insofar as my intention directs itself towards a fulfillment that will exceed its content. Such content is necessarily formed from my memories, perceptions, and anticipations. But these, by definition, cannot coincide with those of the Other.

Another way to grasp Levinas's position is in terms of the Other's behavior. As I noted above, his behavior has an excessive quality. It exceeds in some measure what I predict on the basis of my own experience. My experience leads me to interpret a given situation in a given way and I act accordingly. Action that is not congruent with mine points, then, to a different interpretation, which indicates a different experience—that is, a different set of anticipations, perceptions, and memories. It does so because, on a basic level, interpretation involves anticipation. If, for example, I interpret the shadows that I see under a bush to be a cat hiding there, I anticipate that as I move forward to get a closer look, I shall get a better view of the features that are now obscure. I thus interpret accordingly the experiences I have in moving closer. My anticipations, of course, grow out of my past experience. I project forward this experience in interpreting what I encounter. Now, neither the memories nor anticipations of the Other are available to me. Thus, neither his interpretations nor the actions based on these can be grasped in terms of their origin. There is, then, an irreducible margin of unpredictability in the Other's behavior. In fact, were I able to completely predict his behavior, he would not be other. Such prediction could only be based on an access to his inner sense, which I do not and cannot have. Thus, the Other necessarily escapes my control. As Levinas puts this, "The 'stranger' also means the free one. Over him I have no power. He escapes my grasp by an essential dimension, even if I have him at my disposal. He is not wholly in my site"

(*TI*, 39). This holds even if I imprison the Other and control his every movement. This limitation of his behavior to what I can predict still does not reduce him to a thing. In an essential dimension—the dimension of his interpretation based on his memories and anticipations—he still remains beyond my grasp.

Yet another, complementary way of understanding the Other's alterity is in terms of the future. The "authentic future" is what does not repeat totally the present. It has an element of the open, the new. As such, it exceeds my interpretations, plans, and so on. I cannot entirely predict it. What I face is not an unpredictability of the natural world, which could, ideally, be overcome with the increase of my knowledge of its processes and, hence, a refinement of my interpretation of what they will result in. Its basis is what, by definition, exceeds this. This is the Other and his interpretation. His action on this basis occasions what I could not foresee on the basis of my interpretation. As Levinas expresses this, given that the "authentic future . . . is what is not grasped," we have to say that "the other is the future."[8] There is, we may note, a certain paradox here. On the one hand, we have to say that the objective world is the world that is there for all of us. This is the world that science appeals to in laying down its necessary laws. Yet the same world, by definition, is filled with Others. By virtue of such Others, however, this intersubjective, "objective" world is never entirely predictable. We cannot entirely anticipate what our Others will say and do.

All these ways of expressing the alterity of the Other point to the irreversibility of the relation between myself and the Other. Only one side of this relation is directly available to me. I must start from myself; and, in intending the Other, I must go beyond myself and my knowledge. Here, as Levinas says, "the relation is effected by one of the terms as the very movement of transcendence, as the *traversing* of this distance" (*TI*, 39–40). Such a traversal is not a question of knowledge, a knowledge that might somehow embrace both terms of the relation. It is a movement beyond this, one where I suspend *my* interpretation and wait for the Other to manifest his understanding of our situation.

Conversation and Ethics

The relation to the Other, Levinas writes, "is primordially enacted as conversation." In this conversation, the same—that is, the I—"leaves itself" to go out to the Other. The concrete situation of the encounter is that of a face-to-face, one where intimacy does not overcome distance. In

Levinas's words, "A relation whose terms do not form a totality can . . . be produced within the general economy of being only as proceeding from the I to the other, *as a face-to-face*, [produced] as delineating a distance in depth—[the distance] of conversation, of goodness, of desire" (*TI*, 39). Thus, talking *with* someone is different than talking *at* them or talking *about* them. In genuine conversation, we do not desire that they simply mirror our sentiments. Our "metaphysical" desire is that they tell us something new, something that hasn't come to mind. Thus, *the face of the Other is a speaking face.*[9] It is not simply totally Other, as some critics have suggested, the way that a bat's face is other.[10] The bat does not speak, but a person does. In speaking with her, I intend her as exceeding my intentions, which are based on what has already been said. I expect she will add something new to the conversation. Once again, my intention intends its own surpassing. In doing so, I suspend my own interpretation to hear her interpretation. I wait for her to "speak her mind." I then respond. But this response calls forth a further response from her as the conversation continues, a response that transcends what has already been said. This transcendence is the breakup of the totality of the "said." Levinas thus writes, "Conversation . . . maintains the distance between me and the other, the radical separation asserted in transcendence which prevents the reconstitution of the totality." This does not mean that in speaking I renounce my egotism. It does, however, mean that "conversation consists in recognizing in the other a right over this egotism." It thus involves the need of "justifying oneself" (*TI*, 40). Thus, in conversation, I admit the right of the Other to "call me into question." I see myself as called to respond to this question.

With this, we have Levinas's definition of ethics. "A calling into question of the same . . . is brought about by the other. We name this calling into question of my spontaneity by the presence of the other 'ethics'" (*TI*, 43). The identification of ethics with the limitation of my spontaneity points to the fact that ethics involves self-limitation. The ethical person does not do all that his free spontaneity suggests—in particular, he does not do all that he has power to do with regard to the Other. To do so would be to treat the person as a thing, as a mere means to his ends. Ethics, in other words, reveals itself in the imbalance of power. A society, for example, shows its ethical aspect in its treatment of the most vulnerable, those least able to resist its action. Nothing limits society's treatment of this class except itself. Its motive for doing so is not the power of this class, but rather the ethical calling into question of its spontaneity.

For Kant, this self-limitation is a matter of reason. Asking myself, for example, if it is proper to lie to get out of a difficulty, I reason out what would happen if everyone did this. I then see that lying would be impossible since no one would believe what people said. The universal standpoint thus confronts my particular one and imposes a limit on it. The same result holds when I universalize the notion of my subjectivity. As a subject I am an end in itself: I am not a means towards an end, but rather the end (the that-for-the sake-of-which) I use things as means. Universalizing this, I realize that everyone else also regards himself as an end and I must treat them as such. I, therefore, reason out that I cannot will for the Other what the Other would not will for himself. For example, given that the Other would not will to be lied to—that is, choose this as his end, I cannot lie to him.[11] As this example indicates, for Kant, the ethical relation is completely reversible. It involves my ability to comprehend both myself and the Other in a concept—namely, that of the subject as an end in itself. The transcendence that lifts the subject outside of himself is provided by reason, that is, by our ability to universalize our proposed courses of action and, hence, strip them of any particular limiting circumstances. For Levinas, by contrast, the ethical relation is irreversible. The transcendence it demands is provided by the Other. It begins with the acknowledgment of the otherness of this Other. What interrupts my spontaneity is the Other's "calling into question of my spontaneity." The result of such calling into question is my need to justify myself, my need to respond to the differing interpretation the Other puts on our situation.

Ethics and Ontology

What prevents the philosophical acknowledgment of such alterity is, in Levinas's eyes, nothing less than Western philosophical thought. Here, he returns to the initial claims he made in the "Preface" about war and philosophy. "War," he wrote, "does not manifest exteriority and the other as other" (*TI*, 20). Neither does philosophy. In his words, "The visage [or aspect] of being that shows itself in war is fixed in the concept of totality that dominates Western philosophy" (*TI*, 21). This is because the ideal of such philosophy is that of gaining a total knowledge, one that, like war, leaves nothing out. Regarded in this light, philosophy becomes ontology, understood as the attempt to grasp being qua being, that is, being in its totality. This can only be done by searching for the *sense* of beings, that is, by knowing them through concepts in their "generality." As Levinas puts this: "For the things the work of ontology consists in apprehending the individual (which alone exists) not in its individuality but in its generality (of which alone there is science). The relation with the other is here accomplished through a third term [the concept] that I find in myself"

(*TI*, 44). The difficulty is that this method, when applied to a person, fails to grasp the person as an individual. In apprehending the person through the generality of a concept, it mirrors on the intellectual level the process of war: it *conceals* the ethical relation, whose focus is on the individual. In Levinas's terms, it reduces this relation to the realm of the "same." It attempts to express it in terms of the "generality" that "I find in myself."

From Socrates to Heidegger, this attempt has characterized the West. In Levinas's reading of the tradition, "Western philosophy has most often been an ontology: a reduction of the other to the same by the interposition of a middle and neutral term that ensures the comprehension of being. This primacy of the same was Socrates' teaching: to receive nothing of the Other but what is in me" (*TI*, 43). His reference is to Plato's doctrine of recollection, where to know is to recall what is already within one. For Levinas, the "ideal of Socratic truth" implied by this is clear. It "rests on the essential self-sufficiency of the same, its identification in ipseity, its egoism. Philosophy is an egology" (*TI*, 44). What links egotism, egology, and the reduction of the Other to the same is, as Levinas elsewhere writes, "the correlation between knowledge and being." The correlation "indicates both a difference [between the two] and a difference that is overcome in the true. Here the known is understood and so appropriated by knowledge." It is thereby "freed from its otherness." As a result, "being as the other of thought . . . becomes . . . knowledge."[12] It becomes the known as it is grasped in the circle of the same which is composed of our concepts.[13] According to Levinas, "modernity" completes this appropriation insofar as it attempts to move from "the identification and appropriation of being *by* knowledge toward the identification of being *and* knowledge."[14] Knowledge is knowledge by an ego. The study of being thus becomes the study of the ego's acquisition of knowledge; it becomes a doctrine of the ego, an "egology." The foremost exemplar of this view is, for Levinas, Heidegger himself. His question in *Being and Time* is not the that of Being (*Sein*), but rather the question of the *meaning* of being (*SZ*, 1). He thus makes Being "inseparable from the comprehension of Being." In doing so, he embraces the same ideal as Socrates. For Heidegger, "Being is already an appeal to subjectivity" (*TI*, 45). As with Socrates, "philosophy is egology." It becomes a study of the senses (and the behaviors that, for Heidegger, underlie such senses) that the ego imposes in its attempts to gain a total comprehension.[15]

Embedded in this view is a particular conception of freedom. Levinas introduces it by writing:

> The relation with Being that is enacted as ontology consists in neutralizing the existent in order to comprehend or grasp it. It is hence not

a relation with the other as such but the reduction of the other to the same. Such is the definition of freedom: to maintain oneself against the other, despite every relation with the other, to ensure the autarchy of an I. (*TI*, 45–46)

Here, the freedom that ontology "promotes" is that of "not allowing itself to be alienated by the other" (*TI*, 42). Implicit here is not just the identification of freedom with autonomy. There is also the equation of autonomy with sovereignty, that is, with power (and rule) over others. The unspoken argument here is that this equation is implicit in any attempt to realize autonomy (or "autarky"). To spell this out, we can say that given our inherently social nature, we need Others to survive. Our autonomy thus depends on them. To maintain itself, it thus demands that we possess sovereignty or rule over them. Thus, freedom implies sovereignty since without it, the autonomy it presupposes cannot be realized. If we grant this, then ontology has a political import. In Levinas's words, "'I think' comes down to 'I can'—to an appropriation of what is, to an exploitation of reality. Ontology as first philosophy is a philosophy of power. It issues in the State and in the non-violence of the totality, without securing itself against the violence from which this non-violence lives, and which appears in the tyranny of the State" (*TI*, 46). The link between this "I think" and the "I can" that issues in tyranny is the suppression of the Other. Freedom, itself, is thought in terms of such suppression. Heidegger's ontology, as exemplifying this line of thought, is equally open to tyranny. Rather than involving any paradigm shift in its raising the question of Being, "Heidegger's ontology, which subordinates the relationship with the Other to the relation with Being in general, remains under obedience to the anonymous, and leads inevitably to another power, to imperialist domination, to tyranny" (ibid., 46–47). What such ontology conceals is what ontology from the beginning has always covered up. This is ethical relation. As long as we make ontology our "first philosophy," the relation to the unique individual that allows him to interrupt us, to call into question our spontaneity or freedom *has no field for its disclosure*. The loss of such, however, is the state of tyranny and war.

To avoid this state, we have to overturn the relation between ethics (understood as "metaphysics") and ontology. We must assert: "Metaphysics precedes ontology" (*TI*, 42). This involves rejecting the equation of freedom, autonomy, and sovereignty. The argument linking the three premises ignores the social relation. It acknowledges our dependence on Others, but does not see this dependence as our natural ontological condition. Instead, it takes it as something to overcome in the "natural" expression of our freedom. Thus, in equating autonomy and freedom, it both asserts and denies our dependence on Others. Doing so, it thinks our *independence* (or autonomy) in terms of the *dependence* of Others, that is, in terms of our power over them. A similar forgetting occurs in the very project of ontology. The role of Others in this project is invoked and forgotten. According to Levinas, "every question we could raise concerning the meaning of [an object's] Being" involves Others in their excess and exteriority. It implies a "relationship with a being infinitely distant, that is, overflowing its idea" (*TI*, 47). The reference here is not to some deity, but to another person.[16] If I want to inquire about the Being of some object, that is, consider it beyond my private subjective apprehensions, I must consult Others. I need their *alternative* perspectives. Only in this way can I get to what is objectively there, that is, there not just for me but for Others as well. If such Others did not overflow their idea, that is, offer me more than my idea of them, they could not play this role. My relation to another person is thus not to a being, whose Being I might inquire about. It is to an interlocutor. In Levinas's words, "One does not question oneself concerning him; one questions him." To forget this is to make ontology impossible. As Levinas continues, "If ontology—the comprehension, the embracing of Being—is impossible, . . . it is because the comprehension of Being in general cannot dominate the relationship with the Other. The latter relationship commands the first. I cannot disentangle myself from society with the Other, even when I consider the Being of the existent he is" (ibid.). The reason for this is that the question of such Being would not even arise without the other person. The horizon in which it would make sense would be lacking. Given this, we have to say, "this relationship with the Other as interlocutor . . . precedes all ontology; it is the ultimate relation in Being. Ontology presupposes metaphysics" (*TI*, 48).

Transcendence

In the final section of part A, Levinas attempts to clarify the notion of transcendence implied by infinity. This is a transcendence that maintains exteriority. Such transcendence, when applied to God, transforms the traditional understanding of his infinity. According to Levinas, "The distance between me and God, radical and necessary, is produced in being itself. Philosophical transcendence thereby differs from the transcendence of religions . . . from the transcendence that is already (or still) participation, submergence in the being toward which it goes" (*TI*, 48). The position he is countering attempts to think of God's transcendence in terms of a conception of infinity that leaves no room for alterity. It takes the infinite as the totally unlimited and, hence, by implication, as absolutely everything. The infinite's transcendence of the finite can thus be thought only as inclusion. The finite is conceived either as a part of the infinite—literally "participating" in it—or as submerged in its totality. In this view, the ultimate religious goal of the individual is merging with God, becoming one with the divine substance.

The "philosophical transcendence" Levinas opposes to this is drawn from Descartes's *Meditations*. In the third of these, Descartes attempts to prove that something else exists beside himself and his "ideas." He believes that he can do so if he can show that at least one of his ideas has an external source—that is, it is an idea that he could not have produced. He finds this in his idea of God, which is that of an "infinite substance."[17] As finite, he could never have generated this idea. The reality it represents exceeds him. The presence of this idea in him is, thus, the first evidence he has that he is not alone, that there is another existent aside from himself.[18] For Levinas, "Descartes's first evidence, revealing the I and God in turn without merging them . . . characterizes the very meaning of separation." Since it is founded in the distinction between the finite and infinite, such separation is "non-contingent, non-provisional. The distance between me and God, radical and necessary, is produced in being itself" (*TI*, 48).

What Levinas is doing here is taking Descartes's proof for the existence of God and reinterpreting it in terms of our experience of the Other. For him, it is from Others that we have the evidence that Descartes sought. Given their excessive quality—that is, the fact that they show themselves as Other than ourselves by exceeding the intentions we have of them—we cannot have produced the "ideas" we have of them. Their source must, in Descartes's terms, be external to us. This, for Levinas, is insight that underpins Descartes's proof. In Levinas's words, "The relation of the same with the other . . . is in fact fixed in the situation described by Descartes in which the 'I think' maintains (with the infinite it can nowise contain and from which it is separated) a relation called [the] 'idea of infinity'" (*TI*, 48). This idea does not have a definite content: "to think the infinite, the transcendent, . . . is . . . not to think an object." Rather "the transcendence of the Infinite with respect to the I, which is separated from it and which thinks it, measures (so to speak) its very infinitude. The distance that separates ideatum and idea here constitutes the content of the ideatum itself" (ibid.). What we think, when we think the ideatum (the reality) of the infinite, is simply its *exceeding* what we think of it; we think its being more than the idea we have of it. This excess is its exteriority. Its infinity is its manifesting such exteriority. In Levinas's words, "The transcendent is the sole ideatum of which there can be only an idea in us; it is infinitely removed from idea, that is, exterior, because it is infinite" (ibid.).[19]

Given its exceeding, what is our actual, practical relation to the infinite? Levinas writes, the effect of "the infinite in the finite, the more in the less" is "Desire" on the part of the finite. This is "not a Desire that the possession of the Desirable slakes." The effect, rather, is a "Desire perfectly disinterested—goodness" (*TI*, 50). Experiencing it, I desire the good of the Other. I desire to become good by exercising goodness. Thus, my desire turns "into generosity, incapable of approaching the other with empty hands" (ibid.). What we have here is a relation to the transcendent, who is understood as the Other person *and as God*. The mediating point is the face of the Other who appeals to my generosity. As Levinas says in *Ethics and Infinity*, "The face signifies the Infinite" (*EI*, 105). It does because the appeal of the face is "insatiable." Its infinity manifests itself in always demanding more, that is, in imposing a non-finite, unending responsibility on me. I bear witness to the infinite in attempting to meet this. My actions, which never can be sufficient, manifest it. In Levinas's words, "one only testifies to the infinite, to God, about which no presence or actuality is capable of testifying" (*EI*, 108) by an action that is never enough and knows itself as never enough.[20]

The relation to God thus maintains exteriority. The desire directed to God is not bent on union; neither the subject nor the object of desire absorbs the Other. As Levinas explains, "in order that the Desire beyond being, or [the desire for] transcendence, might not be an absorption . . . , the Desirable, or God must remain separated in the Desire; as desirable—near yet different, Holy." "This," he adds, "can only be if the Desirable commands me to what is the nondesirable, to the undesirable *par excellence*; to the Other."[21] This undesirable is the person in need, the Other who, in his poverty and privation, lacks everything I might desire. To direct me towards this Other is to make me see the face of God in this person. It is to insist that I see this person's face as signifying the infinite. According to Levinas, the Desirable or God "is Good in this very precise, eminent sense: He does not fill me with goods, but compels me to goodness, which is better than to receive goods."[22] There is no coercion in this compulsion; its only power is that of the appeal of the destitute. Answering the appeal, acting to relieve the Other's destitution, I become good. Becoming good, I manifest God. The manifestation is of God's infinity insofar as I can never sufficiently accomplish it. I do, however, testify to it. In Levinas's words, "It is through this testimony, whose truth is not the truth of representation or perception, that the revelation of the Infinite occurs" (*EI*, 107). Not that someone sees God when he sees me, but my actions do testify to him. "It is through this testimony that the very glory of the Infinite glorifies itself. The term 'glory' does not belong to the language of contemplation" (ibid.). Its referent is not visual. It does not point to any beatific vision, with its union of the seer and the seen. Its field of presence is the ethical. We experience such testimony in the actions of certain individuals like Raoul Wallenberg or Mother Teresa. Their actions exceed what we would normally expect of human goodness, this, even though they themselves felt that they could never do enough. In such cases, as Levinas writes, "The glory of the Infinite reveals itself through what it is capable of doing in the witness" (*EI*, 109).

These, of course, are exceptional cases. Witnessing is not limited to them. The generosity it manifests can occur in conversation. Conversation is a face-to-face affair. In it, my "avidity" can turn into "generosity." Levinas, in fact, defines the face in these terms. He writes: "This relationship established over the things henceforth possibly common, that is, susceptible of being said, is the relationship of conversation. The way in which the other presents himself, exceeding the idea of the other in me, we here name face" (*TI*, 50). The exceeding is that of the saying over the said. Because it speaks, "the face of the Other at each moment destroys and overflows the plastic image it leaves me . . . It does not manifest itself by these qualities, but καθ'αὐτό [*kath'auto*—according to itself] expresses itself" (*TI*, 50–51). Here, "to approach the Other in conversation is to welcome his expression, in which at each instant he overflows the idea a thought would carry away from [the expression]." This overflowing is his adding to the expression, that is, to the said. It is his excessive presence, his exceeding the presence that he has just presented by adding to it. Thus, to "approach the Other in conversation" is also "to receive from the Other beyond the capacity of the I, which means exactly: to have the idea of infinity." To be taught involves just such reception from the Other of what one cannot get on one's own. As Levinas continues: "But this also means: to be taught . . . inasmuch as it is welcomed, this conversation is a teaching. Teaching . . . comes from the exterior and brings me more than I contain" (*TI*, 50). It is in this context that Levinas claims: "The relation with the Other, or Conversation, is . . . an ethical relation" (ibid.). It is ethical insofar as the Other, in teaching us, calls us into question. To be taught, we have to wait upon the Other, on what she has to say, that is, on her interpretation that may not be our own. The "infinity" or excess of this interpretation over our own "puts the spontaneous freedom within us into question. It commands and judges it and brings it to its truth" (ibid.).

What we confront here is "a notion of meaning . . . independent of my initiative and my power" (*TI*, 51). I have to wait. In the first instance, meaning is not a result of my *Sinngebung*—my act of giving meaning, my interpretation. It depends on the Other. In an implicit criticism of Heidegger, Levinas writes that this "signifies the philosophical priority of the existent over Being." For Heidegger, the question of Being is that of its sense. This sense varies historically, each age being marked by a specific understanding of Being that becomes concrete in a specific standard for the real and a corresponding area of relations (*Bezugsbereich*) or place of disclosure set up in accordance with this standard.[23] If, for example, our standard for the real is mathematically quantifiable nature, the area of relations will be given by the modern scientific laboratory with its various instruments. If, as in ancient Rome, the real is the political and the judicial, then the forum and the law courts with their procedures of interrogation and debate will serve as the privileged places of disclosure. They will constitute our way into the "openness of Being." For Levinas, however, "To say that the existent is disclosed only on the openness of Being is to say that we are never directly with the existent as such" (*TI*, 52). This is because the existent's presence is mediated by the standard of disclosure. Levinas's point becomes clear when we try to use the standards of either physics, or biology, or psychology to disclose an individual. In each case, only those aspects of the individual appear that correspond to the particular standards adopted. In no case is the existent allowed to put these standards into question.

Levinas's alternative to this is to place the existent before the standard. It is to respect it in its individuality, that is, to break up the totality that threatens to absorb it—be this the temporal totality of the historical "epochs of Being" with their different standards or the a-temporal totality of absorption in the divine. What he is after, he says, is "a relationship with the Other that does not result in a divine or human totality, [a relation] that is not a totalization of history but the idea of infinity" (*TI*, 52).[24] Transcendence is not to be thought of in terms of "the privileged moments of liturgical mystical elevation, or in dying." Neither is it to be conceived in terms of the end of history, when the truth of its events is finally revealed. Rather, as Levinas writes, "I find in the Other a point that is absolute with regard to history—not by amalgamating with the Other, but in speaking with him . . . When man truly approaches the Other he is uprooted from history" (ibid.).[25]

4

Separation and Discourse

Totality and Infinity, I, B

The Temporality of Selfhood

Levinas in this section is intent on defining "the separation of the same with regard to the other" (*TI*, 53). He begins by remarking that our relations with the Other are marked by a moral asymmetry. In his words, "what I permit myself to demand of myself is not comparable with what I have the right to demand of the Other." He adds, "This moral experience, so commonplace, indicates a metaphysical asymmetry." Phenomenologically, its basis is "the radical impossibility of seeing oneself from the outside" as one can see others and, hence, "of speaking in the same sense of oneself and of the others." The impossibility of applying the same principles to both implies the "impossibility of [the] totalization" that would include both. Equally, it implies "on the plane of social experience, the impossibility of forgetting the intersubjective experience that leads to that social experience" of putting different demands on oneself and Others (ibid.). What I cannot forget is the fact that my self-experience is radically other than my experience of others. Such self-experience constitutes the sphere of the "same." But the same's separation with regard to the Other is at the basis of the infinity and transcendence that mark my intersubjective experience.

To understand this infinity and transcendence, we must, then, give an account of the same in its separation from the Other. Given the "metaphysical asymmetry" of its relation to the Other, the self that is transcended in intersubjective experience cannot be simply the correlate of the transcendent Other. In Levinas's words, "it must not only be the logical rejoinder of that transcendence; the separation of the I with regard to the other must result from a positive movement" (*TI*, 53). The demand here is to conceive it apart from the Other, not just as its correlate. As such, it involves Levinas's fundamental project, which is that of positioning plurality before unity. This requires that we not take individual selves as falling under a common concept. If we do, then they "are one through this concept . . . their multiplicity forms a whole" (*TI*, 59). Similarly, if we say that they differ by some specific difference, "this attribute nowise opposes the unity latent in their multiplicity. This unity will be actualized in the knowing of an impersonal reason, which integrates the particularities of the individuals in becoming their idea or in totalizing them by history" (ibid.). To combat this, we have to grasp what Levinas calls the "psychism" of the self in its radical individuality, an individuality that makes it a member of a "radical multiplicity, distinct from numerical multiplicity" (*TI*, 220).

We can set the stage for Levinas's account of our "psychism" by recalling Heidegger's description of Dasein. For Heidegger, its structures are those of temporality. Its fundamental mode is that of the future since Dasein is always ahead of himself. Ahead of what he presently is, he is there with the possibilities that he projects forward as goals to be accomplished. If he is "inauthentic," then such possibilities are not really his own. They are the hackneyed ones of "*das Man*." They spring from the everyday sort of unexamined opinions that are gleaned from the newspapers, the radio, TV, the gossip on the street, and so on. If Dasein understands his possibilities in these terms, then in projecting them forward, he is actually only daydreaming. He is sleepwalking through life. For these possibilities to be realizable, they must spring from his actual historical situation; they must be possibilities rooted in his time and place. For Heidegger, Dasein's "resoluteness" involves his recognizing this and, hence, his accepting the truth of his situation. This situation, which he did not choose, individualizes him when he roots himself in it. Its "truth" does not just signify the disclosure—the unhiddenness—of his "thrown situation." It also points to a second, etymological sense of truth as αληθήα (*aletheia*). The root, ληθή (*lethei*), signifies "forgetting, forgetfulness, and oblivion." The privative α points to the necessity of *not* forgetting the historical situation that makes one's possibilities real. The resolute person becomes an individual in regarding his situation as it actually is. The future he actualizes is authentically his since it is rooted in the real possibilities his situation offers. As was mentioned in the first chapter, this dependence on the past does not mean that the past determines the future. Rather, the future that we envisage in our projects determines how we take the past. In Heidegger's words, "Dasein 'is' its past in the manner of *its* being, which roughly speaking, occurs from its future. . . . Its own past . . . is always in advance of it" since the future provides the perspective from which we view this past (*SZ*, 20).

Levinas's account mirrors yet differs from Heidegger's in crucial ways. Like Heidegger, he sees our being ahead of ourselves as the essential moment of our self-separation. Speaking of our being as a cogito (as an "I think"), he writes: "this being is not yet—which does not make it the same as nothingness, but maintains it at a distance from itself." This distance is between the self that I presently am and the self that I project forward in my projects. Levinas agrees with Heidegger that this projecting forward affects how I view my past. It makes me take it as material for my projects. What I project, as a not yet, is in Levinas's terminology an "After" or an "Effect." Here, "the *After* or the *Effect* conditions the *Before* or the *Cause*" (*TI*, 54). It does so because we view the *Before* in terms of the not-yet, that is, in terms of the "Effect" we want to accomplish. Levinas also agrees with Heidegger that we are rooted in the past, in a situation, which Levinas calls the "site." Where he differs with Heidegger is in his emphasizing how our being ahead of ourselves *frees us from the "site" of the past*. According to Levinas, we transcend this site by virtue of the interpretation we give to it. In his words, "Likewise, by virtue of the psychism [or thought], the being that is in a site remains free with regard to that site; posited in a site in which it maintains itself, [the self] is that which comes thereto from elsewhere"—this "elsewhere" being its future as determined by its projects (ibid.).

This emphasis on transcendence transforms Heidegger's view of authentic Dasein as integrated into his situation, as resolutely accepting "the past of its 'generation.'" According to Levinas, "In reality it is so integrated only once it is dead. Life permits it an as-for-me, a leave of absence [from the situation], a postponement [of its determination], which is precisely its interiority" (*TI*, 55). Such interiority involves the "existent's being set up and having its own destiny to itself." Here, "interiority institutes an order . . . where everything is pending, where what is no longer possible historically remains always possible" (ibid.). For Heidegger, what is no longer possible historically is *impossible*. To accomplish a future, we must choose possibilities that are capable of realization. These are given by our historical situation. Being "resolute" is simply accepting our "thrownness" in a given, historical world. For Levinas, however, the I has an interiority in its ability to separate itself from its situation. This ability shows itself in memory. Memory makes the past available to me as material for my future. Its presence is determined by my not yet. In other words, I remember what is useful for my projects. Thus, rather than recording the dead weight of the past that historically determines me, memory gives me the material for my projective freeing myself from the past. In Levinas's words, "By memory, I ground myself after the event, retroactively . . . By memory I assume [the past] and put [it] back into question. Memory, after the event, assumes the passivity of the past and masters it. Memory as an inversion of historical time is the essence of interiority." It inverts it, since the future, rather than the past, is determinative of the self (*TI*, 56).

Why is not the future just the projection forward of the possibilities given by the past? When Heidegger asserts, "Pastness originates in a certain way from the future," he also stresses the fact that the future is the standpoint from which we interpret the past. This, however, does not give Dasein the power to alter the possibilities the past makes available to it, that is, to escape "the past of its 'generation.'" For Levinas, however, the notion of such an inescapable past is simply another variation of "totalization." What it ignores is the fact of the plurality of selves, each with their own memories and corresponding anticipations. This can be put in terms of his assertion, "The Other is the future." With his different past and corresponding interpretation, the Other introduces a transcendent element into the future that we share. For this to occur, the Other's interiority must, of course, be different than mine. It must not be given by a common, determining historical situation. Levinas's focus is, thus, on the fact that we all have our private histories springing from our individual, embodied perspectives. The memory that accesses this presents each of us with what is uniquely our own as an essentially private interiority. Our unique futures are projected forward from these different bases.[1] The result is our radical separation. In Levinas's words, "This separation is radical only if each being has its own time, that is, its *interiority*, if each time is not absorbed into the universal time" (*TI*, 57). This implies that "psychic life . . . does not exhibit itself in history; the discontinuity of the inner life interrupts historical time." In fact, the reality of history has to be interpreted not just in terms of the givenness of common determining situations. One also has to view it "from interior intentions, from the secrecy that interrupts the continuity of historical time." This is because "only on the basis of this secrecy is the pluralism of society possible." In fact, "the inner life is the unique way for the real to exist as a plurality" (*TI*, 58). It is, in other words, on the basis of this inner life that humans form a "radical multiplicity, distinct from numerical multiplicity."

The ultimate basis of this multiplicity is the unique embodiment that through sensation shapes our interiority. This will become a theme of later chapters. For the present, it is sufficient for us to be clear about Levinas's purpose. He wants to contest Heidegger's historical determinism by establishing the unique interiority of Dasein. In a certain sense, Heidegger's Dasein has no interiority. It exists realizing its projects and is disclosed as such. This means that its ontological status is that of being-in-the-world. Each Dasein has its reality as a person who has accomplished or is engaged in accomplishing projects involving the world. As being-in-the-world, each is essentially outside of himself *in the world*. Ontologically, each already involves transcendence. As such, Dasein has no need of Others to transcend himself. Levinas, with his emphasis on the metaphysical relation of transcendence (the transcendence brought on by the Other) must argue against this position. He has to establish interiority as the site from which transcendence occurs.

One clue to his intent is given by his defining the resulting separation of selves as "atheism." He writes: "One can call atheism this separation so complete that the separated being maintains itself in existence all by itself without participating in the Being from which it is separated . . . one lives outside of God, at home with oneself; one is an I, an egotism. The soul, the dimension of the psychic, being an accomplishment of separation, is naturally atheist" (*TI*, 58). To call this separation atheism points, on the one hand, to the association of God with the Other. As we shall see, there is a certain sense in which the I, in its interiority, has no need of the Other to be. On the other hand, it points to the fact that biblical creation is not an emanation from the divine; it is not the production of a level of the divine being. It is the creation of a separate being. In Levinas's words, "The great force of the idea of creation such as it was contributed by monotheism is that . . . the separated and created being is thereby not simply issued forth from the father, but is absolutely other than him" (*TI*, 63). Only on this basis, according to Levinas, is a relation to a *transcendent* God possible.

Truth

How does the notion of truth fit in with the themes of exteriority and separation? Levinas asserts, "Without separation, there would not have been truth; there would have been only being." Truth, insofar as it makes a claim about something, implies a distinction between the claim and its referent. The claim risks being proved wrong by the situation referred to. For Levinas, this possibility of error means that "truth . . . in the risk of ignorance, illusion and error, does not undo 'distance,' does not result in the union of the knower and the known, does not issue in totality" (*TI*, 60). It does not result in these since in asserting a truth, the subject has to go outside of himself. He cannot make the truth. Insofar as the truth of what he asserts is in the hands of what he speaks of, there is the "risk of ignorance, illusion and error."

To understand this position, we must, once again, draw a contrast with Heidegger. According to Heidegger, truth is manifestation. It signifies "disclosedness, uncoveredness" (*SZ*, 261). Such disclosedness occurs through Dasein's disclosive behavior, that is, through his practical activities as he uses things to gain his ends. Such activities are driven by his needs. When Heidegger asserts that Dasein is the being for whom being is an issue,[2] he means that Dasein cannot take such being for granted. He needs the things of the world to accomplish his projects and maintain his being-in-the-world. Thus, in his "circumspective concern" (*umsichtige Besorgnis*), he is constantly regarding such things in terms of his projects. Such concern reveals them by disclosing their "what is it for" (*Wozu*), their usefulness for these projects. It is against such a view that Levinas remarks, "[The knowing subject's] aspiration to truth is not the hollowed-out outline of the being it lacks." It is not an aspiration based on need. On the contrary, "to seek and to obtain truth is to be in a relation . . . because in a certain sense one lacks nothing" (*TI*, 61). For Heidegger, such truth, understood as manifestation, is a consequence of our being-in-the-world as need. We are rooted in the world by our concerns. Levinas, however, asserts: "Despite the theses of the philosophy of existence, this contact [of the knower and the known] is not nourished from a prior enrootedness in being" (*TI*, 60). It is not a function of our need for the things the world offers.

The danger Levinas sees in this view is the fact that truth, so defined, would be part of a totality. If the knower and the known were united by need, both would form part of a system. The truth that expressed this union could not contradict it. It would be included within it. This is why he also asserts that truth is not a function of participation. Thus, while we might assert that "the quest for truth unfolds in the apparition of the forms," this does not obviate the fact that "the distinctive characteristic of the forms is precisely their epiphany at a distance" (*TI*, 60). His point is that the relation of the knower to the known is not a participation in the known. It is not a relation where somehow, as Plato thought, I become the known—where, for example, I become eternal in knowing eternal things.[3] Were we to accept this, then the eternal forms would express a totality, one that included the knower and the known.

Levinas's alternative to such positions is that the search for truth is one where "in a certain sense one lacks nothing." He clarifies this by saying that such seeking is a "going towards the other in Desire." This means, he adds, "the idea of exteriority which guides the quest for truth is possible only as the idea of infinity." Both infinity and exteriority are needed since what I seek exceeds me and, as such, is external to me. My relation to truth is, in this description, rather like Descartes's relation to the idea of God. This idea, Descartes argues in the third of his *Meditations*, is not, in its infinity, something that he could have generated. It is also not conceived as the negative of the finite.[4] It thus points to a reality external to him. Similarly, for Levinas: "The idea of infinity does not proceed from the I, nor from a need of the I gauging exactly its own voids;

here the movement proceeds from what is thought and not from the thinker" (*TI*, 61). Levinas's point is that if my relation to truth were based on my needs, on my "own voids," then it is relative to me. My needs determine my projects, which determine what I disclose and how I disclose it. They thus determine truth as disclosure in the Heideggerian sense. In Levinas's words, "To recognize truth to be disclosure is to refer it to the horizon of him who discloses. . . . The disclosed being is relative to us and not καθ'αὐτό [*kath'auto*—according to itself]." The result, then, is that "we disclose only according to a project" and not according to the object in itself (*TI*, 64). Given this, the disclosed world cannot resist us. It is not "objective" [*Gegen-ständlich*] in the etymological sense of being able to "stand against" the truth claims we make. What we have, here, is, thus, truth without "the risk of ignorance, illusion and error." To conceive of truth as involving risk, we have to distinguish "between desire and need: desire is an aspiration that the desirable animates; it originates from its 'object'; it is revelation—whereas need is a void of the soul; it proceeds from the subject." This is why, as motivated by desire, "truth is sought in the other, but by him who lacks nothing" (*TI*, 62).

Levinas's critique of Heidegger's pragmatic account of truth has a parallel in the ancient view that pragmatic action lacks the disinterestedness of theory (*theoria* in the Greek sense). As Aristotle argues in the beginning of the *Metaphysics*, the theoretical sciences are different from the practical ones because they "are not directed either to our pleasure or to our necessities. They appeared first in those places where men had leisure. Hence it was in Egypt that the mathematical arts were first developed" (918b22–25). Such sciences, he writes, begin not in need but in wonder. They are "cherished on their own and in the interests of knowledge" (982a16). One engages in them "in the pursuit of knowledge and not for some useful end" (982b20). He adds, the other sciences are more "necessary," but not more "excellent" than these (983a11). There is a profound difference between being necessary and being excellent. The former refers to us, the latter refers to the object.[5] Thus, for Aristotle, these more excellent (theoretical) sciences begin when one is free from need, when one has leisure. Their motivation is not some advantage but simply the truth. Such truth is correlated to our freedom to inquire—a freedom that implies freedom from need.

Levinas's corresponding claim is that this relation to the truth, which is not based on need, is motivated by our "metaphysical desire." Rather than using the other, I let it put me into question. Instead of thrusting my interpretation on it, I let it guide me. The attitude of such desire in this regard is, perhaps, best captured by Simone Weil in her essay, "Reflections on the Right Use of School Studies with a View to the

Love of God." As she observes, "All wrong translations, all absurdities in geometry problems, all clumsiness of style, and all faulty connection of ideas in compositions and essays, all such things are due to the fact that thought has seized upon some idea too hastily, and being thus prematurely blocked, is not open to the truth." The counter to this is to attend to the object. Such "attention consists of suspending our thought, leaving it detached, empty, and ready to be penetrated by the object."[6] It involves "waiting" on the object, keeping our own knowledge ready, but in the background, and responding to what the object shows us. The moral aspect of this occurs, she remarks, in our relations to other people. What is crucial is to know how to look at them. In her words, "This way of looking is first of all attentive. The soul empties itself of all its own contents in order to receive into itself the being it is looking at, just as he is, in all his truth."[7]

For Levinas, this moral side of the search for the truth is apparent in conversation. He writes, "Truth arises where a being separated from the other is not engulfed in him, but speaks to him. . . . Separation and interiority, truth and language constitute the categories of the idea of infinity or metaphysics" (*TI*, 62). The broad claim here is that truth is like a conversation, one where one lets the Other have his say. Thus, in posing a question to nature, one is open to a response that may, in fact, put one's categories into question. This involves a self-transcendence that has a different orientation than need. The relation is theoretical rather than practical, which means that to engage in it, one has to surpass oneself and one's needs. The "desire" that animates this self-surpassing, Levinas claims, "marks a sort of inversion." It becomes "preoccupied with another being." There occurs "a fundamental inversion not of some one of the functions of being, a function turned from its goal, but an inversion of its very exercise of being, which suspends its spontaneous movement of existing" (*TI*, 63). The inversion is in Dasein or human existence. The human existent no longer directs itself towards the affirmation of its own being; it is intent on the affirmation of the other. This, according to Levinas, is what makes us capable of truth.

Discourse and Truth

According to Levinas, to know the object absolutely, we "would have to maintain the other being καθ' αὐτό [*kath'auto*—according to itself]" (*TI*, 65). He adds that this "manifestation of the καθ' αὐτό [*kath'auto*] . . . does not consist in its being disclosed, its being exposed to the gaze that would take it as a theme for interpretation" (ibid.). Apart from its relativity, the difficulty with such disclosure, Levinas writes, is that it results in a "world that has lost its principle, anarchical, a world of phenomena." Such an anarchical world "does not answer to the quest for the true." It only "suffices for enjoyment" (ibid.). The criticism, here, is that pragmatic disclosure only reveals things' utility, for example, their suitability for our enjoyment, rather than their "truth." To attain such truth, something more is needed: a principle that would give order to the anarchy of projects and resulting disclosures. This, according to Levinas, is the Other. What the Other does is allow us to call into question such disclosures. Faced with the Other's different interpretation, we are called to justify the interpretations that guide our own disclosures.

The point can be put in terms of the question of reason. This is the question why something is the way it is rather than some other way. It asks for a reason or a "ground" for things being the way they are. To raise such a question, one needs, of course, an idea that they could be different. No one asks, for example, why a triangle has three sides. To raise the question of something's ground is to conceive of it, not as necessary, but as possible. It is to range it along a series of alternatives and ask why this particular alternative has been realized and not some other. For Heidegger, this question is raised when we confront our freedom, when we see that the projects that disclose the world are a matter of our choices.[8] Freedom, he writes, is, thus, the "origin itself of 'ground.' Freedom is the ground of ground [*Grund des Grundes*]," that is, the origin of reason.[9] It is the principle that orders the phenomenal world. For Levinas, by contrast, what prompts the question of the ground is the Other. The Other's having different projects raises the question of our own modes of disclosure. The call is for us to explain ourselves, to give reasons for our choices.

There are, here, two very different approaches to freedom. For Heidegger, there is nothing behind our freedom; it stands behind ("grounds") the search for grounds or reasons. "As *this* ground," he writes, "freedom is the abyss [*Ab-grund*] of Dasein."[10] For Levinas, by contrast, the Other that stands behind the search for grounds *calls this very freedom into question.* He interrupts one's spontaneity, one's self-affirmation. Doing so, he first opens up the question of the validity of disclosure—both his and our own. This is the question of the relation of disclosure to the καθ'αὐτό (*kath'auto*) of the object. With this comes the conception of "a being telling itself to us independently of every position we would have taken in its regard, expressing itself." Such "telling" "is present as directing this very manifestation—present before the manifestation, which only manifests it" (*TI*, 65). The result is a kind of moral relation to the object. We let it take the lead. We assume it is present before the manifestation, directing the manifestation. We disclose it not according to our needs, but rather according to the way it shows itself to our attentive regard. Such regard, as I cited Simon Weil, refrains from initially imposing on it our conceptions—in particular, those drawn from our practical needs.

How is the Other able to ground the theoretical attitude? How does he open us up to it? Levinas's answer is that he does so through his face. The face of the Other presents us with a continuous example of the distinction of the καθ᾽αὐτό (*kath'auto*) and disclosure. The face appears as a physical "form." It is present as the face of someone. But it "is a living presence; it is expression. The life of expression consists in undoing the form in which the existent" appears. What this means is that "the face speaks. The manifestation of the face is already discourse. He who manifests himself . . . at each instant undoes the form he presents" by adding to it. The Other, in speaking "comes . . . to his own assistance" (*TI*, 66). He directs the manifestation καθ᾽αὐτό (*kath'auto*)—that is, *according to himself* as he corrects our interpretations. What we experience in discussing with him is not disclosure, but "revelation." As Levinas remarks, "to disclose, on the basis of a subjective horizon, is already to miss the noumenon" or the thing in itself according to itself (*TI*, 67). Disclosure, as based on a subjective horizon that is set by my needs, only gives me the phenomenon, not the noumenon. To gain the "pure experience" of the in-itself of the Other, I have to speak to him. As Levinas describes this:

> The interlocutor alone is the term of pure experience, where the Other enters in relation while remaining καθ᾽αὐτό [*kath'auto*], where he expresses himself without our having to disclose him from a "point of view," in a borrowed light. . . . What presents itself as independent of every subjective movement is the interlocutor, whose *way* consists in starting from himself, foreign and yet presenting himself to me. (*TI*, 67)

There are two claims here. The first is that the phenomenon-noumenon distinction announces itself in the encounter with the Other. For Levinas, this is also the distinction between disclosure and the καθ᾽αὐτό (*kath'auto*). The Other, as other, is distinct from his appearance as set by our interpretative horizon.[11] This is why he has to correct it. The second, which is implicit, is that the contrast between the appearance and the καθ᾽αὐτό (*kath'auto*) is what is required for the theoretical attitude, that is, for the classic conception of truth. The possibility of a truth claim being falsified is not contained in Heidegger's account of disclosure. It is, however, manifest whenever someone corrects our claims regarding himself.

The exteriority that makes truth possible is also behind signification. The distinction between a truth claim and what it refers to is the exteriority that signification bridges without denying. The claim signifies a fact, but is not the latter. My words signify both my mental intentions (what I have in mind) and also what I am speaking about. But my words are not these realities, nor do they, themselves, intuitively present them. As Levinas puts this, "to signify is not to give. Signification is not . . . analogous to the sensation presented to the eye. It is preeminently the presence of exteriority." It is "an original relation with exterior being" (*TI*, 66). This relation is, in the first instance, to the speaking Other. Without Others, there would be no one to speak to. What makes language necessary is their exteriority. What they have in mind is not directly (intuitively) present to us. It can only be signified.

For Levinas, the very presence of the Other's exteriority is through his words. It is the way he gives meaning to his presence as other. As Levinas writes, "To give meaning to one's presence is an event irreducible to evidence. It does not enter into an intuition; it is a presence more direct than visible manifestation, and at the same time a remote presence—that of the other" (*TI*, 66). The temporality of such presence is the reverse of that of the normal flow of time, where it comes to the present from the future and then moves on to the past. Here, "his speech consists in 'coming to the assistance' of his word—in being *present*. This present is not made of instants mysteriously immobilized in duration, but of an *incessant* recapture of instants that flow by"—this "by a presence that comes to their assistance, that answers for them" (*TI*, 69). In correcting himself, the Other *redoes the past*. Doing so, it is as if "the presence of him who speaks inverted the inevitable movement that bears the spoken word to the past state." This means that the "present" of the speaking Other "is produced in this struggle against the past" (ibid.). What we have here is a temporality of conversation, which is radically different than that of the normal flow of time. It is also distinct from that of Heidegger's disclosure, where time flows from the future through the past, which is interpreted in the light of the future, and from thence to the present. The temporality of conversation is that of correction, of the Other overcoming his dissimulating appearances by going backwards, as it were, to amend them. This, according to Levinas, is also the temporality of truth, where the object takes the lead and corrects the misapprehensions we have been laboring under.

There are all kinds of discourse; and, as Levinas remarks, "not every discourse is a relation with exteriority" (*TI*, 70). Rhetoric, for example, attempts to subvert this relation. Levinas puts this in terms of the Other's being "the free one" (*TI*, 75). His freedom manifests itself in his having his own interpretation of a given situation. Acting on this, he is not under our sway. According to Levinas, "the specific nature of rhetoric (of propaganda, flattery, diplomacy, etc.) consists in corrupting this freedom" (*TI*, 70). Rhetoric attempts to manipulate the Other. It does not just solicit his ascent. It tries to control it through emotional appeals. Doing so, it corrupts the truth. Its use undercuts the Other's calling into question the claims about some subject and, thus, the possibility of this subject appearing καθ'αὐτο. Now, according to Levinas, to "let [the Other] be, the relation of discourse is required." In the back and forth of conversation, where claims are interrogated and tested, this Other is "let be" in the sense of being allowed to show himself καθ'αὐτό (*kath'auto*). He adds, "*We call justice this face-to-face approach, in conversation*" (*TI*, 71). As Levinas also expresses this: "Truth is thus bound up with the social relation, which is justice. Justice . . . is access to the Other outside of rhetoric, which is ruse, emprise, and exploitation" (*TI*, 72). This definition does not just situate rhetoric as "violence, that is, injustice" (*TI*, 70); it also implies "justice coincides with the overcoming of rhetoric" (*TI*, 72).

Why should we call the free, nonmanipulative relation with the Other "justice"? What is its connection with the classical conception of this term? One answer can be found in Aristotle's conception of justice. Over and beyond the general sense of justice as the "lawful," there is, he notes a special sense of justice as fairness. In this sense, we "regard as unjust . . . a man who is unfair and takes more than his share."[12] The unjust person is, thus, greedy. He suffers from πλεονεξία (*pleonexia*)—the desire of always wanting more, of never having enough. The virtue he offends against is justice understood as a fair exchange. This is an exchange freely agreed on, without manipulation or constraint, by the parties involved.[13] The unjust person manages to get more out of this exchange than the others. He comes out ahead either by manipulating or coercing others. Now, as Aristotle notes, money is the general medium of economic exchange, since it equalizes in terms of price objects that are not naturally equal: for example, the products of a farmer and a shoemaker. One can through money express how many bushels of wheat equal a pair of shoes. Injustice most commonly involves such economic exchanges. Given that the state was founded to make up for our individual deficiencies, each member supplying through his work what the others need but cannot produce for themselves, justice as economic fairness is absolutely fundamental for its functioning. Injustice, when sufficiently widespread, particularly when it affects the relations of classes of citizens, undermines the original reason for the state's being called into being. At this point it becomes a form of "violence." Rhetoric, particularly, political rhetoric, when it corrupts the processes of fair exchange, can, in this sense, be considered as injustice and violence. Although Levinas was, perhaps, not thinking in these terms, it is clear that in this context, "justice" as fairness "coincides with the overcoming of rhetoric."

Discourse and Ethics

Apart from rhetoric, with its coercive emotional appeals, there is, of course, another way of establishing agreement. Reason, taken as "universal thought," has traditionally been considered as the philosophical alternative to rhetoric. Rational agreement, in this view, arises from following the universal rules of such thought. In fact, it is only by following such rules that speakers are rational. As Levinas expresses this position: "Separated thinkers become rational only in the measure that their personal and particular acts of thinking figure as moments of this unique and universal [rational] discourse" (*TI*, 72). The difficulty that Levinas has with this view is that it leaves no room for exteriority and, hence, the communication that bridges external beings. In his words, "A universal thought dispenses with communication. A reason cannot be other for a reason. How can a reason be an I or an other, since its very being consists in renouncing singularity?" (ibid.). Examples of the "universal thought" Levinas is criticizing are not hard to find. Their basis is the fact that to the point that my assertion is true, it coincides with all other assertions having the same content. As a speaker of the truth, therefore, I am not distinct from others expressing the same truth. The same holds with regard to my use of the correct forms of inference. Using them to link my truths and generate new truths, I am no different from anyone else who does this. Such thoughts lead to the notion of a totality of true statements and correct inferences connecting them. Leibniz thought of actually generating this coherent totality through a rational calculus—the distant ancestor of the modern predicative calculus. The "thought" that would actually think this totality would not be plural, but rather something like Aristotle's self-thinking thought. Each separate thinker participates in (or is but a moment of) this thought when he has a true insight. As Levinas notes, "to make of the thinker a moment of thought is to limit the revealing function of language to its coherence . . . In this coherence, the unique I of the thinker volatizes" (*TI*, 72–73).

In Levinas's mind, this view gets things backwards. It places the coherence of agreement prior to those who engage in it. It thus forgets that "language presupposes interlocutors, a plurality." As such, it "implies transcendence, radical separation, the strangeness of the interlocutors, the revelation of the other to me" (*TI*, 72–73). In a word, the initial setting of language is that of the "exteriority" of the speakers. This means that it "is spoken where community between the terms of the relationship is wanting, where the common plane is wanting or is yet to be constituted" (*TI*, 73). We speak, in fact, to constitute this plane.

Levinas mentions three elements of this constitution. First there is the freedom of the interlocutors. Each is free to have his own interpretation of their situation; each is free to assent to or deny the interpretations of his others. This is the freedom that is inherent in their exteriority. In Levinas's words, "Free beings alone can be strangers to one another. Their freedom, which is 'common' to them, is precisely what separates them" (*TI*, 73–74). The second element is the individuality of what they speak about. This individuality is, first of all, a matter of individualizing circumstances that are distinct from a thing's form. In Levinas's words, "The perception of individual things is the fact that they are *not* entirely absorbed in their form; they then stand out in themselves." He adds, "breaking through, rending their forms, [they] are not resolved into the relations that link them up to the totality." Beyond this, individuality involves "the surplus of [a thing's] being over its finality. It is its absurdity, its uselessness" (*TI*, 74). The thing, καθ'αὐτό, is not reducible to its usefulness—the *Wozu* of Heidegger's pragmatic disclosure. There is a surplus beyond this. The third of the elements is the ethical relation of the participants. It takes account of their individuality insofar as the focus of this relation is the face of the Other. This face is neither a form nor a use value. It exists *outside the totality* and, as such, is *destitute* with regard to what the totality contains. This implies, "existence καθ'αὐτό (*kath'auto*) is, in the world, destitution" with regard to the world. Thus, "the nakedness of the face is destitution" (*TI*, 75). Since it has nothing to give, our relation to it must be one of generosity. As Levinas writes, "To recognize the Other is to give" (ibid.).

This generosity is at the heart of the constitution of the "common plane." Engaging in it, I obligate myself to give a response to the Other, to open myself up to his perspective. The result is the reverse of the position that Levinas is criticizing. This position begins with conceptualization, with general terms that are already constituted. It sees the relations of the speakers in these terms. For Levinas, however, "the generality of the Object is correlative with the generosity of the subject going to the Other, beyond the egotist and solitary enjoyment" (*TI*, 76). Constituting such generality, I move in my discourse from the world that is there just for me to the world that is there for both myself and the Other—the world that has common or general objects. I do so by going outside of myself to the Other when I speak to him. Thus, in Levinas's view, language is universal because it is the medium by which I speak to the Other, generously offering my views and accepting his. In his words,

> Language is universal because it is the very passage from the individual
> to the general, because it offers things which are mine to the Other.
> To speak is to make the world common, to create commonplaces. Lan-
> guage does not refer to the generality of concepts, but lays the foun-
> dations for a possession in common. . . . The world in discourse is . . .
> what I give: the communicable, the thought, the universal. (*TI*, 76)

All this, however, presupposes that I take up an ethical relation to the
Other. This does not just mean giving him my views, but also seeing what
his perspective is so as to learn from him. The sharing that results has
a number of levels. Pragmatically, it involves teaching and learning one
another's projects and, hence, sharing the senses they disclose. Theoreti-
cally, it entails investigating together in a spirit of free inquiry. There is no
question of an "economy" here. Each side, in the face-to-face encounter,
is motivated by generosity towards the Other. The point is "to establish,
by gift, community and universality" (*TI*, 76). As Levinas also puts this:
"The relationship between the same and the other, my welcoming of
the other, is the ultimate fact and in it the things figure . . . as what one
gives" (*TI*, 77).

To call this the ultimate fact is to return to Levinas's basic claim that
ethics is "first philosophy." This means that ethics precedes epistemology
as it precedes all other sciences. It is prior to the science of knowing as it
is prior to metaphysics or the science of being. I do not, in Levinas's view,
relate to the Other through a timeless realm of ideas or stable meanings
coherently ordered. Such meanings are rather generated through our
common actions and investigations. If we accept this view, there is a difference between technocratic and democratic governments. One must
proceed through the give and take of democratic discourse to establish
the common world of the community and the actions that are appropriate to it. To leave this to technocrats, under the assumption that they
have an unmediated access to the way things are, is to freeze the common
world into a coherent, stable totality. In Levinas's eyes, it is to rob it of the
newness that alterity alone can give.

Exteriority and God

I mentioned above that Levinas's book proceeds in a kind of spiraling
motion, returning in different contexts to the same themes to further
clarify them. In the section, "The Metaphysical and the Human," he re-
visits the theme of the transcendence of God in the context of the "face-
to-face." For Levinas, the face-to-face is the ultimate relation. It, rather

than the Greek notion of participation, designates our relation with the divine. This means that "the comprehension of God taken as a participation in his sacred life, an allegedly direct comprehension, is impossible because participation is a denial of the divine and because nothing is more direct than the face-to-face" (*TI*, 78). Participation is a denial of the divine because the divine is the Other. As exterior, it cannot be "shared" or participated in. God, as the Other, appears in the face. He appears as the call to generosity, which signifies that the primary relation to God is ethical rather than ontological. As Levinas writes, "To posit the transcendent as stranger and poor one is to prohibit the metaphysical relation with God from being accomplished in the ignorance of men and things. The dimension of the divine opens forth from the human face. . . . It is here that the Transcendent, infinitely other, solicits us and appeals to us." This means that "God rises to his supreme and ultimate presence as the correlative to the justice rendered unto men" (*TI*, 78). This presence, as I earlier noted, is that of our witnessing to him through our generosity. In calling on us to be generous to "the stranger and the poor one" and to render "justice" to them, God calls on us to manifest his goodness.

Levinas's position on the sacred recalls Kant's celebrated remark that "thoughts without [sensible] content are empty, intuitions without concepts are blind."[14] Kant means that we need concepts to order and classify our sensible, intuitive experience, but such concepts, as ways of understanding this experience, have no content (are "empty") without such experience. Levinas, in warning against conceptions of the divine that are "accomplished in the ignorance of men and things," has a similar point in mind. He writes: "Metaphysics is enacted in ethical relations. Without the signification they draw from ethics, theological concepts remain empty and formal frameworks. The role Kant attributed to sensible experience in the domain of the understanding belongs in metaphysics to interhuman relations" (*TI*, 79). Given that God manifests himself in our ethical relations, to talk about God without reference to this is to have empty theological concepts. Interhuman relations give such concepts their content. For theology, then, "ethics is the spiritual optics . . . 'vision' here coincides with this work of justice" (*TI*, 78). This work is the "sensible experience" that we need in order that our concepts of the divine not be empty. In the absence of human relations that witness to him, the concept of God reduces itself to the strictly formal notions of "first cause," "summum bonum," "pure being," and so on of classical metaphysics.

We can put Levinas's position in terms of the conception of metaphysics as onto-theology—that is, as the study both of the *onta* (the *beings* in their being) and of the *theos* (the *God* that is the highest being). Both themes appear in Aristotle's *Metaphysics*, Leibniz's *Discourse on Metaphysics*, and other classical metaphysical texts. The connection between the two is quite natural: a study of being leads to the question of the highest being, understood as the entity that possesses in an exemplary way that which makes beings be. Now, if we say that "metaphysics is enacted in ethical relations," then we have to say that the study of both being-as-being and the highest being must draw their content from such relations. Take, for example, the metaphysical assertion that objective being, the correlate of objective truth, is that which is accessible to everyone. Ethics would assert that there is a social relation that must be presupposed before we can arrive at this concept. People must be willing to compare their experiences and frankly discuss them. The priority of ethics demands that the concept of the objectively true cannot deny or ignore the social relation. To do so would involve us in a performative contradiction—we would be denying or leaving out of account what we implicitly presuppose. This point holds for all conceptualization, whether it involves metaphysics, theology, the social or the physical sciences. It cannot deny or undercut the ethics it presupposes. For Levinas, "The establishing of this primacy of the ethical . . . is one of the objectives of the present work" (*TI*, 79).

With regard to religion, the primacy of the ethical means that "everything that cannot be reduced to an interhuman relation represents not the superior form but the forever primitive form of religion" (*TI*, 79). When we strip out these interhuman relations we return to "the violence of the sacred," the "numinous," "the infinite" that would "burn the eyes that are lifted unto [God]" (*TI*, 77). In Levinas's view, the philosophical expression of this primitive form of religion is the Greek conception of "participation" in the divine, which involves our somehow coming to share the divine essence through prayers or practices. Levinas writes in this regard:

> Transcendence is to be distinguished from a union with the transcendent by participation. The metaphysical relation, the idea of infinity, connects with the noumenon which is not a numen. This noumenon is to be distinguished from the concept of God possessed by the believers of positive religions ill disengaged from the bonds of participation, who accept being immersed in a myth unbeknown to themselves. (*TI*, 77)

The criticism here is that the positive religions that accept the doctrine of participation are, unbeknown to themselves, still ensnared in the myths of more primitive forms of religion.

What distinguishes biblically based religion from such forms is its doctrine of creation from nothing. This doctrine assumes God's existence before creation and, hence, his independence of the created world. Given this, neither his action nor his nature can be defined in its terms. He is not part of its "economy" understood as the system of exchange that characterizes its elements. Such exteriority contrasts sharply with the pagan view that conceived the gods as part of the world—as "immortal mortals" in Heraclitus's phrase. Since they were part of the world, images could be made of the pagan gods. They could be conceived and visualized in worldly terms. The biblical prohibition about making images of God is meant not just to distinguish him from his pagan alternatives, but to emphasize his alterity. For Levinas, it is this very alterity that stands in the way of using participation to express our relations to the divine. We are not and cannot be a part of the divine substance. We can only "witness" to it. For the Greeks and the "positive religions" that adopt their philosophical framework, the possibility of participation is guaranteed by the fact that the gods and the world form a totality. We can participate in the "highest being" insofar as it is simply an exemplary case of the being that we all share. The "myths" that make God part of the world are, thus, implied in the notion of participation in the divine.

One of the consequences of the above is that Levinas's stress on "interhuman relations" as providing the experiential content for our theological concepts does not reduce his conception of the divine to an anthropomorphism. These interhuman relations are to "the widow and the orphan," the "stranger and the poor one." As I cited Levinas, "It is here that the Transcendent, infinitely other, solicits us and appeals to us." The identification of "the Transcendent" with the stranger and the poor comes from their lack of worldly goods and power. They have nothing to offer the earthly economy. The stranger cannot call on its social relations, the poor have no ability to participate in the exchange of its material goods. They have nothing to exchange. As exterior to this economy, they manifest the transcendent God in his transcendence. Such a God cannot appear in the world as part of the world—and, hence, as participating in its economy—without falsifying his transcendence. His only alternative, if he is to appear in the world *as he is*, is to appear as exterior to its economy, that is, as the widow, the orphan, the poor, and the stranger. This is why Levinas associates the face with God. The reference is not to its particular features or form, but to its "nudity" and "destitution." These constitute its transcendence. In Levinas's words, "The transcendence of the face is at the same time its absence from this world into which it enters, the exiling of a being, his condition of being [the] stranger, destitute, or proletarian" (*TI*, 75). To speak of God in these terms is not to engage in anthropomorphism. It is actually a way of expressing the "relation without relation" that Levinas defines as "religion" (*TI*, 80). Anthropomorphism, in speaking of God in human terms, implicitly assumes that he is part of the world and can be defined in its terms. Levinas, in speaking of God as the stranger, the destitute person, and so on, is expressing the counter position. The relation here is to what is outside the world's economy, to what inherently transcends it.

5

Truth and Justice

Totality and Infinity, I, C

Freedom and Knowing

Modern philosophy is marked by the assumption that epistemology rather than metaphysics is the "first science." Its view is that the first question is not, "what does it mean to be?" but, rather, "what does it mean to know?" While the ancients focused on the fact that things must be in order to be known, the modern position is that we cannot grant being to what we are not certain of. Thus, prior to any discussion of what exists, we must ask what our standards are for certainty. Descartes, for example, takes it "as a general principle that everything which we conceive very clearly and very distinctly is wholly true."[1] This means that in considering the properties of a thing, "all that I clearly and distinctly recognize as characteristic of this thing does in reality characterize it."[2] His standards, then, for being are the clarity and distinctness of our perceptions. Kant also assumes the priority of epistemology when he proposes his "Copernican revolution." "Previously," he writes, "it was assumed that all our knowledge must conform to the object." It was objects that set the standards for knowing. His "revolution" is to "make trial whether we may not have more success in the tasks of metaphysics by supposing that objects must conform to our knowledge."[3] For Kant, the subjective conditions by which we know objects determine what we can rationally posit as existent. Given that epistemology studies such conditions, its study must be first. As Husserl expresses this assumption: "Naturally epistemology must not be understood as a discipline that follows metaphysics or even coincides with it, but rather as one which precedes metaphysics just as it precedes psychology and all other disciplines."[4] Even Heidegger, in his attempt to reawaken the question of Being, fails, according to Levinas, to break away from this tradition. Not only does he reduce the question of Being to that of the meaning of being, he also attempts to explicate this meaning in terms of the temporal structures of Dasein. Concretely, this means explicating it in terms of the ways in which Dasein understands its world as it makes its way within it. The fact that such understanding is pragmatic does not change the fact that such understanding determines what we take a being to be.

If we do take epistemology as preceding "all other disciplines," then its priority extends to ethics. The question of ethics becomes that of knowing what right conduct consists in. Such knowing can be conceived in terms of the Kantian "thought experiment" of asking what would happen if everyone engaged in a certain action. It can also be conceived empirically, as when we ask with Mill what action would produce the greatest amount of happiness. "Happiness" in utilitarianism is taken as a knowable (and, even, a measurable) condition; we know what is moral when we know what increases it.[5] For Levinas, the problem with such views is that if epistemology is prior to ethics, then knowing is independent of it. It must, then, set its own standards and follow them independently of the other sciences, ethics included. This implies that one can engage in research independently of any ethical standards. One could conceivably, then, become a Dr. Mengele or, indeed, any of a number of Nazi scientists who seized on the opportunity to experiment on the human subjects that the concentration camps provided. No one today believes this is permissible. We object, not because such scientists violated the epistemological standards for good research—standards involving such things as careful observation and recording of data—but because they violated our ethical standards. We believe that such standards should guide our research. For Levinas, the philosophical premise of this belief is that ethics, itself, is "first philosophy." To subordinate research to ethics is to make it precede not just metaphysics but also epistemology.

Levinas's strategy for positioning ethics as prior to epistemology is to argue that epistemology is possible only when we let the things we seek to know call us into question. What is called into question is our dealing with them as we will. It is our very freedom with regard to them. The self-restraint this imposes is, for Levinas, the essence of ethics. He begins by asserting that "the concern for intelligibility . . . signifies . . . a certain respect for objects." Such respect opposes the view that our "spontaneity" in dealing with them "is not to be put into question, that free exercise is not subject to norms, but is itself the norm." This is because "for the object to become a fact that requires a theoretical justification [that is, for epistemology as a science to get started], the spontaneity of the action that surmounts it had to be inhibited, that is, itself put into question. It is then that we move from an activity without regard for anything to a *consideration* of the fact" (*TI*, 82). In other words, it is then that we can engage in questions of how and why we know this fact. As Levinas adds, "Knowing becomes knowing of a fact only if it is at the same time critical, if it puts itself into question, goes back beyond its origin." The question of what is *beyond* the origin of knowing will concern us in a moment. First, however, we have to be clear that this origin involves the restraining of our freedom. The freedom needed for inquiry is not a pure spontaneity, but rather a freedom that "does not abandon itself to its drives, to its impulsive movements, but keeps its distances" (ibid.).

Given this, modernity's emphasis on knowing would seem to involve an equal emphasis on the limitation of our freedom. This, however, is not the case. In the modern period, "the spontaneity of freedom is not called into question" (*TI*, 83). In fact, "its limitation alone is held to be tragic and is held to be a scandal." Thus, for modernity, the problem of political theory is to ensure "by way of knowledge of the world, the most complete exercise of spontaneity by reconciling my freedom with the freedom of others" (ibid). What is needed is the *knowledge* of how to do this through the appropriate constitution and laws of a state.[6] The only thing that can call freedom into question in this context is a failure to reach our goals. But, with our emphasis on knowing, this is understood as a failure of knowing how to reach such goals. As such, it can only be recognized and corrected by knowledge. Overcoming failure for modernity thus "proceeds from knowledge of the world, is already born from a knowledge, the knowledge of failure" (ibid.).

What prevents it from going beyond knowledge to raise the issue of our freedom is, in fact, its implicit identification of knowledge and spontaneity. On a formal level this occurs with Kant's identification of knowing with synthesis and his seeing synthesis as a matter of our free spontaneity.[7] Pragmatically, it occurs with our seeing knowing as a form of pragmatic disclosure and, hence, as an exercise of our practical freedom. Freedom in this context is seen as the freedom to choose our projects and the disclosures that they entail. Failure, here, does not call into question this freedom. It is, rather, seen within the context of disclosure. Thus, for Heidegger, it is when I fail to achieve my goal that I examine my instruments for achieving it—for example, the hammer that does not work. I then disclose the hammer as it is "in itself," but only to see why it is not functioning in order to repair it. Once repaired, the hammer again reveals itself in hammering. The problem with this view is that we never proceed beyond disclosure, beyond knowledge in the pragmatic sense, to get at what it presupposes. What it presupposes is *not* the freedom that modernity understands in terms of knowing. It is rather our ability to call freedom into question.

To talk about our ability to call freedom into question seems paradoxical. Does not such ability itself presuppose freedom? Does not freedom still remain an unquestioned ground? This holds if the freedom to call freedom into question arises from ourselves, that is, if it is a function of our own ability. For Levinas, however, this ability points "beyond" the origin of knowing since it comes from the Other. I experience the Other as having alternative standards and, hence, as calling my standards (my freedom to set them as unquestionably valid) into question. This experience of the Other, Levinas writes, "is the revelation of a resistance to my powers that does not counter them as a greater force, but calls into question the naïve right of my powers, my glorious spontaneity as a living being" (*TI*, 84). With this, we have a moral basis for epistemology. This "morality begins when freedom, instead of being justified by itself, feels itself to be arbitrary" (ibid.). Feeling itself to be arbitrary, it is open to the truth. In fact, Levinas's claim is "the freedom that can be ashamed of itself founds truth" (*TI*, 83). It is what allows us to move from the practical to the theoretical or contemplative stance.

This can be expressed in terms of Levinas's reworking of Kant's "critical philosophy." He agrees with Kant that "critique or philosophy is the essence of knowing." He adds, however, that "what is proper to knowing is not its possibility of going to an object, a movement by which it is akin to other acts." Rather, "its prerogative consists in being able to put itself into question in penetrating beneath its own condition" (*TI*, 85). For Kant, the notion of critique is required to understand what we contribute to the action of knowing, this being the spontaneity of our syntheses. For Levinas, however, what is at issue is not such spontaneity but rather "penetrating beneath [knowing's] own condition" by seeing how this is given by the Other. Here, "to philosophize [critically] is to trace freedom back to what lies before it, to disclose the investiture that liberates freedom from the arbitrary." What such philosophy discovers is that "knowledge as a critique, as a tracing back to what precedes freedom, can arise only in a being that has an origin prior to its origin" (ibid.).

As I indicated, this origin that is prior to us and our abilities is the Other. In introducing us to a new perspective, the Other allows us to distance ourselves from ourselves by regarding ourselves from the Other's point of view. The self-separation that this results in means that we are not necessarily prey to our impulses, that we can pause and consider where they might lead. We become, in our ability to reflect on ourselves, a "for-itself." The freedom implied in this becomes apparent when we realize that this alternative perspective relativizes our own. It shows that our present situation as disclosed by our current projects is not necessary, but rather something that could be otherwise. Rather than necessarily determining us, it is something that, were we to adopt the perspective and projects of the Other, could be changed. With this, we have the freedom that Sartre describes when he writes:

> For man to put a particular existent out of circuit is to put himself out
> of circuit in relation to the existent. In this case he is not subject to it;
> he is out of reach; it cannot act on him, for he has retired *beyond a noth-*
> *ingness.* Descartes, following the Stoics, has given a name to this possi-
> bility, which human reality has, to secrete a nothingness which isolates
> it—it is *freedom.*[8]

For Levinas, the secretion of nothingness is essentially social. It cannot
occur without the alternatives that Others present us. Given that in presenting us with alternatives, they give us, as it were, the space for our freedom, they provide us with an "origin prior to" our "origin" as free beings.[9]
With regard to critical philosophy, this means that "if philosophy consists
in knowing critically, that is, in seeking a foundation for its freedom, in
justifying it, it begins with conscience, to which the other is present as the
Other, and where the movement of thematization is inverted" (*TI,* 86).
The inversion of thematization is where I let the Other thematize (or set
the interpretation) rather than attempting myself to thematize the situation that faces us. Here, "to welcome the Other is to put in question my
freedom" (*TI,* 85). Rather than exercising it by imposing my interpretation, I wait for the Other to provide me with hers. Welcoming it, I question my own freedom. With this, we have the moral basis of knowing.
Insofar as knowing involves self-restraint, it has a moral foundation. This
foundation involves my relation to the Other insofar as she "liberates freedom from the arbitrary," thus making it capable of free inquiry (ibid.).[10]

Consumption and Discourse

Levinas's account of the moral basis for knowing stands in sharp contrast
to Heidegger's largely pragmatic account. Heidegger, as we have seen,
discusses knowing in the context of disclosure. Disclosure occurs in terms
of our projects, where things show their meaning as their "*Wozu,*" their
"what is it for." Thus, for Heidegger I really "know" the hammer in its
being when I use it. Its very being as a hammer is disclosed as I hammer.
If the hammer breaks, then I regard it apart from the context of rela-
tionships in which it functions, seeing it as a thing with its own internal
structure. Since all human meaning involves human projects, the hammer in itself (as opposed to the hammer to be repaired) is meaningless.
It has no context of functioning in which its meaning could be disclosed.
What sets this context are our needs. It is to satisfy these that we have our
projects. Now, for Levinas, this pragmatic process destabilizes the mean-

ings it supposedly discloses. It reveals them only to conceal them. This is because, pragmatically regarded, the signification of the object, its "what it is for," ends once we reach our goal. It is concealed in the enjoyment that comes when we satisfy the need that animated our project. Thus, were we to accept this view, "the reference that signification implies [as a 'what is it for'] would terminate where the reference is made from the self to the self—in enjoyment" (*TI*, 94). The two "selves" referred to here are the self engaging in the project and the self at the goal enjoying the accomplishment of the project. When these two coincide, then we are at the goal and the reference of the object to the goal vanishes. This means, "the outcome is the point at which every signification is precisely lost" (ibid.). Thus, as long as things do have a use value, that is, as long as they serve as the means for accomplishing my project, they have a "what it is for"—a signification or meaning in Heidegger's sense of the term. In his view, Levinas writes, "beings take on or lose their signification as means according as they are situated on the way that leads to [the outcome] or away from it." The problem is that "the means themselves lose their signification in the outcome" (*TI*, 95). They no longer refer beyond themselves to a future state. Having served their purpose, they have no purpose or "what it is for."

The point of these remarks is to question the Heideggerian "priority of care over contemplation." Heidegger advocates "the enrootedness of cognition in a [pragmatic] comprehension that opens upon the 'worldhood' of the world and opens the horizon for the apparition of the object" (*TI*, 94). Levinas's question is: "Is practical significance the primordial domain of meaning?" (ibid.). Can it be such, given that its focus is consumption rather than contemplation? The difficulty, as he sees it, is that objectivity, where being is proposed to consciousness, is not a residue of finality. "The objects are not objects when they offer themselves to the hand that uses them, to the mouth and the nose, the eyes and the ears that enjoy them" (*TI*, 95). For objectivity to arise, one needs to interrupt the process of their consumption. This interruption is more than the breaking down of a tool. What one needs is "the breach of the ultimate unity of the satisfied being" (ibid.). This breach, he claims, is provided by discourse. Thus, in opposition to the view that the object "in itself" appears when it is separated from its context of relations, Levinas writes: "Objectivity is not what remains of an implement or a food when separated from the world in which its being comes into play. It is posited in a discourse, in a conversation which proposes [or posits] a world" (*TI*, 96).

To understand this, we have to remember that objectivity and intersubjectivity are correlative notions. The objective world differs from the private, subjective world by being there for more than a single person

Thus, if I doubt that something is objectively real, I ask someone else if he sees what I see. If he does not, then I assume that what I see is a subjective illusion. I have to ask: given that I cannot see out of another person's eyes, I can find out only by asking him what he is seeing. He replies through language. What he says, for example, "a book," is my only access to the object as there for us both. Without discourse, then, there is no intersubjective, no objective world. Discourse, language, is the medium of its presence. If we accept that the presence of the intersubjective world is linguistic, then we have to say with Levinas, "the objectivity of the object and its signification [as objective] come from language" (*TI*, 96). Language, of course, does not do this by itself. It requires speakers who speak of the world they experience. As Levinas writes, in our ongoing discourse, "the Other, the signifier, manifests himself in speech by speaking of the world and not of himself; he manifests himself by proposing the world, by thematizing it" (ibid.). I do the same. Together we talk about the world, which in our discourse becomes the world for both of us, the objective world with its significances.

What is crucial is that this discourse is ongoing. Because it is, "the proposition that posits and offers the world does not float in the air, but promises a response to him who receives this proposition." One doesn't just receive the proposition from the Other, one also receives "the possibility of questioning" him (*TI*, 96). Ongoing discourse is, thus, "an ever renewed promise to clarify what is obscure in the utterance" (*TI*, 97). As such, it maintains the presence of the objective world. It stands at the origin of its objectivity because it continually impinges on my viewing it simply in terms of my private projects. The restraint on my freedom that comes from the Other's correcting my perspective thus gives a space for the object to show itself as it objectively is. Here, the in-itselfness of the object does not, as in Heidegger, imply the loss of its significance. It does not involve the abstraction of the object from the context of relations that give it a meaning. Such in-itselfness is rather present in the ongoing signifying of discourse.

Levinas's opposition to Heidegger is thus clear. It is that "the signification of beings is manifested not in perspective of finality [of the 'what is it for'—the *Wozu*—of beings], but in that of language" (*TI*, 97). In his eyes, the problem with Heidegger's view is that "disclosure . . . implies the solitude of vision" (*TI*, 99). The ground of disclosure is care; the object of care is my being; I disclose in relation to it. But then what I disclose is only there for me. It is not objective. For Levinas, by contrast, "to put speech at the origin of truth is to abandon the thesis that disclosure . . . is the first work of truth" (ibid.). The first work of truth is being attentive to the Other. According to Levinas, "Attention and the explicit thought it makes possible are not a refinement of consciousness, but consciousness itself. Attention is attention to something because it is attention to someone" (ibid.). "Consciousness" is here thought of in its basic sense as "consciousness of" something. Consciousness is such because it goes out of itself to intend what is not itself. It is intentional because it attends to what transcends it.[11] The assertion that such attending presupposes attention to someone follows from the role the Other plays in our experience of transcendence. The Other, in proposing a world to me, makes me attend to it as transcendent since he presents it as there for more than me. This "more than me" is the Other in his exceeding me. Without his alterity, there would not be an objective world, a world that is there both for him and for me. It is, in fact, from the alterity of the Other that we get the distinction between appearance and reality, between the object as it appears and the object "in itself." This is because the Other who appears is not the Other in himself, not the Other in his inner thoughts and intentions. My only access to the latter is through his signifying them. Even such significations, insofar as they appear, are not what he is "in himself." In himself, he is only present in his ongoing coming to the aid of what he said, that is, in his qualifying and adding to it. This very "excess" of the saying over the said means that the object in its objectivity can never be reduced to its linguistic presence as what has been said. As intersubjectively maintained, it shares in the excessive character of the interlocutors who make it linguistically present.

For Levinas, then, it is the speaking presence of Others that breaks up what he calls the "silent world"—the world in which there are no others to call into question my ways of viewing the world. Without them, I am trapped in Cartesian doubt. I cannot know whether the world I experience might not be the product of some *malin genie* bent on deceiving me. The world produced by such a deceptive spirit is one where I cannot distinguish the true-for-me from the true-in-itself, where there is no distance, no separation between the sign and the signified. It is one where the signified does not have the objectivity—the "in-itselfness"—to call the sign into question, to assert that it signifies incorrectly. What breaks this spell is the speaking Other. His alterity is what puts an unbridgeable distance between the sign and the signified preventing their collapse into one another. The signified, as there for the Other as well as for me, can never be reduced to my signification of it. It cannot because its presence for both of us depends not just on my speaking, but also on my attending to and responding to the Other.

The back and forth of discourse does not mean that my relation to the Other is simply the reverse of his relation to me. If it were, I could start out equally from either side. But this would mean that my interpretation would not be questioned. I would already have both sides (both interpretations) at my disposal. In point of fact, "our relations are never reversible" (*TI*, 101). According to Levinas, the "reciprocity of dialogue" hides "the profound essence of language," which "resides in the irreversibility of the relation between me and the other" (ibid.). This is because "he who speaks to me . . . retains the fundamental foreignness of the Other who judges me." Judging me, "he remains beyond the system [of my interpretations], he is not on the same plane as myself." Only as such can he come to me from outside and call my interpretations into question, thus forcing me to respond by attending to the world "in itself" that is the subject of our discourse.

6

Separation and Absoluteness

Totality and Infinity, I, D

In the final part of the first section of *Totality and Infinity,* Levinas affirms that "the positions we have outlined oppose the ancient privilege of unity which is affirmed from Parmenides to Spinoza and Hegel." In this tradition, "[s]eparation and interiority were held to be incomprehensible and irrational" (*TI,* 102). Parmenides, for example, asserts this "privilege of unity" by claiming that we can only speak of being. Non-being or that which "is-not" is not a possible subject of discourse. Thus, he writes that there are two "ways of inquiry . . . the one way, that it is and cannot not-be, is the path of Persuasion, for it attends upon Truth; the other, that it is-not and needs must not-be, that I tell thee is a path altogether unthinkable. For thou couldst not know that which is-not (that is impossible) nor utter it; for the same thing can be thought as can be."[1] The injunction here is to think about the "it is," not about the "is-not." The correlation between thinkability and being means that non-being cannot be thought. The "is-not" can neither be philosophically known nor uttered. From the beginning, then, the limits of philosophical inquiry are those of being. As for being itself, it forms a totality. Since everything that exists *is,* being is one according to Parmenides. It is an undivided, knowable, speakable whole.

This view reaches its culmination in what can be called the "one substance" theory. According to it, to be a substance is to be able to exist on one's own. It is to have one's own source of being. Now, everything exists either by itself or by something else. If it exists by itself, then it has its own source of being and cannot not be. Its essence as specified by its definition includes its existence. The being is a necessary being. If it exists by another, then it is contingent; it is dependent on something else to give it being. It is not, properly speaking, a substance. Everything, except God, identified as the necessary being, is dependent. This means that its essence does not demand its existence. We can know this essence, that is, what the thing is, without knowing whether it is. This existential neutrality is what allows us, for example, to apply the definition of man both to Socrates and to ourselves regardless of the fact that Socrates has ceased to be and we continue to exist. Nothing in the definition as such demands that the individuals it defines actually exist. In other words, to specify the concept "man" is not to determine that the individuals falling under the concept actually exist. The same holds for all the finite entities that we can think of. Since they can be thought of as not actually existent, they are contingent. As capable of not being, they must be brought into being by something else. Taken as a whole, they thus point back to the necessary being, which is God. Thus, everything is dependent on God. As having their being from God, finite entities are not, properly speaking, substances, but rather part of God's being. It follows, then, that there is only *one substance*, one being capable of existing on its own, namely, God.[2] Whatever one thinks of this argument, it shows how "the ancient privilege of unity" works to collapse beings into being.

As Levinas points out, the view of the Bible stands in sharp contrast to this tradition which runs from Parmenides to Spinoza and Hegel. In the Bible's account of creation, God works by separating. He begins with a formless, empty waste and creates light. Light, which is the condition of separate things' being seen, is then separated from the dark, creating day and night. This is followed by the separation of the original watery waste by the dome of the heavens into the waters above and the waters below—that is, into the clouds from which the rain comes and the ocean below. Next the earth is separated from the ocean so that there is the division between dry land and the sea. The list of separations, which are successively pronounced "good," continues with the distinction of the lights in the sky into the sun and the moon, the distinction of living from the nonliving with the creation of vegetation, and the three-fold distinction of animals into creatures of the sea, air, and land. It ends not just with the creation of man, who is distinguished from the animals, but also with the separation of man into male and female. This preference for difference does not end with creation. It continues with the society of man. Thus, God acts to undo the fact that, as men multiplied, "the whole earth was of one language, and of one speech." As opposed to the wish of the first people to "build a city and a tower . . . lest we be scattered abroad upon the face of the whole earth," God looks with disfavor on the fact that "the people are one and they have all one language." He remarks, "Go to, let us go down, and there confound their language, that they may not understand one another's speech" (Gen. 11:3–9). Such examples could be multiplied, but their point is clear. Creation for God is a matter of separation and division. He does not maintain "the ancient privilege of unity."

For Levinas the biblical account provides a paradigm for understanding being. The paradigm is the "paradox of creation." This is "the paradox of an Infinity admitting a being outside of itself which it does not encompass." It is the paradox of an Infinity "accomplishing its very infinitude by virtue of this proximity of a separated being" (*TI*, 103). What we have here is "an infinity that does not close in upon itself . . . but withdraws . . . so as to leave a place for a separated being" (*TI*, 104). In other words, creation is not just the separation and limitation of created beings, it is also their separation from the infinite God, who creates by limiting himself. This means that "society with God is not an addition to God nor a disappearance of the interval that separates God from the creature" (*TI*, 104). My relation to God does not result in my being added to him or being absorbed by him. Rather, the biblical vision is one where the infinite shows its perfection by creating beings that are distinct from itself. In Levinas's words, "multiplicity and the limitation of the creative Infinite are compatible with the perfection of the Infinite. They articulate the meaning of this perfection" (*TI*, 104).

Behind this assertion is the distinction between desire and need. In Levinas's view, the ontology of the ancients conceived of separation as a privation because it knew of "no other separation than that evinced by *need*" (*TI*, 102). Desire, however, is "the need of him who lacks nothing, the aspiration of him who possesses his being, who possesses his being entirely" (*TI*, 103). "Here, the relation [of desire] connects not terms that complete one another and consequently are reciprocally lacking to one another, but terms that suffice to themselves" (ibid.). The relation is not one of absorption or annihilation of the alterity of the other, but rather of self-surpassing. This holds even for God in his infinity. In Levinas's words, "Infinity . . . starting with the separated being turned toward it, surpasses itself. In other words, it opens to itself the order of the Good" (ibid.). This self-surpassing is acting not for one's own sake, but for the sake of the other. It marks the move from an ontological to an ethical relation, that is, from the order of being to that of the good. God, engaged in the relation of desire, manifests his generosity. He acts for our sake. We have the same relation to God. This, as we have noted, is possible because of God's presence in the widow and the orphan. He "solicits us and appeals to us" through them. We witness or bear testimony to this presence in our acts of generosity. In this relation, God does not give us good things. He calls on us to *be good*, which, as Levinas remarks "is better."[3] This relation of desire is possible because the biblical creation from nothing "expresses a multiplicity not united into a totality." The dependence of the creature on the creator is not that of a part to a whole. Separation is not some wound in the unity of being. In Levinas's words, "the creature is an existence which indeed does depend on an other [the creator], but not as a part that is separated from it." This is because "creation ex nihilo breaks with [every totalizing] system." It "posits a being outside of every system" (*TI*, 104). As Levinas also writes, "the dependent being draws from this exceptional dependence . . . its very independence, its exteriority to the system." One has a "separation from the infinite" that is "not simply negation" (*TI*, 105).

It is possible to take the story of Abraham and Isaac as illustrating this relation, which is based on desire. Initially Abraham's relation to God appears as one of exchange, as part of an economy in which each would get from the other what he needed. God promises to cure Abraham's wife Sarah of her barrenness, thus fulfilling his need for descendants. In fact, he promises to make him the father of a "great multitude" of people inhabiting a "promised land." Doing so, God fulfills his own need to create a "chosen people" for himself. Abraham's child, Isaac, mediates this relation since it is through him that Abraham's descendents will come and God's purpose will be achieved. Thus, when God asks Abraham to sacrifice Isaac, the economic basis of their relation disappears. That Abraham continues towards Moriah, that he proceeds to the point of raising his knife, signifies that his relation is actually *with God himself*, not with any benefit that God provides him. In other words, in not acting out of need, he shows that he actually acts for God's sake. This, of course, is God's relation to Abraham. He really does not need him to accomplish his purposes. He has always acted for Abraham's sake.

God does not let Abraham actually kill Isaac. When Abraham, facing Isaac, picks up the knife, he hears the command, "Do not raise your hand against the boy or do anything to him" (Gen. 22:12). From a Levinasian perspective, it is possible to combine this command with the face of Isaac, the face that Abraham regards as he holds the knife. The face is that of the helpless victim, of a person bound and about to die. For Levinas, God's command comes from this face. "Thou shalt not kill," he writes, is "the first word of the face."[4] He writes: "It is an order. There is a commandment in the appearance of the face, as if a master spoke to me. However, at the same time, the face of the Other is destitute."[5] Rather than offering one something in terms of the economy, it pulls one out of it. For Levinas, "in the access to the face there is certainly also an access to God."[6] This implies that the relation between Abraham and Isaac is that of accessing God through the face of the victim. Abraham hears the command of God seeing Isaac's face. With this, we return to God's presence in the widow and orphan. God in such presence, as we cited Levinas, does not give us good things, does not fill our needs; rather, he calls us to be good.

It is interesting to note that Abraham, in having the same relation to God, also calls on God to be good as he pleads with him not to destroy the cities of Sodom and Gomorrah. Progressively getting God to spare these cities if he finds 50 or 45 or 40 or 30 or 20 or finally only 10 just men living there, he reminds God repeatedly, "far be it from you to do such a thing, to bring death upon the innocent as well as the guilty . . . Shall not the judge of the earth deal justly?" (Gen. 18:25). As the other of God, he can call God to account. Moses also does this when at Mount Sinai, he persuades God not to destroy the Israelites who have been worshiping the Golden Calf. God, on seeing them, cries, "leave me be that my wrath may flare against them, and I will put an end to them." But Moses restrains him, saying, "Remember Abraham, Isaac, and Israel your servants, to whom you swore by yourself and spoke to them, 'I will multiply your seed like the stars of the heaven'" (Exod. 32:10, 13). God, hearing this, gives way. What such biblical accounts indicate is that the relation with the divine is that of discourse. God creates creatures who in their separation can call not just one another to account; they can as well call God to account as Job does to God when he presses him to explain why the innocent suffer and the wicked prosper (Job 21:1–15, 24).

7

Interiority and Economy

Totality and Infinity, II, A–B, C §§1–2

Need and Embodiment

Section 2 of *Totality and Infinity* is devoted to the "analysis of the relations that are produced within the same" (*TI*, 110). These are the relations of enjoyment and egotism that the ethical relation interrupts. For beings to engage in an ethical relation they must be separate and enjoy a measure of autonomy. Only thus can the ethical desire that extends beyond need appear. For Kant, we act ethically when, rather than acting to fulfill our needs, our motive is simply to do the right thing. The Levinasian parallel to this is our acting not out of need, but out of generosity to the Other. Doing so, we are motivated by desire for the Other; we transcend our egotism by acting for his sake. Such an action is an interruption of our egotism and, as such, presupposes it. More precisely, it presupposes our "interiority," our "separation as inner life" (ibid.). Levinas's focus on this life is meant to counter Heidegger's analysis of Dasein as being-in-the-world, that is, as inherently outside of itself and, hence, as lacking any real interiority, any self-sufficient sphere of private enjoyment. Levinas's goal is to show that real transcendence comes from Dasein's relation to the Other; it comes from the Other's interruption of our interiority.

Levinas begins by asserting that he will not found the ethical (or "metaphysical") relationship "on being in the world, the *care* and *doing* characteristic of the Heideggerian *Dasein*" (*TI*, 109). Acting ethically, we act out of desire rather than need. But, for Heidegger, according to Levinas, everything is based on need. His ontology continues the tradition that knows "no other separation than that evinced by *need*." Such need "indicates a void and lack in the needy one . . . the insufficiency of the needy being precisely in that it does not entirely possess its being and consequently is not strictly speaking *separate*" (*TI*, 102). For Heidegger, this tradition appears in Dasein's insufficiency with regard to the world, an insufficiency that makes Heidegger include the world in Dasein's definition as being-in-the-world. It also appears in the fact that for things to disclose themselves as what they are, they must be correlated to our needs. They

then show themselves as means for our purposes, as tools. The result is
an all-pervasive utilitarianism that ignores their status as objects of enjoyment. For Levinas, however, "the things we live from are not tools . . . in
the Heideggerian sense of the term. Their existence is not exhausted by
the utilitarian schematism that delineates them as having the existence of
hammers, needles, or machines. They are always in a certain measure . . .
objects of enjoyment" (*TI*, 110). Food, for example, is not just a means
for living. While "hunger is a need," eating is "enjoyment" (*TI*, 111). In
fact, one is nourished by *all* the contents that fill one's life. In Levinas's
words, "nourishment, as a means of invigoration, is the transformation
of the other into the same, which is the essence of enjoyment: an energy
that is other . . . becomes in enjoyment my own energy, my strength, me"
(ibid.). The general phenomenon is that of "living from" what sustains
one. As Levinas defines it, "living from . . . is not a simple becoming conscious of what fills life. These contents are lived: they feed life." "Living"
them, one enjoys them.[1] Such "enjoyment is the ultimate consciousness
of all the contents that fill my life—it embraces them" (ibid.).

Enjoyment is here conceived as an alternative to Heidegger's concept of "care." "Care," for Heidegger, is care for our own being. On the
one hand, the concept indicates that our being is a matter of our own
choices. We have to decide what we will be. On the other, it points to
the fact that such choices are driven by our needs. For Levinas, by contrast, "Life is not the naked will to be, an ontological *Sorge* (care) for this
life. . . . Life is love of life, a relation with contents that are not my being
but more dear than my being: thinking, eating, sleeping, reading, working, warming oneself in the sun" (*TI*, 112). The contrast between the two
views can be put in terms of existence. Etymologically, "existence" comes
from two Greek words, *stence* from the word signifying "standing" and *ex*
from the word for "out."[2] For Heidegger, Dasein's "standing out" is a matter of its standing outside of itself in its being ahead of itself as it engages
in its projects. This standing out or existence precedes its essence—the
description of what it is—since the latter is the result of its projects. For
Levinas, by contrast, "Life is an existence that does not precede its essence." Its essence, as enjoyment, as happiness, is first. It is because I want
to be happy that I engage in my projects, that I go out of myself, that I
ex-sist in Heidegger's sense. As Levinas puts this: "happiness is not an ac-
cident of being, since being is risked for happiness" (ibid.).[3]

We can find an ancient parallel to Levinas's position in Aristotle's
account of happiness and its relation to life. According to Aristotle, "Life
is in itself good and pleasant. We can see that from the very fact that
everyone desires it."[4] That they desire it implies that they are aware of it.
In fact, our life or "existence is perceiving or thinking" and this includes

self-perception. Thus, "in perception, we perceive that we perceive, and in thinking we perceive that we think." All our activities are, in fact, accompanied by self-awareness. Given that life is itself pleasant, this presence to ourselves of ourselves gives us pleasure. Thus, "to perceive that we are living is something pleasant in itself."[5] The general doctrine here is that living is functioning and that pleasure is the self-presence of this functioning. Such functioning ranges from the general sense of well-being that we have when our organism is functioning well—that is, when we are healthy—to our pleasure in seeing, hearing, moving, and so on. It also includes the pleasure we have in thinking, that is, in reasoning, talking, and figuring things out. Aristotle adds that "life is desirable especially for good men, because existence [or the activity of living] is good and pleasant to them."[6] This is because the good man is defined as the person that can function well at a high level. The enjoyment that is the self-presence of this functioning increases with the level of this functioning.

Levinas reflects this view when he writes "action itself . . . enters into our happiness. We live from acts . . . What I do and what I am is at the same time that from which I live. We relate ourselves to it with a relation that is neither theoretical nor practical . . . The final relation is enjoyment, happiness" (*TI*, 113). This happiness, he emphasizes, is not a mood in the Heideggerian sense. It is not how I find myself—my *Befindlichkeit*. It is not my "bearing in being, but already the exceeding of being; being itself 'befalls' him who can seek happiness" (ibid.). In other words, happiness is not the result of the care for my being; it is what moves me to care for my being. It, rather than need, is the ultimate motive for my engaging in projects so as to acquire my being in the Heideggerian sense. Thus, echoing Aristotle's assertion that "we always choose happiness as an end itself and never for the sake of something else,"[7] that, in fact, it is the "one end for all that we do,"[8] Levinas writes, "happiness is a condition for activity" (ibid.).

This fact of happiness affects our relations to our needs and, hence, the ontology that is based on this. We are not driven by our needs. They do not put the lie to our autonomy. On the contrary, as Levinas writes, "What we live from does not enslave us; we enjoy it . . . The human being thrives on his needs; he is happy for his needs" (*TI*, 114). Their satisfaction provides him with enjoyment. Our relation to our needs is not just a sign of our dependence, it is also the way we establish our independence. As Levinas expresses this: "The paradox of 'living from something' . . . is . . . not a mastery on the one hand and a dependence on the other, but a mastery in this dependence" (ibid.). In the activity of "living from," the same "acquires its own identity by this dwelling in the 'other' (and not logically, by [a formal] opposition to the other)" (*TI*, 115). This means that we do not gain our independence by denying our needs, but rather in our ability to satisfy them. The Platonic notion that independence comes from abstention is an error similar to that which Kant indicates when he writes that "the light dove, in free flight parting the air with its wings might imagine, when it feels the resistance of the air, that its flight would still be easier in empty space."[9] The dove forgets that it only flies by pushing against the air. Similarly, according to Levinas, our dependences when converted into needs make possible our independence. Needs, he writes, "constitute a being independent of the world, a veritable subject capable of ensuring the satisfaction of its needs, which are recognized as material, that is, as admitting of satisfaction. Needs are in my power; they constitute me as the same and not as dependent on the other" (*TI,* 116). The ontological consequence of this is to reconfigure the relation between need and ontological independence. In the traditional view, need is understood as a condition of dependency pointing to the underlying unity of being. The doctrine of being from another is seen as ultimately leading to the position that there is only one being, one independent substance. Against this, need is now seen as the basis of independence.

To state the obvious, we have needs for material things because we are embodied. But this very embodiment gives us, through our bodily "I can," the means to fulfill our needs. As Levinas expresses this, "The body is the very self-possession by which the I, liberated from the world by need, succeeds in overcoming the very destitution of this liberation" (*TI,* 117). The liberation is from the dependency on the world that would reduce us to the world. We overcome the "destitution" of this, that is, the impoverishment of having our needs unfulfilled, through our bodily actions. Our uniqueness arises through this fulfillment. It is not the uniqueness that comes through a conscious choice of what we will be, but rather one that arises in our *preconceptual* bodily experience of the world. Thus, for Levinas, "the I is not unique like the Eiffel Tower or the Mona Lisa. The unicity of the I does not merely consist in being found in one sample only, but in existing without having a genus, without being the individuation of a concept" (*TI,* 117–18). It is, in fact, a uniqueness that arises by the "refusal of the concept" (*TI,* 118). This refusal of the concept is the I's "interiority." Such interiority evinces the uniqueness of enjoyment. As Levinas writes, the I "is an existence for itself . . . as the 'famished stomach that has no ears . . . is for itself . . . The self-sufficiency of enjoying measures the egotism or the ipseity of the ego" (ibid.).

Although Levinas does not mention this, it is interesting to note that the uniqueness of the ego's ipseity is a function of the privacy of the body in its organic functioning. Such privacy signifies that no one can eat for you, sleep for you, breathe for you, or perform any of a host of functions. The functioning of the body is non-substitutable, irreplaceable. While someone else can go to the bank for you, no one else can go to the bathroom for you. Indeed, the fact, which Heidegger stresses, that no one can die for another, that is, the privacy of our deaths, is traceable to the same privacy of our organic functioning. Now, the uniqueness of the I in its interiority comes from this functioning. When we bite into a fresh peach, we have an experience that is not public, not disclosable as there for everyone. The result is an interiority that "refuses the concept" since there is no plurality of public examples to draw the concept from. Without this non-conceptual interiority of the I, we cannot have a human plurality. Thus, "when the I is identified with reason . . . it loses its very ipseity . . . reason makes human society possible; but a society whose members would be only reasons would vanish as a society . . . Reason has no plural; how could numerous reasons be distinguished?" (*TI*, 119). Rather than reason, embodiment distinguishes us, which means that "for the I to be means to enjoy something" (*TI*, 120).

What is crucial is the fact of human plurality, which has now been approached from two different sides. The last part of the first section approached it from the side of God by defining creation as the ability of God to create beings separate from himself. The first part of the new section approaches the same plurality from the side of the creature by focusing on his ability to be by himself—that is, be a substance in the traditional sense—this, even though, as finite, he has needs. In both cases, what Levinas wants to do is to open a space for the ethical relationship. This is a relationship requiring plurality, requiring the distinction of the same and the Other.

Intentionality and Embodiment

Levinas begins part B with a pair of questions. He asks: "Is not enjoyment, as the way life relates to its contents, a form of intentionality in the Husserlian sense, taken very broadly, as the universal fact of human existence?" He specifies this by adding: "The thesis that every intentionality is either a representation or founded on a representation dominates the *Logische Untersuchungen* [the *Logical Investigations*] and returns as an obsession in all of Husserl's subsequent work. What is the relation between the theoretical intentionality of the objectifying act, as Husserl calls it, and enjoyment?" (*TI*, 122). To grasp Levinas's response to these questions, we first have to briefly examine Husserl's account of intentionality and the objectifying act.

Intentionality is the property consciousness has of being "of" some object; the intentional relation is between it and its object. As Husserl stresses in the *Logical Investigations*, the relation is not a causal one since it is not between two realities.[10] On the most basic level, it is a relation between consciousness and the object's perceptual sense. Husserl's account of constitution, which, in the *Logical Investigations*, is an account of the objectifying act, is meant to show how consciousness gets this perceptual sense. The function of the objectifying act is interpretative. In perception, it interprets the multiple sensations that consciousness receives as sensations of some one thing—namely, of an appearing object that is there for consciousness. For Husserl, then, it is "in the animating interpretation of sensation that what we call the appearing of the object consists."[11] As Husserl stresses, we do not *per se* "see" our sensations. What we see are the *objects of which* we have sensations. For example, we see one and the same box however it may be turned. The perceived object remains the same, although the actually experienced contents shift with each turn of the box. In Husserl's words, "Very different contents are thus experienced, but in spite of this the same object is perceived. Thus, to give a general principle, the experienced content is not itself the perceived object."[12] The difference between the two arises through the objectifying act. It interprets the sensations comprising the experienced content. The result of its interpretation is the perception of the object. As Husserl sums up this position:

> It belongs to perception that something appears within it, but *interpretation* makes up what we term appearance—be it correct or not, anticipatory or overdrawn. The *house* appears to me through no other way but that I interpret in a certain fashion actually experienced contents of sensation. I hear a *barrel organ*—the sensed tones I interpret as *barrel organ tones*. Even so, I perceive via interpretation what mentally appears in me, the *penetrating joy, the heartfelt sorrow*, etc. They are termed "appearances" or, better, appearing contents precisely for the reason that they are contents of perceptive interpretation.[13]

Another example of what he is pointing to is the experience we have when we regard optical illusions. The same sensuous data or experienced content is present, but the perceptual object shifts as we regard the picture. Is the arrow we see pointing towards us or away from us? Are we seeing a goblet or two faces? Is the picture that of an old woman or a young girl? We have all had similar experiences where the appearing object shifts between two alternatives. For Husserl, these illusions are created by making the data support two different interpretations. What we experience with the shift of the visual object is actually the shift in our objectifying act from one interpretation to another.

According to Husserl, interpretation is a constitutive "making sense" of what we experience. Sense is a one in many and we make sense of the contents we receive by placing them in an interpretative framework of unity in multiplicity. Thus, we identify objects by noticing how certain patterns of perceptions, namely those that give us perspectivally arranged series, fit together. We then assign them a common referent, a unity to which their multiplicity refers. In asserting that we see this unity, rather than the different perceptions that present it, we are actually asserting that the perceptual object is a sense, a one in many. If we didn't do this, we would mistake a single perception—say that captured in a photograph—for the object. In reality, however, we never take the photo as equivalent to the actual object.

For Husserl in the *Logical Investigations*, what we confront here is "the fact that all thinking and knowing is directed to states of affairs whose unity relative to a multiplicity of actual or possible acts of thought is a 'unity in multiplicity' and is, therefore, of an ideal character."[14] The ideal character of its object is what distinguishes the intentional relation from a real (causal) relation. Thus, according to Husserl, consciousness transcends the real influence of the real object on itself—that is, the real presence of contents of sensation—by virtue of the interpretation it places on this real influence. In his words, what appears is not a "real part of my concrete seeing."[15] It is an "ideal intentional content," that is, the content of the object grasped as a sense. Husserl, as Levinas notes, maintains this doctrine throughout his career. Thus, thirty years after the writing of the *Logical Investigations*, he still maintains this presence of the object as a sense. In the *Cartesian Meditations*, he describes it as follows: "This in-consciousness [of the perceptual object] is a completely unique being-in. It is not a being-in as a real, inherent component; it is rather a being-in as something intentional, as an appearing, ideal-being-in [*als erscheinendes Ideell-darin-sein*]. In other words, it is a being-in as the object's objective sense. The object of consciousness, in its self-identity throughout the flowing of experience, does not come from outside into such flowing; it is rather present within it, determined as a sense."[16]

How do we know that we get this sense correctly? What tells us that we are mistaken? Common experience supplies the answer. Suppose I notice what seems to be a cat crouching under a bush on a bright sunny day. As I move to get a better look, its features seem to become more clearly defined. One part of what I see appears to be its head, another its body, still another its tail. Based upon what I see, I anticipate that further features will be revealed as I approach: this shadow will be seen as part of the cat's ear; another will be its eye, and so forth. If my interpretation is correct, then my experiences should form a part of an emerging pattern that exhibits these features, that is, that perceptually manifests the object I assume I am seeing. If, however, I am mistaken, at some point my experiences will fail to fulfill my expectations. What I took to be a cat will dissolve into a flickering collection of shadows and my interpretation of what I am seeing will shift accordingly. As this example indicates, not every interpretation is fulfilled. There is, in fact, a dialectic between interpretation and fulfillment, one where every perceptual sense is present through my interpreting, objectifying act, but not every interpretation advanced by this act results in the ongoing perceptual presence of this sense. I experience this dialectic as I constantly propose and adjust my interpretations to match the content that I experience.

The dialectic of intention and fulfillment is Husserl's attempt to assure the objectivity of the senses we grasp—that is, to make them more than simply our constituted products. Levinas, however, disputes the success of this endeavor. In his language, which he borrows from the later Husserl, our interpretative acts are called "noesis," while the intentional objects that result from these acts are called "noemata." The latter are also referred to as "representations." Since consciousness in the objectifying act actually *makes* sense of what it experiences, this sense, he argues, must be considered something made or constituted and, hence, our "product." For Levinas, then, "the Husserlian thesis of the primacy of the objectifying act . . . leads . . . to the affirmation . . . that the object of consciousness, while differing from consciousness . . . is, as it were, a product of consciousness, being a 'meaning' endowed by consciousness, the result of a *Sinngebung*" (*TI*, 123). *Sinngebung* (sense-giving) is Husserl's later term for the bestowal of meaning that the interpretative, objectifying act engages in when it interprets what it experiences as perceptions of one and the same object. The fact that this process results in a unity of sense certainly distinguishes the intentional relation from a real causal one. In Levinas's words, "The intentional relation of representation is to be distinguished from every other relation," especially that of "mechanical causality." But the price of this is to make it our product. In this relation, as he says, "it is always the same that determines the other" (*TI*, 124).[17]

Levinas can call on a number of Husserl's assertions to support his view.[18] Husserl, for example, asserts that "pure consciousness in its own absolute being . . . conceals and constitutes in itself all worldly transcendencies."[19] For Husserl, this means that the presence of a transcendent object is only a correlate of a specific type of connection among our experiences, namely, the type that allows us to posit through our objectifying act a unity in multiplicity. Levinas sees a number of problems with this position, all revolving around the fact of our embodiment. If, indeed, as Husserl asserts, "all real unities are unities of sense,"[20] then our body must also be considered such a unity. Taken as something that we represent to ourselves, that is, as intentional object, it is just a meaning. But it is because we have bodies that we have a position in the world, our body being at the center of our world. In Levinas's words, "The body naked and indigent identifies the center of the world it perceives." When, however, we represent it, "it is thereby, as it were, torn up from the center from which it proceeded" (*TI*, 127). It becomes, as a sense, our product. It is not "here," but "there," over against us as an intentional object. Furthermore, senses are not exposed to the world, but the body, as naked, is. As indigent, it lives from the world. Such living from indicates the dependence of our embodied consciousness on the world. We must eat in order to live, and we must live in order to represent. Given this, the body points to life as prior to representation. In fact, as Levinas writes, "The body naked and indigent is the very reverting, irreducible to a thought, of representation into life" (ibid.).

Another difficulty in taking the intentional presence of our body as a sense is the fact that senses are not physically exterior to each other. Yet to have a body is to assume exteriority—the exteriority of the world one physically depends on. This, however, is to assume a mutual determination. It is "to enter a relation with [the other] such that the same determines the other while being determined by it" (*TI*, 128). I am determined by the other insofar as I "live from" the other. Here, the constituted object, "reduced to its meaning overflows its meaning, becomes within constitution the condition of the constituting, or, more exactly, the nourishment of the constituting" (ibid.). For example, the meaning-bestowing subject has to eat. I can *think* that food and eating condition my consciousness. But food and drink are not reduced to such a thought. In Levinas's words, "The surplus over meaning is not a meaning in its turn, simply thought as a condition . . . The aliment [or food] conditions the very thought that would think it as a condition" (ibid.). As Levinas also expresses this, "the surplus of the reality of the aliment over every represented reality . . . is the way the I, the absolute commencement, is suspended on the non-I" (*TI*, 129). This "surplus" is the reality of the world I live from. It is also the reality of my body as non-representable. Like the ego it sustains, my body exists "without having a genus, without being the individuation of a concept" (*TI*, 118). My body is myself in my non-substitutable, irreplaceable organic functioning.

So conceived, the body "is a permanent contestation of the pre-rogative attributed to consciousness of 'giving meaning' to each thing" (*TI*, 129). It contests this in its being non-representable.[21] It also contests consciousness's prerogative in its very indigence. This indigence reverses the constitutive intentionality that proceeds from consciousness to its object given that the embodied subject "lives from what it thinks." Here, "the very movement of constitution is reversed" since it proceeds from the reality of what is thought to the body. All this affects consciousness's relation to the world. In Levinas's descriptions, it appears as intertwined with the world in Merleau-Ponty's sense. As Merleau-Ponty observes, we naturally believe that, as embodied, we are in the world and also that, as represented, the world is in us. Holding on to "both ends of this chain," the "'natural' man" asserts: "I am in the world and the world is in me."[22] Levinas's version of this runs: "What the subject contains represented is also what [externally] supports and nourishes its activity as a subject" (*TI*, 130). In other words, as representing the world, I contain it. As nourish-ing my activity, it contains me. This mutual containment is a mutual deter-mination. Thus, as representing the world, I determine it. I give it sense. As living-from the world, it determines me. This is because the relation of living-from involves my embodiment. But "to posit oneself corpore-ally is to touch the earth, to do so in such a way that the touching finds itself already conditioned by the position, a foot settles in the real . . . as though a painter would notice that he is descending from the picture he is painting" (*TI*, 128). The picture being painted is our representation of the world. Our being in it is our being in this world through our embodi-ment. Thus, the relation in question is like that of a painter being both outside of his painting and within it as living from it. This intertwining is our being-in-the-world. To be in the world is both to represent it and live from it. Both are included in the concept of our enjoyment of it.

Being-in-the-World as Bathing

Levinas now turns to an even more elementary level of our being in the world. While still correlated to our enjoyment, it is prior to our repre-sentation of the world. This is the level of our immersion, our "bathing" in the elemental aspects of the world. Again he draws a contrast with Heidegger. For Heidegger, as we have stressed, we are in the world by disclosing its objects through our projects, the ultimate project being the care we have for our own being. The things of the world are thus taken as implements and materials needed for our projects. In this view, Levinas writes, "the world, as a set of implements forming a system and suspended on the care of an existence [a Dasein] anxious for its being . . . attests labor, habitation, the home and economy." Everything, even food, is disclosed as a means to a goal. Thus, this world "bears witness to a particular organization of labor in which 'foods' take on the significance of fuel in the economic machinery." The difficulty with this picture is that Heidegger "does not take the relation of enjoyment into consideration." He has set up a world in which "the implement has entirely masked . . . the satisfaction" that its use brings (*TI*, 134). To counter this, Levinas turns to a level of our being in the world that he terms "bathing."

He writes, in introducing this concept, "in enjoyment the things are *not* absorbed into the technical finality that organizes them into a system. They take form within a medium in which we take hold of them. They are found in space, in the air, on the earth . . . The medium remains essential to things . . . it has its own density." This medium, he adds, is "a common fund . . . earth, sea, sky, city . . . Every relation or possession is situated within the non-possessible which envelops or contains without being able to be contained. We shall call this the elemental" (*TI*, 130–31). For Heidegger in *Being and Time*, the earth, sea, and sky appear only as means to my ends. Wind is disclosed as wind for my sails if I need to cross the lake in a sailboat. The sea is there to support my craft. The earth appears as that on which I make my way as I walk towards my goal. Each has its sense in terms of a *Bezugsbereich*, an area of relations that is correlated to my projects. For Levinas, by contrast, the "medium is not reducible to a system of operational references and is not equivalent to the totality of such a system" (*TI*, 131). The medium is not objectively representable since "the element has no forms containing it; it is content without [objective] form." This is because I only experience the element from a side. I can regard only "the surface of the sea and of the field." I can feel only "the edge of the wind." I cannot represent the whole of the element. Rather, as Levinas writes, "one is steeped in it, I am always within the element" (ibid.). As immersed in it, "the adequate relation with the element is, precisely, bathing" (*TI*, 132).

Enjoyment on the sensuous level exemplifies this relation of bathing. When I bite into a fresh peach, its sensuous presence in my mouth has no sides. As I warm myself in the sun, I do not feel its presence as an object. "In enjoyment," as Levinas writes, "things revert to their elemental qualities" (*TI*, 134). We live from them, enjoying them. Even tools, according to Levinas, offer us enjoyment. In his words, "As material or gear, the objects of everyday use are subordinated to enjoyment" (*TI*, 133). I enjoy using my lighter to light my cigarettes. Its sensuous presence pleases me. The same holds for "furnishings, the home, food, clothing." They are not just *Zeuge* or tools. They have their purposes, but "we enjoy them or suffer from them; they are ends." In fact, he concludes, "to enjoy without utility, . . . this is the human" (*TI*, 133). Only Heidegger's all-pervasive utilitarianism makes him forget this. In fact, as Levinas remarks, "Food can be interpreted as an implement only in a world of exploitation" (*TI*, 134). In such a world, both enjoyment and ethics are masked. This is because the concealing of enjoyment leaves no place for *the ethical understood as the interruption of enjoyment*. It prevents my accessing the level on which I feel the hunger of the other "as the bread snatched from my mouth."

The relation of ethics to embodiment that Levinas is drawing brings together a number of factors. We have, first of all, the sense of the body as "existing without having a genus, without being the individuation of a concept." This is the body as unrepresentable, the body in its unique singularity, a singularity expressed in the fact that no one else can perform your bodily functions for you. This non-representability is the "surplus" of the lived body over the representation of it. We also have the tie of this unique singularity to our interiority, an interiority expressed in the "famished stomach that has no ears." The body is here thought of as the basis of "the egotism or the ipseity of the ego." Then there is the fact that the enjoyment that the body makes possible ties us to the present. For Heidegger, we are always in advance of ourselves in our being in the world. For Levinas, we are not ahead of ourselves at the moment of enjoyment. Our being in the world involves enjoying the present moment in its sensuous affective presence. Such enjoyment manifests the world in its "elemental" character. This aspect of the world does not appear perspectivally. It comes to presence in enjoyment as something we bathe in, something in which we are immersed. The water we drink does not have a side, neither does the smell of a rose, nor the chocolate in our mouth. In this, they are like the air, water, earth, and air. They do not appear perspectivally.

All these factors enter into the ethical relation. This relation, according to Levinas, is to a unique other. But such uniqueness is the function of the body. The ethical relation is to the Other in his or her need: to the widow, the orphan, and the stranger. But the body is the condition of their indigence and, indeed, of our own generosity. Furthermore, the ethical relation presupposes our own interiority as that which we transcend in relating to the Other. This, however, is given to us by our embodiment, that is, by the sensuous affective presence it affords us. Finally, the ethical relation is to the Other as exceeding our representation. It is to the Other as immeasurable, as in-finite. But this exceeding is founded on the "surplus" of the body with regard to its representation. It is based on the body in its non-representable singularity. Thus, the embodied Other confronts us with an immeasurable interiority, one that is irreplaceable and, hence, of non-finite value. The same holds for the world that the embodied Other brings to presence. It is also unique and irreplaceable. Thus, he who saves another person "saves a world." The appeal coming from this Other is to preserve this irreplaceable world.

Sensibility and Striving: Comparisons

Levinas's view of sensibility and striving can best be brought out by a series of comparisons, the most obvious of which are to Heidegger. Thus, much of what we have just covered can be seen as focusing on an area that Heidegger ignored in his existential analytic. Against Heidegger's view that being is disclosed in terms of our projects as tools and materials for accomplishing our goal, Levinas introduces the idea of the element. We do not use the element, we "bathe" in it. Against the conception that care is the most basic state of Dasein, Levinas brings in the notion of enjoyment. Enjoyment does not spring from our care for our being, that is, for what we will be through our choices. It is a present condition. It does not fit into the for-the-sake-of or the in-order-to of projects. We do not enjoy things for the sake of something else. We enjoy them for their own sake in the present. All of this is very Aristotelian. Aristotle makes the argument that if we did everything for the sake of something else, "our desire would be futile" since we would never get to the end of the process.[23] In fact, we do a number of things just for themselves. These are things in which the activity contains the goal in itself. For example, we see beautiful objects just to see them, we hear music just to hear it, and so on. Doing so we have pleasure. We enjoy life. For Aristotle, such enjoyment is the self-presence of our functioning. More precisely, it is the presence of the activity of our being-alive to this very activity.

Levinas also speaks of sensibility as finding itself "immediately at the term," as expressing "the relation with the end as a goal" (*TI*, 136). The relation he has in mind, however, is not with our functioning, but rather with the "elements" we "bathe" in: air, water, light, the sights and sounds of a city, a landscape, and so on. In each case, we do not possess what we sense. We are immersed in it. Corresponding to this basic view, Levinas defines "sensibility" not as representation, not as belonging to the order of thought, but rather as "the affectivity wherein the egotism of the I pulsates" (*TI*, 135). He adds: "One does not know, one lives sensible qualities: the green of these leaves, the red of this sunset" (ibid.). This living is not an intentionality. As our remarks on Husserl's account of intentionality indicate, we do not intend to see our sensations as objects. We live through them. Levinas echoes this when he writes, "Sensibility does not constitute the world, because the world called sensible does not have its function to constitute a representation" (ibid.). According to Husserl, we represent something by interpreting our sensations as sensations of some object. What Levinas is asking is that we consider sensibility not as material for the interpretative, objectifying act, but rather as it is in itself. When we do, we think of it as affectivity. The sensible affects us. This affection is generally pleasurable. As an example of this non-objective, affective relation, think of biting into a fresh peach and having its flesh dissolve in our mouth. As you chew it, it affects you without being an object, without having sides, without showing itself perspectivally like some spatial-temporal reality. It is there as an "element." Here, as Levinas writes, "sensibility establishes a relation with a pure quality without support, [it establishes a relation] with the element. Sensibility is enjoyment" (*TI*, 136).

In affirming that sensibility is enjoyment, Levinas opposes Plato's view that pleasure and pain inevitably go together—for example, the pleasure of drinking with the pain of being thirsty when one quenches one's thirst. Plato, he writes, "fails to recognize the originality of the structure . . . living from." Describing this structure, he adds: "An existence that has this mode [of living from] is the body—both separated from its end (that is, need), but already proceeding toward that end without having to know the means necessary for its obtainment, an action released by the end, accomplished without knowledge of means, that is, without tools" (*TI*, 136). Thus, the structure of living from is that of our embodied being in its action of satisfying its needs. Plato's argument about the coupling of pleasure and pain comes in a context in which he asserts that our true independence involves our separation from the body and its needs. For Levinas, by contrast, our very identity as an ego or self involves embodiment and its needs. In living from, the self "acquires its own identity by this dwelling in the 'other'" (*TI*, 115).

Husserl, we should note, also speaks of the ego's identity as involving the sensuous content that affects it. He writes, for example, "One can say that the ego of the cogito is completely devoid of a material, specific essence, comparable, indeed, with another ego, but comparable only as an *empty form* that is 'individualized' through the stream: this, in the sense of its uniqueness" (Ms. E III 2, p. 18, my italics). In other words, what makes the ego unique is the content that affects it. Apart from this, as James Edie remarks, the ego is "an impersonal, necessary, universal, eidetic structure," one that, "is lived in and through each unique consciousness, each ego-life."[24] In a striking turn of phrase, Husserl talks about the sensuous or "hyletic" data that individualize the ego as waking it up. In his words, "The ego is awakened by affection from the non-egological because the non-egological is 'of interest,' it instinctively indicates, etc.; and the ego reacts kinesthetically as an immediate reaction" (Ms. B III 3, p. 5a). This means that we cannot abstract the "awake ego" from the impressions (the "non-ego") that awaken it. In his words, "The ego is not something for itself and the non-ego something separate from the ego; between them there is no room for a turning towards. Rather, the ego and its non-ego are inseparable" (Ms. C 16 V, p. 68a). There is, in fact, a certain identity between the two. It is one where we can say: "What from the side of the hyletic data is called the affection of the ego is from the side of the ego called tending, striving towards" (Ms. B III 9, pp. 70a–70b). This striving manifests itself in the striving to continue to have the affecting contents.

Such striving, Husserl emphasizes, occurs without any knowledge or representation of the goal. It occurs on a very basic level of our organic, affective life. Before considering his remarks on this score, it would be helpful to bring up another point of comparison, one provided by Hans Jonas's description of our organic life. As Jonas observes, an organic being is both totally composed of matter and yet, in its form, different from it. This is because the matter composing the organism "is forever vanishing downstream," which means that it constantly has to be replaced. Thus, to maintain itself, it must reach outside of itself for new matter. It must engage in metabolism—in the exchange of material (*Stoffwechsel*) with the world. Although the organism is "independent of the sameness of this matter, it is dependent on the exchange of it."[25] Thus, in contrast to the inorganic, the organism's material state cannot be the same for any two instants. Were it to be the same, that is, were its metabolism to cease altogether, it would die. It would become inorganic. Since it is organic, it *needs* the influx of new material. In Jonas's words, "This necessity (for exchange) we call 'need,' which has a place only where existence is unassured and its own continual task."[26] Such need expresses its relation to the future. Thus, a living body has a future insofar as its continued being is a result of its doing[27] and such doing stretches beyond the now of its organic state to what comes next. Here, its "will be"—the intake of new material—determines the "is," that is, determines the nature of its present activity. Insofar as the organism exists by directing itself beyond its present condition, it is ahead of itself. In other words, the organism, as need, as the necessity for exchange, is already stretched out in time as a striving to acquire the material it continuously needs.

Such striving may be viewed in Levinas's terms as "both separated from its end (that is, need), but already proceeding toward that end with-

out having to know the means necessary for its obtainment" (*TI*, 136). So
regarded, it is a blind, instinctual striving that does not know its object,
that does not represent to itself a future state in its striving. Its temporal
stretching out is not a conscious one—not one involving a project with a
given goal. What we have, instead, is "the overflowing of sensation by the
element" that "takes on a temporal meaning," one that by overflowing
"escapes the gentle mastery of enjoyment" (*TI*, 141). It escapes it because
the element is not yet a thing. We cannot master it as we can a thing. For
Levinas, we should note, this primitive relation to the elemental that
Jonas designates as metabolism occurs in sensuous contexts where there
is no apparent exchange of materials. We sit in the sun and warm ourselves. We do not control the warmth. We feel the cool of the wind, we
do not control the wind. In Levinas's words:

> the blue of the sky above my head, the breath of the wind, the undula-
> tion of the sea, the sparkle of the light do not cling to a substance. They
> come from nowhere. This coming from nowhere . . . appearing without
> there being anything that appears—and consequently coming always,
> without my being able to possess the source—delineates the future of
> sensibility and enjoyment. This is not yet a representation of the future.
> (*TI*, 141)

This non-representational sense of the future is felt as striving. This is because "the sense datum with which sensibility is nourished always comes
to gratify a need, responds to a tendency," a striving (*TI*, 136).

Husserl's account of this tendency or striving occurs as part of an
extended series of manuscripts devoted to our instinctual life. In his view,
on the most basic level, striving is instinctively directed toward some goal.
This occurs even though the organism can neither represent the goal beforehand nor know beforehand the means to it. What we have, instead,
are a series of motivating sensuous cues. For example, the infant placed
at the breast is first motivated by smell, then by touching the nipple, then
by the kinesthesia of sucking and swallowing before the goal of the drive
towards nourishment appears. In Husserl's words,

> When the smell of the mother's breast and the sensations of moving
> one's lips occur, an instinctive directedness towards drinking awakes,
> and an originally paired kinesthesia comes into play. . . . If drinking
> does not immediately occur, how does it happen? Perhaps the smell
> alone awakens something else, an empty apperception, so to speak,
> which has no "conscious" goal. If touching occurs, then the way to
> fulfillment is first properly an ongoing instinctive drive, which is an

unfulfilled intention. Then, in fulfillment, [there are] the movements of swallowing, etc., which bring fulfillment, disclosing the instinctive drive.[28]

The general principle here is that "striving is instinctive and instinctively (thus, at first, secretly) 'directed' towards what in the 'future' will first be disclosed as worldly unities constituting themselves."[29] This parallels Levinas's remark that on the most basic level of our egological life, we confront "an action released by the end, accomplished without knowledge of means" (*TI*, 136). On this level, then, Husserl and his two former students (Jonas and Levinas) are asserting that there is a striving prior to that asserted by Heidegger's existential analytic of Dasein as care. It is a striving that does not depend on representation. At its basis is simply the fact of our having a living, organic body.[30]

Husserl came to this position rather late in his career. The C and B manuscripts I have been citing date from the 1930s. For Levinas, however, this fact is fundamental for understanding the basic level of our self-relation. In his words, the "patterns of my primary relation with myself, of my coincidence with myself" in "nowise resemble idealist representation" (*TI*, 138). They concern not my representing myself to myself, but rather my embodiment. For example, my "position, the act of standing" is bodily. So is my having a distinct position in the world since it is a function of my bodily standing in one place rather than another. The same holds for my interiority. "Sensibility," Levinas writes, "enacts the very separation of being—separated and independent" (ibid.). Such "separation" is "accomplished as enjoyment, that is, as interiority" (*TI*, 139). In fact, "only in enjoyment does the I crystallize" (*TI*, 144). The I becomes one thing (my I or ego), rather than something else (your I) in enjoyment since the interiorization that shapes it is accomplished through my distinct embodiment. Thus, I take food and eat it and it becomes mine. Once it enters my mouth, it is withdrawn from the public sphere. The fact that nobody can eat for me conditions my having a sphere interior to myself. So does the fact that nobody can breathe for me, sleep for me, and so on. In fact, as we have seen, the whole field of the bodily sensible as bodily sensible designates the private. For example, the object that I see out there is common to me and others. My bodily experiences, the feeling of the sun's warmth, the sense of food as I chew it, and so on, are not common objects. They are accessible to me but not to you. The book that is over there on the table is a public object. It has features that can be publicly discerned. We can, for example, all agree on its color. But "taste is not disputable." It is already, as enjoyment, an interiorization. As Levinas sums up this position: "The interiorization of enjoyment is separation in itself, is the mode according to which such an event as separation can be produced in the economy of being" (*TI*, 147). Another way to express this is to note that sensibility is precisely our *not* being outside of ourselves— that is, our not being out there with the things. For Husserl, to access them, we have to transcend ourselves by interpreting our sensations as sensations of something. But, in itself, sensibility is prior to this. In itself, it is pure interiority. A parallel argument can be made for Heidegger. Sensibility and the interiority it defines are prior to all pragmatic disclosure of things as means and tools. To say that Heidegger overlooks this feature of human existence is to affirm that he has no place for the fundamental reality of human plurality. Over and beyond the obvious fact, as Arendt writes, that it is not man, "but men that inhabit the earth,"[31] such plurality points to the interiority that makes us something more than instances of a species. It indicates the unique singularity of such instances.

Dwelling and Freedom

Totality and Infinity, II, C §3–E §3

The Freedom of Created Being

For Levinas, as we saw, not every sense of being is the result of our posit-ing or representing an object. Our organic being is prior to this, being what grounds the ego in its interiority. The fact that no one can perform our organic functions for us gives us an irreplaceable singularity, one that we experience in the phenomenon of enjoyment. This enjoyment is a pre-objective, non-representable experience. It expresses neither the subject's relation to an object nor Dasein's projective relation to its world. The relation is rather that of the ego's being immersed or "bathing" in the element. The interiority or being-in-oneself that results is before our being-in-the-world. It is distinct from selfhood conceived as being-for-oneself since the latter involves a self-separation or an inner distance. For the existentialist, this distance is between the choosing self and the self that we choose, the latter being the result of the choices we make, the projects we engage in. Levinas's claim is that there is an individuality prior to this, one that comes simply from our embodiment, that is, from its ir-replaceability. This difference can be put in terms of human freedom. For the tradition of German idealism, which the existentialists continue in their emphasis on choice, freedom is what separates the choosing and the chosen self. For Kant, such freedom is rational autonomy. It is what makes us capable of being, in the moral sphere, a self-caused cause. For Levinas, however, there is "a freedom, referring to happiness, made of happiness, and consequently compatible with a being that is not causa sui, [a freedom compatible with a being] that is created" (*TI*, 148). This is the freedom of the autonomy of the self in its sensuous interiority. It is the freedom of the self that lives from the world. Like the bodily individu-ality it presupposes, it is prior to the freedom the existentialists describe.

Levinas begins his account of this prior freedom by noting that sen-suous enjoyment depends on the continual arrival of enjoyable contents. This dependence means that enjoyment has a certain fragility in that its source can fail. Thus, the sun that warms me goes behind a cloud; the summer warmth itself departs with the season, and in winter, the fruit that I gather is no longer available. All these examples point out the fact that "the I . . . is enjoyment of something else, never of itself" (*TI*, 143). Because of this, "enjoyment is without security" (*TI*, 142). For Levinas, as we saw, this very insecurity gives the I its underlying temporal direction. In his words, "the overflowing of sensation by the element . . . takes on a temporal meaning" (*TI*, 141). The contents "come from nowhere." I cannot, as long as I remain on the level of sensibility, "possess the source." Thus, I am stretched out beyond myself to the future without owning it. Such stretching out "delineates the future of sensibility and enjoyment" (ibid.). This future is prior to and foundational for the projecting forward of the possibilities of the self that characterizes the existential sense of Dasein's futurity. What motivates this prior projecting is the very fact that "the I . . . is enjoyment of something else, never of itself."

Levinas's alternative to Heidegger's existential analytic builds on these insights to develop the concepts of labor and the home, both as crucial for the genesis of the freedom that lives from the world. Before we consider the details of his account, it would be well to sketch its outline. For Levinas, our projecting forward of our possibilities occurs in the context of labor. Labor is what assures the future. In Levinas's words, "labor, by mastering the uncertainty of the future and its insecurity and by establishing possession, delineates separation in the form of economic independence" (*TI*, 150). Labor requires a place to store its products, so the first action of labor is establishing a home. Within it, there are the things I need for enjoyment. Possessing them, I establish the basis of my autonomy. Such autonomy, understood as freedom from immediate need, is, of course, not absolute since it involves the world that supports my labor. Within the context of this autonomy, a second sense of autonomy arises from the fact that the infant is raised in a home. More specifically, its genesis is the infant's experience of the home in the context of the mother (or caregiver). The ego of the infant, established in the interiority of bodily pleasure, gradually becomes aware of the fact that the continuance of pleasure is not under its control, but rather that of the caregiver. It thus opens itself to this person as first Other. In Levinas's account, this is the mother. The home appears to the child in "the gentleness of the feminine face" (*TI*, 150). The mother (or caregiver) supplies the infant's needs. In this relation, "the other precisely reveals himself in his alterity not in a shock negating the I, but as the primordial phenomenon of gentleness" (ibid.). Autonomy enters the picture here since with this "welcoming of the face," we have the "unquenchable Desire for Infinity." The child enjoys the mother but cannot possess her. She is not elusive like the element (which we cannot possess since it has no sides and, hence, cannot be encompassed). She is elusive because of her excessive presence, her offering more than the child can anticipate or intend. With the relation to the mother, we have a new form of dependence, a new form of non-representability, and a new form of separation. The result is an autonomy or freedom that does not deny, but rather builds on the dependence, non-representability, and separation that sensation establishes. The dependence on the element becomes dependence on the caregiver; the caregiver's non-representability substitutes for that of the element; and the separation of interiority becomes the basis for the separation of the same from the Other. The full fruition of the autonomy that the welcoming Other prepares us for comes in the self-separation that arises when the Other calls us into question. In responding to her, we have to go outside of ourselves and see the world from the Other's perspective. Here, the Other "calls into question and puts at a distance from itself, the I itself" (*TI*, 172). With this, she provides us with the freedom implied by this inner distance. Such freedom, as we shall see, includes the possibility of refusing her call.

In giving this argument, Levinas attempts at each stage to meet apparently opposing demands. On the one hand, "the [sensuous] interiority that ensures separation . . . must produce a being absolutely closed over upon itself." On the other, "this closedness must not prevent egress from interiority, so that that exteriority [namely, the exteriority of the Other] could speak to it." The demand then is that "in the separated being, the door to the outside must be at the same time open and closed" (*TI*, 148). The account of sensuous existence must be both closed into itself as interiority and yet open to the Other. It is, as we shall see, in the balance of these two that our human freedom has its ethical genesis.

Dwelling and the Feminine

Heidegger rarely uses the term "ego," since Dasein is, in its very foundations, being-in-the-world. It is in terms of this relation to the world that our existence is defined. For Levinas, however, my being-in-the-world—as manifested by my active disclosure of the objective world—is situated in relation to my dwelling, which he takes as an extension of my "I" or ego. There is, then, a reversal of the way we normally think of the relation of our dwelling to the world. For Levinas, "the dwelling is not situated in the objective world, but the objective world is situated in relation to my dwelling" (*TI*, 153). Normally, we say that the objective world is situated in relation to the ego, the ego being taken as the zero point in space and time from which a person views the world. When we make this claim with regard to the home, we imply that the home, itself, is an extension of the ego. It extends the ego's interiority to a part of the objective world: the home becomes the extended 0-point. Levinas expresses this as follows: "the consciousness of the world is already consciousness through the world [i.e., through the home that is part of the world]. Something of the world that is seen is an organ or an essential means of vision." This organ is the home. The home is "the incarnation of consciousness and . . . in-habitation." The reference here is "to existence proceeding from the intimacy of a home, the first concretization" [of the ego in the world] (ibid).

There are two complementary ways to express this concretization. The first is to note with Levinas that through its windows, the home "makes possible . . . a look of him who escapes looks, the look that contemplates" (*TI*, 153). This means that the home manifests on an extended level the privacy of our interiority. The Other can see a person's body. He cannot see the seeing that takes place within it. Similarly, he sees the outside of a person's home, but neither its interior nor the person who looks out from it is available to his gaze. In an extended sense, then, "interiority [is] concretely established by the home" (*TI*, 154). A second, more profound sense of this establishment involves our relation to the elemental. When we simply bathe in the elemental, our attention is immediately directed outward. With the home, however, there arises the possibility of recollection. There is "a suspension of the immediate reactions the world solicits in view of a greater attention to oneself, one's possibilities, and the situation" (ibid.). Because of what we have stored there, we do not have to continuously look to acquiring what we need. The distance from the elemental that the home permits opens up, for the first time, the possibility of the inner distance that characterizes the for-itself. One can reflect on oneself through the physical interior that one has constructed.

Recollection, for Levinas, involves more than the familiar surroundings of the home. It involves the "feminine . . . as one of the cardinal points of the horizon in which the inner life takes place" (*TI*, 158). In, perhaps, the most controversial or, rather, "politically incorrect" passages of *Totality and Infinity*, Levinas takes the home and the recollection it affords as embodying the feminine principle. For him, "the woman is the condition for recollection, the interiority of the home, and inhabitation." This is because her face is not just present, but is "revealed, simultaneously with this presence, in its withdrawal and in its absence." What we have in woman "is the very essence of discretion. And the other whose presence is discreetly an absence . . . is the woman." She is the one who accomplishes the "hospitable welcome that describes the field of intimacy" (*TI*, 155). Whatever one thinks of this particular characterization,

Levinas's general conception is clear. He conceives the home as a place of intimacy, a place whose presence involves withdrawal from the world. This withdrawal is associated with women. Not everyone, of course, will make this association. Levinas, himself, seems to qualify it when he writes, "there is no question here of defying ridicule by maintaining the empirical truth or counter-truth that every home in fact presupposes a woman . . . The feminine has been encountered in this analysis as one of the cardinal points of the horizon in which the inner life takes place— and the empirical absence of the human being of 'feminine sex' in a dwelling nowise affects the dimension of femininity which remains open there, as the very welcome of the dwelling" (*TI*, 157–58).

What precisely is this "cardinal" point? Levinas indicates an answer when he writes, "The Other who welcomes in intimacy is not the you [*vous*] of the face that reveals itself in a dimension of height, but precisely the thou [*tu*] of familiarity: a language without teaching, a silent language, an understanding without words, an expression in secret" (*TI*, 155). This welcoming Other is not that of the face that calls us into question. It is of the face "whose presence is discreetly an absence." Levinas refers here to the I-Thou relation of Buber. This relation, he writes, is "not with the interlocutor." Rather, it "is situated on another plane than language."[1] This does not mean that its expression is "truncated . . . On the contrary, the discretion of this presence includes all the possibilities of the transcendent relationship with the Other." Levinas sees this as a relation "with feminine alterity" (ibid.). One can, however, also think of it in terms of our relation to God. Just as God limits himself in order to leave a space for creation, so the welcoming Other limits himself. He or she withdraws so as to leave a space for the Other to express himself, to grow and develop. This is creating an environment, a nourishing space for the Other. A gardener does this for her plants by weeding, watering, and fertilizing the soil. A mother and a father do this for their children in the intimacy of space that they create in their home.

One can also think of this in terms of incarnation, of providing the flesh (in the extended sense of a nourishing environment) for the Other to come to be, grow, and develop. Such incarnation involves the empathy that allows one to take up the other person's standpoint. In the parent-child relation this incarnation through empathy is twofold. First of all, in his loving his parents, the child takes up their standpoint. Through empathy, he takes on their flesh and, hence, their loving gaze as they regard him. Doing so, he incarnates himself through this gaze. Seeing himself as they see him, he *incarnates himself in the world* of things, not as a thing, but *as his parents' child* with all the human content this involves. The same model applies not just to sight, but also to touch. Touching, for example, his mother, a child touches himself. Her return of his touching allows him to incarnate himself as a located touching. The same may hold for our other senses, such as hearing and smell. If it does, then the result of this incarnation is the located selfhood of the sensing individual. Given this, when the child is deprived of this relation with his parents or caregivers, he becomes placeless. Deprived of this double incarnation through the Other, he feels lost. The important point here is that such placing involves the "welcome of the dwelling." It does not involve "the you [*vous*] of the face that reveals itself in a dimension of height" and issues commands, "but precisely the thou [*tu*] of familiarity" (*TI*, 155). Its result is not a moral imperative, but rather the space that allows us to grow into a moral being.

Labor

Turning to describe the home, Levinas describes its "primary function" as "breaking the plenum of the element." The space it encloses "makes labor and property possible" (*TI*, 156). Thus, having found a home, we can through labor withdraw things from the elemental—the fruits from the earth, the fish from the sea, and so on. In the home, we are no longer exposed to the elements; we no longer just live from and enjoy their common products. Instead, we postpone enjoyment. Rather than immediately eating what we gather or capture, we put it into storage, taking concern for the morrow. In Levinas's words, "the labor that draws the things from the elements . . . put[s] [them] in reserve, deposited in the home." The home, in other words, "founds possession." It, itself, "is not a possession in the same sense as the . . . goods it can collect and keep" (*TI*, 157). It is what makes possible such goods. The possessions we acquire by labor become distinct goods since with a home we no longer immediately have to consume what we gather. By contrast, "possession by enjoyment is one with enjoyment; no activity precedes sensibility" (*TI*, 158).

The point that Levinas is making is subtly different from that of John Locke, who sees the origin of property in our action of withdrawing goods from the common store of nature. For Locke, the labor that we extend, which is proper to us, makes the goods we gather our property.[2] Levinas agrees with this, but adds that "labor" as the "energy of acquisition . . . would be impossible in a being that had no dwelling" (*TI*, 159). Gathering, in other words, would not make any sense, if I had no place to store what I gathered. Storing it, I keep it for myself. It becomes mine, not just from the labor I expended acquiring it, but also from the fact that I withdraw it from the common world to place it in my dwelling, conceived as an extension of my "I." This withdrawal into my extended I makes labor "egotistical." We normally do not recognize this since its private actions are concealed by its public products—namely, by the "wastes" and "works, this movement of acquisition . . . leaves in its wake . . . city, field, garden, landscape" (ibid.).[3] In spite of its seizure and acquisition, labor, he adds, is not "violence" since it is applied to the elemental, that is, to "fathomless obscurity of matter" that is "faceless" (*TI*, 160).

For Levinas, our projecting forward of our possibilities in our projects occurs in the context of labor. Our relation to the future involves mastering its insecurity "by establishing possession." It is, then, through the pragmatic disclosure of labor that the beings of the world first emerge for us. As Levinas expresses this: "The hand delineates a world by drawing what it grasps from the element, delineating definite beings having forms." The labor of the hand is "the informing of the formless," its result being the emergence of the "existent, [the] support of qualities." This means that labor is responsible for "the substantiality of the thing" (*TI*, 161). In making these assertions, Levinas distances himself from Aristotle, who asserts that some things are by art (that is, labor), but others have their forms naturally—such as living beings and natural bodies with their inherent tendencies.[4] The real point of contrast is, however, with Heidegger. In his account of Dasein's disclosure of the world through his projects, Heidegger mentions neither labor nor the home. For Levinas, by contrast, pragmatic disclosure occurs through labor, and "the dwelling conditions labor." This is because "the hand that acquires is burdened by what it takes." It needs home to store it (ibid.). In making these assertions, Levinas returns to the original sense of the Greek word for being or substance, which is *ousia*. Originally, the word meant "property."[5] In English, this sense of substance is maintained in expressions like "a man of substance" and a "substantial sum." Levinas preserves this sense when he asserts that "substance refers to the dwelling." This implies that "possession alone touches substance; the other relations with the thing only affect attributes" (*TI*, 162). If we accept this, then *Being and Time*, which mentions neither labor nor the home, does not account for the disclosure of beings. Its focus on the disclosure of things as useful for our purposes does not touch their substance. Rather, as Levinas writes, "the function of being [an] implement . . . imposes itself . . . as [only] one of the attributes of these beings" (ibid.). Now, it is because substances are property that they can be bought and sold. As such, they can be converted into money (ibid.). With this, we have the thought that, lacking any discussion of labor, *Being and Time* has no conception of an economy. It cannot since the fundamental fact of an economy is labor's transformation of the elemental into property. More importantly, *Being and Time* fails to grasp the fact that the fundamental sense guiding our pragmatic disclosure of beings—the sense of the being of beings—involves dwelling. It thus misses the point that an ontology of disclosure must take account of ethics—in particular, the ethical relations that underlie the intimacy of the home.

Embodied Freedom

Both dwelling and labor presuppose our embodiment. The body allows us to labor and, thus, to separate from the elemental the space of the dwelling that our embodied being requires to survive. Given its fundamental role, the body, Levinas writes is "not an object among other objects." Rather, it is "the very regime in which separation holds sway." It appears as "the 'how' of this separation and, so to speak, as an adverb rather than as a substantive" (*TI*, 163). This "how" is the "I can" that our living body affords us. As such, it mediates between our sensuous interiority, which is itself a result of our embodiment, and the outward labor and acquisition that embodied action makes possible. It thus appears as "a node where a movement of interiorization meets a movement of labor and acquisition" (ibid).

To understand this encounter we must return to Levinas's assertion that "only in enjoyment does the I crystallize" (*TI*, 144). This is because such enjoyment is a matter of our embodied sensibility and, hence, of the interiorization that is accomplished by our embodiment. Such interiorization is, through this embodiment, open to the world. The bodily enjoyment that informs it "is wholly nourished by the outside it inhabits" (*TI*, 163). Yet, in spite of this, such enjoyment "manifests its sovereignty, a sovereignty as foreign to the freedom of a *causa sui*, which nothing outside could affect, as [it is foreign] to the Heideggerian *Geworfenheit*, which, caught up in the other that limits it and negates it, suffers from this alterity" (*TI*, 163–64). This is because, in enjoyment, "the distinction between activity and passivity is undone." In enjoyment, we do not face the choice between the sovereignty of being a completely active *causa sui* or the passivity of being submitted to our "thrown situation" or *Geworfenheit*. Rather, in enjoyment, "sovereignty and . . . submission . . . are simultaneous" (*TI*, 164). They are such because the body, which through its "I can" gives us our sovereignty, exists at the "cross-roads of physical forces" (ibid.). It both actively uses the latter and passively submits to them. According to Levinas, "the existence of this equivocation [between sovereignty and submission] is the body" (ibid.). In other words, this equivocation is "the 'how' of [the] separation" that the body affords us, the *independence* of our embodied interiority being maintained by our embodied *dependence* on the world. For Levinas, then, "corporeal existence" is the ability "to be at home with oneself in something other than oneself, to be oneself while living from something other than oneself" (ibid.). Such existence "affirms its independence in the happy dependence of need." In fact, "their simultaneity constitutes the body" (*TI*, 165).

The ambiguity of the body in being both independent and dependent, both active and passive, gives Levinas a schema that allows him to integrate embodiment and consciousness. According to Levinas, "the ambiguity of the body is *consciousness*" (*TI*, 165). This is because consciousness is the outside-of-itself of temporality. It is our "openness upon duration" (ibid.). One way to express this is in terms of our earlier discussion of metabolism, which made the link between "need" and futurity. The futurity of immediate enjoyment—of sheer "living from"—extends only to the next incoming content. As a tendency, it has no real extension beyond the present. The temporal extension that opens up the "apartness" of consciousness occurs when, by laboring, I suspend this immediate enjoyment, thereby postponing futurity that is its correlate. Doing so, I get the stretched-out quality of time we call duration. Levinas's claim is that the enjoyment that postpones itself puts enjoyment at a distance and, hence, opens up time. In his words: "Enjoyment, as the body that labors, maintains itself in this primary postponement, [it maintains itself] in that which opens the very dimension of time" (ibid.). Postponing one's enjoyment for a future time is presupposed in every projecting ourselves forward, every project we undertake to secure our possession of that which we live from. It is at the root of the outside-of-itself of temporality and, hence, of consciousness.

This transformation of Heidegger's concept of our temporalization leads Levinas to emend the definition of Dasein's freedom as "finite freedom." He asserts, "Freedom as a relation of life with an other that lodges it . . . is not a finite freedom" (*TI*, 165). It is not, as Heidegger thought, a freedom of limited choices coming from my "thrown situation" in the face of the limited time available to me before my death. It is, rather, "virtually a null freedom. Freedom is, as it were, a by-product of life" (ibid.). It is the result of the laboring body in its ambiguity as both dependent and independent. Laboring, we postpone enjoyment, thereby opening the temporal space that is both consciousness and our ability to free ourselves from the immediate pressure of our needs. The labor of gathering and storing that postpones enjoyment, while not denying our needs, frees us from their opportunity. Having constructed a world where we have what we need, we have the time to "recollect" ourselves. For Levinas, then, "to be free is to build a world in which one could be free" (ibid.). "Consciousness," as realized in this world, is "a postponing," one that is "produced" not as an "abstraction," but "as all the concreteness of dwelling and labor" (*TI*, 165–66). This is because dwelling and labor allow us to distance ourselves, not just from our needs, but also from those things that satisfy them. When we gather these things and store them, we treat them as not yet present—that is, as things whose availability is reserved for the future. In Levinas's words, "To be conscious is to be in relation with *what is*, but [to be this] as though the present of what-is were not yet entirely accomplished and only constituted the future of a recollected being" (*TI*, 166).

The temporality that opens up consciousness is distinct from Heidegger's conception of our standing outside of ourselves through our projects. As Levinas writes: "To be conscious is precisely to have time—not to exceed the present time in the project that anticipates the future" where one is ahead of oneself awaiting oneself at the goal. It is, rather, "to have a distance with regard to the present itself, to be related to the element in which one is settled as to what is not yet there" (*TI*, 166). This treating the present as if it were the future has its basis in our bodily being understood in its adverbial sense. So understood, such being is a result of its doing, that is, of its acting to postpone its demise. All organic beings do this by living from what they need to maintain their organic structure. Humans supplement this by the labor of gathering and storing.[6] Doing so, we relate to the element, understood as that from which we live, as if we did not live from it. Rather than consuming it, we reserve it. Laboring, we thus "make use" of our time, creating the apartness of our consciousness. Here, as Levinas remarks, "the indetermination of the element, its future, becomes consciousness, [it becomes] the possibility of making use of the time" (ibid.). The temporal apartness that is our consciousness comes to be in this embodied making use of our time. Thus, we conceive the future in terms of forestalling its exigencies. We do this in the context of labor since "to labor is to delay its expiration" (ibid.). Because of my labor, the future, the time when I will be in need, does not come. The time between my present enjoyment and my future neediness does not expire. The duration, the temporal apartness of my life, is thereby maintained by my labor. Now, such "labor is possible only in a being that has the structure of a body" (ibid.). Thus, in distinction to Heidegger, Levinas explicitly bases the temporal structure of Dasein on its embodiment. His position is that, without embodiment, there is no labor and, hence, no time in the apartness of our concretely lived duration.

Levinas insists that the futurity that labor grasps is not something that we plan out in advance as we examine the possibilities that our given situation affords us. Faithful to his position that "the ambiguity of the body is *consciousness*," he assets that "the end is not caught sight of as an end in a disincarnate aspiration" (*TI*, 167). Rather, "the conception of an end is inseparable from its realization; an end does not attract, is not in some measure inevitable, but is caught hold of, and thus presupposes the body qua hand" (ibid.). This presupposition means that realization and representation go on together. This holds in particular for our first projects. We gained our initial concepts through our enacting, under the guidance of our caregivers, the bodily projects that realize them. Thus, our concept of "spoon" came from the project of eating with it, that of a "triangle" from our first attempts to draw three straight lines enclosing a space. The same holds for the more elaborate concepts built on these. This means that "in reality the 'representation' of the end and the movement of the hand that plunges towards it through an unexplored distance, preceded by no searchlight, constitute but one and the same event and define a being . . . that inhabits the world, that is, that is at home with itself in it" through its embodiment (*TI*, 168). Such a being exists through his doing. This doing encompasses both the representation and the realization of its ends in the same process. Thus, its being as representing the end is one with its doing in realizing this end. The same holds for its temporal being. It, too, is the result of its action—namely that of postponing its demise by delaying the time when its needs are not met.

Levinas's concept of our embodied freedom is not just distinct from the Heideggerian notion of finite freedom; it also stands in sharp contrast with Kant's conception of our autonomy. The result is a radical transformation of Kantian ethics. For Kant, the ethical relation involves treating the Other as an end in himself, that is, as someone capable of setting his own goals or ends as objects of his will. He is such insofar as he engages in rational choices. This means that reason rather than his needs determine his choices. The person does the right thing simply because his reason convinces him that it is the right thing *in and of itself* independent of any external circumstances. The individual thereby is autonomous in his willing. He is a free being since he knows "that reason is independent of purely subjective causes which collectively make all that belongs to sensation."[7] This argument implies that respect for the Other (that is, treating him as an end and not simply as a means) is conditioned on the Other existing as a rational agent in abstraction from the sensuous world. Levinas, by contrast, sees autonomy as a function of our embodiment. Its genesis involves sensuous interiority, living from, labor, and dwelling. As such, our autonomy is an independence rooted in our dependence on the world. As based on the body, it implies its vulnerability. This means that the ethical relation to the Other as autonomous must take this vulnerability into account. For Kant, respect for the Other's autonomy means that we should act such that the Other could authorize our actions. The other, for example, would not normally will that he be lied to. Respecting the autonomy of his will thus implies refraining from this action. For Levinas, the ethical relation moves beyond this in its focus on the vulnerability of the Other. This means that in respecting the Other's freedom, one also respects the bodily basis of this. The attention of ethics is on "the widow, the orphan, and the stranger" and the demands they make on us. Kant, of course, has a general command of benevolence. I must be benevolent to the Other insofar as I cannot will universal non-benevolence and still will that Others aid me when I am in need. In Kant's words, "a will that decided in this way would be in conflict with itself, since many a situation might arise in which the man needed love and sympathy from others."[8] Levinas goes beyond this utilitarian view. His view of helping the Other, though based on the explicit assumption that we do have needs, ultimately transcends any utilitarian economy.

Ethics and Ontology

Levinas's existential analytic of the person is advanced as an alternative to Heidegger's account in *Being and Time*. In his treatment of enjoyment, labor, the body, the feminine (the welcoming Other), and recollection, he positions ethics as prior to ontology. For Heidegger, what is prior is Dasein. It gives us the privileged point of access to the question of being. Thus, being is disclosed through Dasein's "understanding of being" (*Seinsverständnis*) as exemplified by its choice of projects. Such projects evince Dasein's structure as "care." The "Heideggerian analyses of the world" thus lead us to think that care, with its self-regard, "ultimately conditions every human product" (*TI*, 170). This view of our human existence, which takes it as "care" in the "situation" of our finite thrownness, lacks an essential element according to Levinas. His question is: Why does it not include the ethical in its structure? Why does not the ethical inform Dasein's understanding of being? His answer is that Heidegger understands care as care *for one's own being*. In your "thrownness towards death," that is, in the finitude of existence that confronts you when you face the fact that you will die, you become aware of what Heidegger terms the "call of conscience." This is a call to take up the task of living—that is, to "care," through your choices, for your being. Such care is more important than care for the Other. The call of conscience that evokes it is, accordingly, more fundamental than the call or appeal that comes from the face of the Other. Now, for Levinas, "the first word of the face" is the command, "Thou shalt not kill."[9] This is also the first word of ethics. Thus, Levinas's answer to the above question is that Heidegger privileges care for one's own life over care for the Other's life. This means that in Heidegger's analytic "the fear of being a murderer cannot overcome the fear of dying."[10]

The point of Levinas's counter-analytic is to avoid this conclusion—not because it is distasteful, but because it is false. It is based on an understanding of Dasein that abstracts from such factors as enjoyment, labor, the body, and family life. In doing so, it gives us a false conception of our autonomy. For Heidegger, this autonomy is based on our lack of any determinate nature that could limit our choices. This means that "as projection, [Dasein] is itself essentially null [*nichtig*]." This essential nothingness is our openness to the possibilities our situation affords us. In Heidegger's words, "the nothingness meant here belongs to Dasein's being-free for its existential possibilities."[11] For Levinas, by contrast, such freedom is rooted in our nature as embodied social beings. The tracing of its genesis from the care that springs from our embodied sociality is the essential task of his analytic.

Freedom and Representation

Having discussed the role of the body, labor, and dwelling in this genesis, Levinas now turns to the part played by the Other. This is not "the Other who welcomes in intimacy," who expresses herself in "a silent language, an understanding without words, an expression in secret" (*TI*, 155). While "the discretion of this presence includes all the possibilities of the transcendent relationship with the Other," the Other whose role he now analyzes expresses herself openly. She engages us in conversation, calling us into question. To see how this gives us our human freedom, Levinas turns to her role in making "representational thought" possible.

He first notes that such thought is usually taken as foundational in the sense "that in order to will it is first necessary to represent to oneself what one wills; in order to desire, to represent one's goal to oneself; in order to feel, to represent to oneself the object of the sentiment; in order to act, to represent to oneself what one will do" (*TI*, 168). This position stems from Descartes who claims that "when I wish, or fear, or affirm, or deny . . . I conceive something as the object of the action of my mind, but I also add something . . . to the idea which I have of the entity." The result is the object as wished for, feared, and so on.[12] The difficulty with this view, which Levinas calls the "intellectualist thesis," is the artificiality of separating off the representation from the acts that follow it. Such representation would be an impassive contemplation; but as Levinas asks: "how would the tension and care of a life arise from impassive representation?" (ibid.). Heidegger's counter-position, which attempts to derive "the freedom of contemplation" (the contemplation of the object in itself) "from commitment, from action, from care" is no less unsatisfactory. He takes "representation as the misfire of action" (*TI*, 169). For example, it is when my action is interrupted by the breaking of a tool that I am open to regarding this in its own structure rather than simply as means for my end. As we earlier noted, such a view would have representation cease just as soon as the implement was repaired. The regard to it as broken would not be to it as it is in itself, but rather as something needing to be repaired so that our action could continue.

Returning to his critique of the "intellectualist thesis" that makes representation foundational, Levinas notes that it "subordinates life to representation" (*TI*, 168). The "life" referred to is the life we live in the acts that are supposedly founded on representation. Yet, in order to represent, we first must live. This includes living from the elemental, which we cannot represent."Representation," then, "is conditioned. Its transcendental pretension is constantly belied by the life that is already implanted in the being representation claims to constitute" (*TI*, 169). The "transcendental pretension" referred to here is the assumption that representation is constitutive of the sense that being has for us. Since what constitutes is distinct from what it constitutes, this places the constituting subject outside of the sense of the world it constitutes. At this point, we forget that this subject is "implanted" in the world. We assert, on the contrary, that whatever sense it has must be distinct from that of the world—distinct, in fact, from the "worldly subjects" that we encounter there. Husserl, in his idealistic phase, is a good example of this position. He writes that the transcendental, constituting subject, correctly understood, "loses that which gives it the value of something real in the naively experienced, pre-given world; it loses its sense of being a soul of an animal organism which exists in a pre-given, spatial-temporal nature."[13] It becomes, instead, a separate realm, "a connection of absolute being into which nothing can enter and from which nothing can slip away, a connection which has no spatial-temporal outside."[14]

Representation, however, is a function of the life that is implanted in the subject. It is posterior to the reality of the life that it claims to constitute. In spite of this, it "claims to substitute itself *after the event* for this life in reality, so as to constitute this very reality" (*TI*, 169). Levinas's question is: How is this possible? How do we come to reverse the dependence between representation and life? As Levinas observes, since "representational thought . . . nourishes itself and lives from the very being it represents to itself" (*TI*, 168), it is "produced *after the event*" of such living from (*TI*, 169). His question is: how can we "account for this constitutive conditioning accomplished by representation," which takes the subject as a separate, absolute realm?

Levinas's reply returns us to the concrete facts of our embodied life—in particular, to the fact that we first separate ourselves off from the elemental by constructing a dwelling. He writes: "That representation is conditioned by life, but that this conditioning could be reversed after the event—that idealism is an eternal temptation—results from the very event of separation" (ibid.). We do engage in representational thought in our separated existence. Such thought, in fact, "refers to an exceptional possibility of this separated existence" (*TI*, 168). But the "event of separation" is not my being separated absolutely as a constitutor of sense. It is, rather, my establishing a home through my labor. It results from my "having limited a part of this world and having closed it off, having access to the elements I enjoy by way of the door and the window" (*TI*, 169–70). As for "exceptional possibility of this separated existence," it is simply my being able to look through its windows and "see without being seen like Gyges" (*TI*, 170). Doing so, I have a sovereignty with regard to the world that is *prior* to the world (as represented) even though it is *posterior* to the world (in fact). Thus, my sovereignty is "anterior to the world to which it is posterior" (*TI*, 170). What we have here is, then, another example of independence built on dependence. It is only when we forget this dependence that our independence is taken to be an unlimited sovereignty. We forget that the home that extends the interiority of our ego is still a dependent part of the world. Taking the independence and separation that it affords us as absolute, we take ourselves as a separate realm.

Heidegger also forgets that representation is conditioned by our having a home. For him, representation is a matter of pragmatic disclosure and having a home is thought of in terms of such disclosure. As Levinas asks, "In *Being and Time*, the home does not appear apart from the system of implements. But can the 'in view of oneself' characteristic of care be brought about without a disengagement from the situation, without a recollection . . . without being at home with oneself?" (*TI*, 170). Levinas's point is that care for one's being involves recollection. It requires disengagement from the situation and a reflection on oneself (*Selbstbesinnuung*). This, however, *cannot arise without the home*. Having a home is a necessary condition for care. Thus, when you are homeless, you are immediately exposed to the elements. You have no time or place to plan ahead or have projects. You cannot labor, since you have nowhere to store the results of this labor. For the same reason, you cannot have property. Given this, the "care" that concerns itself with what sort of being you will be is deprived of the possibilities that open up its choices. Its "thrown situation," lacking a home, becomes an empty one. With this, the very possibility of representation as pragmatic disclosure loses its foundation.

Levinas brings up representation in his analysis of freedom because of their close connection. Representation, he writes, is "a determination of the other by the same, without the same being determined by the other." This definition excludes "representation from reciprocal relations, whose terms meet and limit one another." This means that representing something is "equivalent to remaining exterior" to its determining you (*TI*, 170). It is, in fact, overcoming its real causal influence on you. This position should be familiar to us from our earlier remarks on Husserl.[15] According to Husserl, our relation to the objects we represent—"intentional objects" in his terminology—is a relation to the *senses* of such objects. Since such senses are not physical things, the intentional relation is not a real, causal relation. For Husserl, then, we overcome the real influence of real objects on ourselves by representing their senses. Since the relation of senses to one another is not causally determined, our ability to represent objects as senses gives us our freedom of thought. This is what makes the world of the consciousness of such senses a "separate" realm.

While agreeing with the position that representation involves our "remaining exterior" to what we represent, Levinas has his own derivation of the separation and, hence, the freedom that representation affords us. Separation begins with my living from "the elements in which I am steeped." It continues with the dwelling that separates off a place within the elemental. Here, even though "I cannot quit the space in which I am steeped . . . I can indeed recollect myself in the midst of my life, which is life from" (*TI*, 170). Such recollection, however, is incomplete. With the home comes the possibility of possessions, but the "recollection which draws me out of submergence" is "not a simple echo of possession" (ibid.). The gathering of things in the home, which makes them "mine," does not separate me from them. Even "the relation with the Other who welcomes me in the Home" is insufficient. I need to "be able to free myself from the very possession that the welcome of the Home establishes . . . in order that I be able to see things in themselves, that is, represent them to myself" (*TI*, 170–71). This means, I need to "know how to give what I possess." I do this when "I welcome the Other who presents himself in my home by opening my home to him" (*TI*, 171).

What does this Other bring that allows me to engage in representation? What does my welcome of him involve? According to Levinas, my encounter is not with "the discreet present of the Feminine," but with "the indiscrete face of the Other that calls me into question" (*TI*, 171). The encounter with this calling into question *is* language. As Levinas defines language: "This calling into question of the I, coextensive with the manifestation of the Other in the face, we call language" (ibid). Now, the action of language is to present the intersubjective, the objective world that is there for everyone. Since our seeing is embodied, we cannot see out of another person's eyes. Thus, it is only by asking Others if they see what we see that we can assume that the object is present not just to ourselves but to Others as well. If they agree, then we assume that the object is real—that is, it is there for all of us to see. But this means that its "real" presence is that of language. Since we can only confirm its intersubjective presence through language, the objective world that is there for everyone is present only through language. As Levinas expresses this, "the universality a thing receives from the word . . . extracts it from the *hic et nunc*" (here and now). The "language, which designates it to the other, is a primordial dispossession," one where "the generality of the word institutes a common world" (*TI*, 173). This dispossession is the thing's being dispossessed of my here and now, my sensuous interiority. It is its relocation to the realm of language and the common communicative world.

This world is the object of "representational thought." We do not have a material relation to it. Composed as it is of linguistic symbols, it does not materially (i.e., physically) determine us. Thus, for Levinas, we transcend the physical world's real influence on us by transforming it into linguistically present senses or meanings. This position is, of course, similar to Husserl's. What distinguishes it is its emphasis on language and, hence, on conversation with the Other. The "freedom" that representation affords us thus has a moral basis. In Levinas's words, "representation derives its freedom with regard to the world that nourishes it from the essentially moral relation with the Other" (*TI*, 172). This moral relation is provided by language, that is, by the sincerity and generosity that speaking and responding openly imply. I have to be generous enough to offer the Other my view of the world, thereby dispossessing myself of it. I also have to sincerely open myself up to the views that Others have of it. This can be put in terms of the "dispossession" that language works on the sensuous presence of the world in us. Its separation of the world from its sensuous representation is accompanied by our self-separation. This is because when the Other calls me into question, I have to go outside of myself. To grasp this call, I have to regard the world from a different perspective than my own. I must engage in the moral stance of putting myself and my own perspective into question. This self-separation opens the possibility of freeing myself from myself, that is, from the prejudices springing from my background and situation. For Levinas, then, "representation derives its freedom with regard to the world that nourishes it from the essentially moral relation, the relation with the Other. Morality . . . calls in question, and puts at a distance from itself, the I itself" (*TI*, 172, translation modified).

This morality is not something abstract. It cannot be, given the constitutive layers that form its genesis: living from, dwelling, the welcoming Other, calling into question, language, and representation. Given that each layer presupposes the ones that precede it, we have to say with Levinas, "the transcendence of the face is not enacted outside of the world" or its "economy" (*TI*, 172). In its broadest sense, this economy can be defined as the system of exchange between ourselves and the world. Our bodily metabolism with its organic needs is an example of this economy; so are our normal, everyday commercial transactions. They point to our dependence on the world, that is, to the fact that we live only through a constant process of exchange with it, of "living from" it in an extended sense. The relation to the Other, as presupposing the earlier constitutive levels, must be in terms of this economy. The moral import of this is that "no human or interhuman relationship can be enacted outside of economy; no face can be approached with empty hands and closed home" (*TI*, 172). This does not mean I give to the Other only if I can expect a return. Rather my action is one of generosity. I speak and I explain myself. I don't just return one coin for its equivalent. I add to the conversation. Conversation is a mode of generosity, of giving to—sharing with—the Other. In Levinas's words, "The relationship with the Other is not produced outside of the world, but puts in question the world [that is privately] possessed." Here, the "first donation," the first gift to the Other "consists in speaking the world to the Other." With language, one makes one's world common, open to oneself and to the Other. This is "a primordial dispossession, a first donation" (*TI*, 173). Such speaking to the Other is a "generalization," a making common. This, Levinas writes, is "the offering of the world to the Other." It is the act "which answers the face of the Other" (*TI*, 174).

It is in terms of this embodied economy that the final factor in the analysis of freedom is portrayed. This is the autonomy of our choosing. I can choose to open my home to the Other; or I can choose not to. Generosity to the Other is not based on need. There is no compulsion in it. It is a voluntary and, hence, an ethical act. Thus, as Levinas says, "the separated being can close itself up in its egoism." This possibility of "banishing with impunity all hospitality (that is all language) from one's home . . . evinces . . . the radicalism of separation" (*TI*, 73). Separation means that my needs are fulfilled. I can live in my home. I can speak my language with those of my home—my friends, my group, and so on—and never open myself up to the language of the Other, to his "teaching me." All this can be done with "impunity" insofar as I do not need anything. Thus, the Other in his demands on me manifests authority without power. The Other is there for me as the author of his words, but I need not listen. I need not respond by offering him my world, my view. Since this is not a power relationship, I am not forced to respond. Were it a relation of power, it would not be a communicative relation, it would not involve mutuality. The underlying point here is that only voluntary actions can be considered to be moral. But these are not actions driven by need. For Heidegger, in Levinas's portrayal, Dasein is driven by need. Dasein has no home. For Levinas, he does; and having a home means that he can choose or not choose to be generous.

The Transcendence of the Face

Levinas asserts that "the transcendence of the face is not enacted outside of the world" or its "economy" (*TI*, 172). But he has also written that "the transcendence of the face is at the same time its absence from this world into which it enters" (*TI*, 75). In affirming both positions, he is claiming that even though this transcendence manifests itself in economic terms, the face that it manifests is not itself an item in the world's economy. The recognition of a face cannot, in other words, be reduced to economic terms.

One example of such a reduction is found in Hegel's *Phenomenology of Mind*, where Hegel describes the dialectical genesis of self-consciousness.[16] According to Hegel, "Self-consciousness . . . is desire as such [*Begierde überhaupt*]." He explains this by saying that, in the state of desire, self-consciousness has a "two-fold object; the first is immediate; it is the object of sensuous certainty and of perception that is marked by the character of negation." This is the negation of desire that wants to consume the object. "The second [object of consciousness] is itself . . . which is present in the first instance only in the opposition of the first object to it."[17] Such self-consciousness is only intermittent in the animal world. It arises as the desiring animal grasps itself as other than the desired object—that is, as the desire that does not yet possess it. The satisfaction of desire is, then, the collapse of this self-consciousness. The human solution to this collapse occurs, according to Hegel, through the recognition of the Other. One does not desire the Other in order to negate him. This would eliminate his recognition. What one desires is the Other's consciousness as desire. One desires to be desired by this desire. Now, animal desire is fundamentally a desire for life. To be desired by this desire is to be recognized by the Other as life. This means being recognized as the *master* of the Other in the sense of having the Other's life completely in one's power. In Hegel's account, this unequal relation is established in a battle where one of the combatants ends by yielding, that is, by refusing to further risk his natural life. Such life, thus, remains for him his highest value. The victor, by contrasts, risks everything. In holding his life as naught, he regards himself as not being determined by the natural desires that focus on life and its preservation. In the recognition he receives from the loser, who assumes the position of the *slave*, the master has his sense of self.

The difficulty with this solution is, as Hegel says, "a form of recognition has arisen that is one-sided and unequal."[18] For the recognition of the slave to mean anything for the master, he must recognize the slave as a person like himself. He cannot, however, do this and preserve the master-slave relationship. Mastery, then, is at a dialectical dead end. Those who labor as slaves, however, can make progress. In their labor, they can recognize themselves in their products; they can see their human selfhood in the human world that they create. They, thus, have a prospect of achieving a self-consciousness denied to those who merely enjoy their products.

From Levinas's perspective, the problem of this view is that the products produced by labor are caught up in an alienating economy. Thus, "the worker does not hold in his hands all the threads of his own action." In the modern world, "works have a destiny independent of the I, are integrated in an ensemble of works: they can be exchanged, that is, be maintained in the anonymity of money." Given this, "the interiority from which the works proceed . . . does not recognize itself in the existence attributed to it by the economy" (*TI*, 176). Levinas's point goes much deeper than the alienation of labor brought about by modern industrial practices. It concerns the difference between the "what" and the "who." When someone asks us, "Who is Mr. X?" and we answer by saying *what* he does, our answer "refers to a system of relations" that refers back to the economy. The *what* is his function within it. Such a function, for example, that of being a doctor, a lawyer, a member of some council, and so on, can be taken up by someone else. As such, it can be alienated from the person performing it. The *who*, however, refers to the "non-qualifiable presence of an existent who presents himself without reference to anything, and yet distinguishes himself from every other existent" (*TI*, 177). The reference here is to something non-replaceable, something that cannot be alienated.

The distinction between the "what" and the "who" is, of course, a crucial one in *Being and Time*. According to Heidegger, "an entity is either a 'who'(existence) or a 'what' (presence-at-hand [*Vorhandenheit*] in the broadest sense."[19] Objects, things with a definite essence or what-character, constitute the latter. As for the former, as Heidegger writes, "The 'essence' of Dasein lies in its existence."[20] Dasein is a "who" rather than a "what" since his essence is not given in advance, but is rather a matter of the choices he makes (and unmakes). As a chooser, Dasein distinguishes himself from his choices. In himself, he has an existence structure consisting of existentialia that are distinct from the ontological categories applicable to objects. As Heidegger observes, we tend to think of ourselves in such ontological categories, describing ourselves as a "what," but this is an error. It does not catch our uniqueness.[21]

For Levinas, the *who* does not designate a chooser, but rather a face. Transcendence is not a matter of the chooser being other than his choices. It is rather a matter of the speaking face. In Levinas's words, "The question *who* [*are you*] ? designates a face . . . here what one asks and he whom one questions coincide" (*TI*, 177). This does not mean that he is identical with what he has said. Rather, he presents himself as "a being who is manifested precisely as absent from his manifestation: a manifestation in the absence of being—a phenomenon" (*TI*, 178). He is present as the "saying" that is *not* the manifest "said." Here, "the signifier, he who gives a sign, is not signified," is not caught by the said (*TI*, 182). In order to be apprehended, he "must present himself before every sign, by himself—present a face." As we have seen, the person speaking transcends the said by his being able to add to it, to come to the defense of his words. To attend to this speaking, adding to and correcting what is said is to attend to "the surplus of spoken language over written language." Recognition of the Other involves this surplus. In Levinas's words, it involves "the surplus that language involves with respect to all the works and labors that manifest a man." This is a surplus that "measures the distance between the living man and the dead" (ibid.).

For Levinas, then, the transcendence of the face is not enacted outside of the world or its economy since it is enacted in speech and works. Such transcendence, however, is its absence from the world into which it enters, since neither speech nor works capture it. This relation between the person and what he says, Levinas suggests, is reminiscent of Kant's phenomenal-noumenal distinction. The noumenal is the thing in itself; the phenomenal is the thing as it appears to us. With regard to the person, the "thing in itself expresses itself. Expression . . . is of itself presence of a face, and hence appeal and teaching, entry into relation with me—the ethical relation" (*TI*, 181). My relation with the noumenal reality of the other person is, then, ethical. It involves attending to the surplus of the saying over the said. The said is the appearance of the Other. It is, as part of the world, within its economy. The surplus of the saying, however, is beyond this. It is here that we attend to the Other as he is in himself. According to Levinas, the same thing can be said with regard to oneself. In his words, "It is only in approaching the Other that I attend to myself . . . The face I welcome makes me pass from phenomenon to being . . . In discourse I expose myself to the questioning of the Other, and this urgency of the response . . . engenders me for responsibility; as responsible I am brought to my final reality." This "final reality" is "my existence as a 'thing in itself'" (*TI*, 178). I manifest this in my responding. Such responding is not a one-time affair but an ongoing process by which I manifest the surplus that is my noumenal being.[22]

Levinas's emphasis on language as manifesting this surplus recalls the Bible's insistence that one cannot represent God through any graven image, but only through the word. The distinction between the Greek religious sensibility and the Hebrew is encapsulated in this. The Greek gods were natural entities in the world. As such they could be represented in terms of the world (its animals, humans, etc.). The Hebrew God cannot. He is in-finite in the sense of not being representable by any finite thing. The Israelites did, of course, have his words. They placed his commandments in the tabernacle. Yet even such words do not capture him as a "living" God, a God that continually added to sacred history by continuing to speak to the prophets.

9

The Face

Totality and Infinity, III, A–B

The Infinity of the Face as Light

Levinas writes in "Diachrony and Representation" that the face is "the rupture of phenomenology."[1] It is such as offering us more than what can be seen, as giving itself as not being able to be given. As Levinas explains this, the "enigma or ambiguity" of the face is that it both "calls forth" and "tears itself away from . . . presence and objectivity."[2] The calling forth occurs in the fact that I can "see" the face of the Other. I can phenomenologically describe and objectively represent its physical features. The face, however, is not a catalog of such features. Insofar as it is grasped as the face of another person, it is grasped as exceeding this. Thus, when I look at the eyes of another person, I see and I do not see. I see the eyes as features of the face. I do not see *what makes them eyes*—that is, their seeing. Both what they *have seen* and *will see* escape me. The other person's memories and anticipations are not public objects. But this means that the interpretations based on these, the senses that the other person makes of the world, are also not public objects; they are not available to the sight and sensibility that directs itself to these objects. Levinas draws a number of consequences from this rupture, the chief of which involve the Other's escape from predictability and, hence, his freedom from my control. In part A of section 3, he considers this rupture in terms of his position that the encounter with the Other is what first gives us a sense of the public realm. Given that it is only in speaking with the Other that we can confirm the presence of publicly available objects, the sense of the seeing that presents such objects depends on what is not seen. The "light" of such seeing must, in other words, have a source other than that of the visible sun.

To make this point, Levinas argues against the traditional views of sensibility and vision. As before, his position has to be understood as a "contestation" of Heidegger's. For Heidegger, "Dasein is its disclosedness." It does not rely on something else to be such. In his words, "It is itself the clearing." It is such in its being outside of itself in its three temporal modes. These are what open up the world so as to let things appear in their intelligible structure as means towards ends. Letting things appear is a function of the light. Heidegger, accordingly, uses the word *Lichtung* or "lighting" for the "clearing." The term refers to a clearing in the forest where the light shines through. The "existential-ontological structure" of Dasein that is its temporal apartness is, he claims, what is meant by the traditional picture of the "light of nature."[3] Such light has been traditionally understood as the light of reason.[4] This conception comes from the *Republic*, where Plato contrasts the physical sun with its intelligible counterpart that is seen once we leave the cave and enter the world of intelligible realities.[5] For Heidegger, this intelligible light is, in the first instance, Dasein itself. This means that, "as being-in-the-world, it is illuminated by itself and not through another being."[6] This, however, does not mean that Dasein is the ultimate source of intelligibility. The clearing that it provides is focused by its "understanding of Being."[7] Insofar as such understanding becomes concrete in a standard for the real, it guides Dasein's disclosure. Thus, the ultimate light is not provided by a being, but rather by Being itself in the form of some given standard.[8] In Levinas's words, "For Heidegger, an openness upon Being, which is not *a being*, which is not a 'something,' is necessary in order that, in general, a 'something' manifest itself" (*TI*, 189). For Levinas, by contrast, the openness of the clearing is a function of the face. It provides the "light" that allows us to see. This involves a different sense of light than that present in the phenomenological thought of Husserl and Heidegger. They think of the clearing in terms of vision, that is, in terms of sensible experience. But for Levinas, "the epiphany as a face determine[s] a relationship different from that which characterizes all our sensible experience" (*TI*, 187). The emphasis on the face shifts the relation from the visual to the ethical. Conversation rather than sight becomes the means of disclosure.

Levinas begins by noting that Husserl's doctrine of intentionality "has compromised the idea of sensation by removing [from it] the character of being a concrete datum" (*TI*, 184). For Husserl, as we recall, the intentional relation to the object involves the interpretation of our sensations. This means that we don't see our sensations, we see the objects that result from such interpretations. As I earlier cited Husserl: "It belongs to perception that something appears within it, but *interpretation* makes up what we term appearance. . . . I hear a *barrel organ*—the sensed tones I interpret as *barrel organ tones*."[9] This means that sensations are always referred to their objects. In Levinas's words, "color is always . . . the color of a dress, a lawn, a wall; sound is a noise of a passing car, or a voice of someone speaking" and so forth (*TI*, 187). The difficulty with this view is that it fails "to recognize the plane on which the sensible life is lived as enjoyment." In enjoyment, we have "sensations whose representational content dissolves into their affective content" (ibid.). Thus, in the bodily experience of eating an apple, our experience is not objectifying but affective. It is one of tastes, textures, chewing, swallowing, the sense of something being within us, and of hunger being satisfied. The words we use to convey this experience seem to be objective, that is, seem to express what is publicly there for everybody. But this is deceptive. The experience that each of us has is private, not open to the public. As entering into the private, non-publicly representable sphere, "enjoyment," Levinas writes, "is endowed with a dynamism other than that of [external] perception" (ibid.). The sensations I have when I eat an apple are "not the subjective counterpart of objective qualities, but an enjoyment 'anterior' to the crystallization of consciousness, [into] I and non-I, into subject and object" (*TI*, 188). In other words, sensations exhibit a "transcendental function *sui generis*," one where the "structures of the non-I are not necessarily structures of objectivity." This is because the sensation of some quality, when regarded in itself, yields this "quality without [the] support or extension . . . [of some] object endowed with qualities" (*TI*, 188). Sensation, then, is neither the I nor reducible to being the sensation of a quality of some object. It is something in itself apart from either the interpretation the I imposes upon it or the objective quality resulting from this interpretation.

Levinas's insistence on this point concerns the body in its uniqueness—in its inability as *my* functioning body—to be substituted for another person's body. Such uniqueness translates into the uniqueness—that is, the non-objective, private quality—of my sensation. In opposing the failure to recognize this, he is opposing the inability of traditional ethical theories to consider our embodiment. This truncates these theories since disembodied beings are not physically vulnerable and do not suffer physical needs. This prevents their understanding responsibility in terms of such needs. In virtue ethics, for example, character is what is important. It is what helps one function well. Thus, Aristotle's *Ethics* has no counterpart to the biblical appeal to aid the widow and the orphan. To the point that the body comes in, it is in terms of its role in our functioning. If one is very ugly, for example, one cannot be happy since one cannot function well socially.[10] In deontology or duty ethics, the body suffers an even greater marginalization. Kant's universal categorical imperative abstracts from all particulars—including those of our bodily particularity. The same failure to account for this particularity occurs in utilitarianism. Its imperative is to pursue the greatest happiness, even if this means sacrificing the happiness of the few for the sake of the many. The fundamental principle of morality is, in Mill's words, that "one person's happiness, supposed equal in degree . . . is counted for exactly as much as another's."[11] The principle, in other words, is summed up in "Bentham's dictum, 'everybody to count for one, nobody for more than one.'" Such a doctrine makes each person, as "one," equivalent to every other one.[12] For Levinas, all such theories fail to recognize our bodily being in its felt uniqueness. Behind this failure is the assumption that vision, which grasps its objects at a distance, determines our access to being. This places the body at a distance from itself. It becomes not the felt, but the seen body.

The schema of vision they employ consists of the eye, the object, and the light. Plato sets the pattern by observing that "besides the eye and the thing, vision presupposes the light. The eye does not see the light, but the object in the light" (*TI*, 189). Light makes the air transparent. It becomes the void through which the object appears. In Levinas's words, "The light . . . makes the thing appear by driving out the shadows; it empties space. It makes space arise specifically as a void" (ibid.). Through it, we have the "openness of experience." We can move our hand through the void. We can see through it. This coming forth from the void" of our experiences of objects is interpreted as "their coming from their origin" in the objects themselves. Levinas adds: "this 'openness' of experience or this experience of openness explains the privilege of objectivity and its claim to coincide with the very being of existents" (ibid.). This is because, in this "schema of vision" that prevails "from Aristotle to Heidegger," the object is public. It is out there in the open available to everyone. It can be in relation to everyone becomes it is in the void. Thus, the privilege of objectivity stems from the fact that "the relation of the subject with the object is subordinated to the relation of the object with the void of openness, which is not an object." In this schema, "to comprehend the object is to apprehend it out of an illuminated site it does not fill" (*TI*, 190).

For modern philosophy, starting with Descartes, this "void of openness" is understood as a "spatial void." Its properties are given by geometry. As a result, geometrical notions impose themselves on our conception of the object. More precisely, objects become understood in terms of their mathematical relations to other objects, such relations being reducible to the mathematical properties of space itself. This view makes the "spatial void a 'something'—the form of all experience, the object of geometry, something seen in its turn" (*TI*, 190). Against this, Levinas argues that our geometrical conceptions "impose themselves upon us from the things seen: the line is the limit of a thing; the plane [is] the surface of an object. It is on the basis of a something that geometrical notions impose themselves." This means that when emptied of its objects, the spatial void becomes nothing. In his words, "considered in itself, illuminate space, emptied by light of the obscurity that filled it, is nothing" (*TI*, 190). This is not an "absolute nothingness," he hastens to add. What we face when confronting it is, rather, the impersonal "there is" that he described in his early work, *Existence and Existents*.[13] This "there is," according to *Ethics and Infinity*, is "neither nothingness nor being" in the sense of an "event of being." It is simply the anonymous background for all occurring, one that leaves us, when we confront it, with a disorientation amounting to "horror and panic."[14] In *Totality and Infinity*, he writes: "The negation of every qualifiable thing allows the impersonal *there is* to arise again, returning intact behind every negation, whatever the degree of negation. The silence of infinite spaces is terrifying. The invasion of this *there is* does not correspond to any representation." We experience it not as something, but rather as a kind of "vertigo" (ibid.).

According to Levinas, "vision," with its focus on *objects* in space, "is precisely the possibility of forgetting the horror of this interminable . . . aperion" (*TI*, 190–91). The same focus makes it also forget the sensuous enjoyment that first allows us to escape this aperion. Focusing on what it takes to be the geometric properties of space itself, vision gives objects their significance, not by referring them to the enjoyment of a subject, but rather "*by reference to* other objects" (*TI*, 190). This means that "vision is not a transcendence. It ascribes a signification by the *relation* it makes possible." The empty space it penetrates "simply ensures the condition for the lateral signification of things within the same" (*TI*, 191). They become things *within* the system of spatial (and temporal) relations (*TI*, 191). They do not refer to anything *beyond* this system. The same lack of transcendence arises in our regard to individual objects. Transcendence implies an interiority that is transcended. But objects, in this view, have no interiority. Taken "in the spatial sense," the interior of a thing is simply a surface that can be exposed. Here, "the depth of the thing can have no other meaning than that of its matter, and the revelation of matter is essentially superficial" (*TI*, 192).

Levinas's concentration on the lived body and its sensuous pleasures is meant to counter this geometric view. The lived body has an interiority. As such, it can sustain a relation of transcendence to something exterior. This is the relation to the face of the Other. It provides the "light." In Levinas's words, "The relation with the Other alone introduces a dimension of transcendence and leads us to a relation totally different from experience in the sensible sense of the term" (*TI*, 193). This implies that Heidegger's *Lichtung* (or clearing) arises through this relation to the Other. The relation provides the transcendence that "clears" space for disclosure. It does so by discourse since the face of the Other is a speaking face. The Other does not just speak, but comments on what he says, adds to it and corrects it. Thus, my relation to him is not just the Heideggerian "letting a being be" through pragmatic disclosure. For Levinas, "Speaking rather than 'letting be' solicits the Other. Speech cuts across vision" (*TI*, 195). It does so because the Other (unlike the object) can actively contest my interpretation. He can dispute what I say about the object. He can also gainsay my interpretation of him when I make him the "theme" of my discourse. What I say "seems to contain the other." "But," Levinas adds, "already it is said to another who, as interlocutor, has quit the theme that encompasses him." This Other rises up "behind the said." "Emancipated from the theme that seemed a moment to hold him," he "forthwith contests the meaning I ascribe" to him (ibid.). Levinas's claim here is that transcendence is inscribed in this relation because of the *infinity* of the Other. Such infinity designates the Other's non-limited character. It signifies his crossing the limits that have been laid down by me in making him my theme. As Levinas defines it: "The *presence of a being* not entering into, *but overflowing the sphere of the same determines its 'status' as infinite*" (ibid.). The "idea of infinity" is that of the "more contained in the less." It is that of excess of the Other over the interpretations that make him my theme.

A good way to describe this excess is in terms of intention and fulfillment. For most things, we recognize something as itself when it shows itself as we intend it, that is, as we expect it to appear given our past experience. The intention, we can say, forms an anticipatory interpretation of a given experience. Here, the givenness of what we intend *matches* our intentions. However, as I noted earlier, there are other possible relations of intention to fulfillment. The givenness of what we intend can be *other* that what we intend. This happens when we are simply mistaken. Such givenness can also be *less*. It can, for example, not offer the detail that was part of our intentions. Suppose, for example, you mistake a mannequin for a person: expecting to meet a person, you can cross a department store to speak with what appears to be a well-dressed salesperson standing near a counter. As you approach, however, you realize your mistake. The mannequin does not return your gaze; when spoken to, it does not respond. Thus, expecting to encounter a person, the mannequin you do experience offers you *less* than you intend. To reverse this, when you expect to experience a mannequin and encounter, instead, a person, you are offered *more* than you intend. When this happens, you feel immediately embarrassed by a lack of the appropriate intentions. You accidentally treated the person as a thing, as incapable of independent observation and action. Because you should have been expecting more, you behaved inappropriately. To behave appropriately, you must intend the person as capable of such independence. But this means intending him in an intention that intends its own surpassing. Doing so, you expect that he will surpass the content of your intention. The point is that we recognize Others as persons by virtue of their behaving as we do, but not in any strictly predictable ways. There is always a certain excess in what they show us. They are not limited to the contents of our intentions, that is, to the anticipations that arise from our interpretations of their situation. They act out of their own interpretations. To intend them as capable of this is, in fact, to intend the inadequacy of our own intentions. Such intentions direct themselves towards fulfillments that will exceed them. Their object is an exceeding givenness. This excess is what manifests the infinity of the Other.

In employing the terms "intention" and "fulfillment," the above description is essentially phenomenological. It may, thus, seem liable to the critique that Levinas makes with regard to all visually based philosophies. Its terms, however, can be put in terms of Levinas's conception of infinity. Levinas contrasts this with Kant's conception. Kant takes the infinite as a regulative ideal. This means, as Levinas writes, it "presupposes the finite, which it amplifies infinitely" (*TI*, 196). The regulative ideal of a free act, for example, is that of an act where the limiting conditions that determine it are removed. Similarly, the ideal of God is that of an absolutely unconditioned condition that we arrive at by removing one by one all the conditions that condition something. In each case, we start off with the finite and gradually approach the infinite by removing limits. Does this procedure actually allow us to generate a conception of the infinite or does it actually presuppose one? Levinas asserts that the latter is the case. For him "this passage to the limit . . . implicates in an unacknowledged form the idea of infinity with all the consequences that Descartes drew from it" (ibid.). Descartes in the *Meditations* asserts that we cannot grasp the finitude of the finite unless we first have the idea of the infinite. The finite presupposes the infinite, not vice versa.[15] The argument, here, is similar to that of Plato in the *Phaedo* where he argues that we cannot say that things are more or less equal unless we have a prior knowledge of a standard for equality (*Phaedo*, 74d-e). We require the positive conception before we can say that something falls short of it.

Levinas's positive conception of the infinite is that of the more in the less, of overflow, of inability to contain the infinite. We presuppose (and, in fact, experience) this in our attempts to grasp another person. In Levinas's words, in "the situation we call [the] welcome of the face . . . the idea of infinity" is experienced as "the overflowing of finite thought by its content" (*TI*, 197). The "finite thought" is the interpretation I have of the Other; the "content" is what the Other presents me with. What we experience in this situation is, then, "the relation of thought with what exceeds its capacity, with what at each moment it learns without suffering shock." This occurs when we converse with the Other, when we are forced to confront views that oppose our own. For Levinas, then, "The idea of infinity is produced in the *opposition* of conversation, in sociality" (ibid.). As we have seen, this is also true of our conception of the objective world. As there for the Other as well as for me, it participates in the transcendence of our relation. It, too, is infinite in the sense that it always exceeds our attempts to grasp it. The fact that the Other sees what I do not see means that the world that is there for us both exceeds each one of us. What this signifies is that, epistemologically, we are social animals. Our attempts to know the world that transcends us are informed by our "sociality."

Another expression of the transcendence inherent in my relation to the Other is the ethical aspect of the face. According to Levinas, "the face speaks to me and thereby invites me to a relation incommensurate with a power exercised" (*TI*, 198). It does not defy my power as an opposing power, but rather it opposes my "ability for power" (*mon pouvoir de pouvoir*). Facing the Other, I face "the very unforseeableness of his reaction"; he can "sovereignly say *no* to me." What resists me is "not the superlative of power, but precisely the infinity of his transcendence" (ibid.). I confront "the resistance of that which has no resistance—the ethical resistance" (*TI*, 199). I cannot get a hold of the Other as other. I can murder him, but then I face a thing. The only possible relation I can have to him *as Other* is to respond to him. This can be put in terms of the excessive presence of the Other. According to Levinas, "if the resistance to murder were not ethical but real, we would have a perception of it." But we cannot see this resistance. It is not some*thing* in the world. It is a presence that exceeds things. Since I am always already with Others, I have to say that this relation to the face is first. In Levinas's words, "the epiphany of the face is ethical. . . . War presupposes peace . . . [war] does not represent the first event of the encounter" (ibid.). By contrast, in Hegel's description of the genesis of self-consciousness, peace presupposes war. It begins, as we saw, in the struggle for recognition. Peace only arises when one side wins. But such peace is temporary. One side is master, the other slave. One side is free, the other not. The result is an inherently unstable situation that works itself out in the class conflicts that mark human history. Only at its end is there mutual recognition and, hence, a stable freedom.

Levinas's opposing view is that freedom is the gift of the Other. It occurs because my encounter with the Other is initially ethical. In conversation, "the being that expresses itself imposes itself, but does so precisely by appealing to me with its destitution and nudity . . . Thus, in expression, the being that imposes itself does not limit but promotes my freedom by arousing my goodness" (*TI*, 200). This, as we have seen, is a goodness that is freely chosen. It completes the genesis of our embodied freedom. Such freedom is essential for learning. If I limit the other's ability to put me into question, if I silence him so that I don't have to respond, then I can learn nothing from him. Furthermore, the question of reason, the question of why something is the way it is can only arise if I confront alternatives. But, as I earlier noted, this happens only when I face the Other as other. Without this, reason, which looks for reasons or grounds, cannot get started. Thus, once again we arrive at the fact that our relation to the Other is the source of our natural light, understood as a light of reason. Given that "the putting into question [of my views of the world] emanates from the other" (*TI*, 195), my conversation with him first opens me up to the light of reason. It does this by the demand that I explain myself, that I give the reasons for my interpretation of the situation confronting us.

Language and Alterity

The arguments by which Levinas links the light of nature to discourse naturally affect his view of discourse. He asserts that "discourse founds signification" (*TI*, 204). This means that we have to understand signification in terms of our relation to the Other and not vice versa. To mean or to signify presupposes this relation. In presenting this position, he rejects a number of alternatives. He refuses, for example, "to assimilate language to activity, to that prolongation of thought in corporeity, the *I think* in the *I can*" (*TI*, 205). Such a view sees language as simply an extension of pragmatic disclosure and, as such, incapable of putting into question the very terms of such disclosure. He also opposes the "nominalism" that seeks "to explain a divergence between thought, incapable of aiming at a general object, and language, which does seem to refer to general objects" (ibid.). In this view, which confuses conceptualization and imagination, we cannot think—that is, imagine—general objects, since all the images we can form are of particulars. The general sense of our words comes from their "symbolism," which, in the original theories, "amounted to association" (ibid.). In other words, we make a term general by associating with it an indefinite number of images. Thus, while we cannot imagine (conceive) a triangle, save that it have a particular size and shape, we can associate the word "triangle" with any number of images of particular triangles, thereby making it a general term.[16] Levinas dismisses this view by referring to Husserl's critique of it, which "showed this divergency [between thought and the general term] to be only apparent" (ibid.). In fact, it disappears once we do not equate conceiving of something with imagining or drawing a mental picture of it. Levinas also rejects the "naturalism" that reduces reason to a bodily function. Here, having similar bodies, similar brains, and so on, would mean that we have a similar "reason." In Levinas's words, "The concordance between consciousnesses would then be explained by the resemblance of beings constituted in the same fashion. Language would be reduced to a system of signs" passing between them (*TI*, 207–8). If we adopt this position, we "run all the risks of naturalist psychologism, against which the arguments of the first volume of the *Logische Untersuchungen* are ever valid" (*TI*, 208). The point of such arguments is that the material categories that this position limits us to cannot account for signification. Signs, after all, are not material things. They have no causal agency. Similarly, linguistic sequences, such as the sentences that form this page, are not causal sequences. It is simply a category mistake to take the sequence, "All A's are B's; all B's are C's; therefore all A's are C's," as asserting that the first two statements (the premises) materially *cause* the third (the conclusion). In citing Husserl's *Logische Untersuchungen*, Levinas does not mean to endorse its view of language. Husserl in this work takes "reason" as "the internal coherence of an ideal order" (ibid.). This is an order between signs that is determined by the formal relations between them and also by their ideal meaning contents. Such formal relations, such as "p implies q," compose formal logic. Relations of various types of content, such as color, extension, loudness, pitch, and so on, make up a logic of content. Its coherence requires that we cannot speak of color without extension or pitch without loudness, and so on.[17] In both types of logic, the individuality of the speakers is completely abstracted from so that one loses the "ipseity of individual consciousness" (*TI*, 208).[18]

What language needs, however, is a plurality of individual consciousnesses. For it to function, these have to be in communication and yet distinct from each other. The primacy of such consciousness means that "it is not the mediation of the sign that forms signification, but signification (whose primordial event is the face-to-face) that makes the sign function possible" (*TI*, 206). In this sign function, I signify something to someone. To signify is to indicate in the absence of something. Its necessity comes from the fact that you cannot see out of my eyes. The only way in which I can indicate to you what I am seeing is to speak. My words function as signs insofar as they stand for (or stand in the place of) what they point to. The same holds for you. I cannot see what you see since I cannot occupy your position in space at the same time as you do. Our embodiment prevents this. In both cases, as Levinas says, "signification is to perception what the symbol is to the object symbolized" (*TI*, 207). The symbol stands for the object, just as signification of our words stands for what we see. With this, we return to the point that the objective (the there-for-everyone) presence of the world is through discourse. The words stand for the objects that we see in common (objects that we never, however, see *through* one another's eyes). Otherwise put: the objective presence of the world is linguistic. It is present in the speech that stands in the place of what each of us individually sees. Such speech presupposes the apartness of our consciousnesses. This holds since were I to directly experience what you see, our perspectives would be the same and our consciousnesses would merge. But then we would not need language to communicate what we are experiencing. Language, therefore, demands the otherness of the Other. It is based on the fact that our consciousnesses do not merge but preserve their individuality. This means, as Levinas writes, "the essence of language is the relation with the Other" (*TI*, 207).

As Levinas stresses, the alterity implicit in this relation cannot be overcome. Thus, I cannot constitute the sense of this Other. I cannot, starting from myself and my experiences, make complete sense of her. She always exceeds the intentions I draw from my experiences. What I face in confronting her, Levinas writes, is "an overflowing of the intention that envisages [intends] by the envisaged [the person I intend]" (*TI*, 207). This implies that "the being of signification consists in putting into question . . . constitutive freedom itself" (*TI*, 206). My freedom to constitute the Other (to make sense of her) is limited since as other, she escapes me, that is, she is not present. I can access neither her present perceptions, nor her memories of her past perceptions nor the expectations that arise for her from what she has seen. This non-presence is, however, precisely what makes language necessary. In the face-to-face, I speak to the Other. We form, in discourse, a "society" that does not dispense with alterity.

In this society, we are obligated to respond to each other. In Levinas's words, "the Other faces me and puts me in question and *obliges* me by his essence qua infinity" (*TI*, 207). The obligation comes from the excess of the Other, that is, from the fact that he sees the world from a perspective that differs from and, hence, exceeds my own. To the point that I take it on, I am uprooted from my perspective, that is, from my consciousness as centered on my point of view. This implies, as Levinas writes, that "the consciousness of obligation is no longer a consciousness, since it tears consciousness up from its center, submitting it to the Other" (ibid.). The result is that I experience a self-separation. I see the world from my point of view; yet, called into question by the other, I also am called to apprehend the world from a different perspective. One perspective (one interpretation of the situation we are experiencing) is overlaid on the other. When I try to combine them, when I try to get the objective world, the world there for everyone, then I detach myself from myself.

Since the work of combining them is through talking with the other, "objectification is produced in the very work of language." The result is that "the subject is detached from the things possessed as though the subject hovered over its own existence, as though it were detached from it." Such "distance is more radical than every distance in the world." This is because, for language, to work, "the subject must find itself 'at a distance' from its own being" (*TI*, 209). Thus, when I express myself, I convert into linguistic signs what I experience. The signs signify or stand in the place of such experience. My linguistic presence in such signs, thus, is distinct from my self-presence as an actual experiencing subject. I am in this linguistic presence "at a distance" from my being as an experiencing subject. As Levinas puts this, "In designating what it possesses to the other, in speaking, the subject hovers over its own existence." This designated possession is linguistically present. Only as such linguistic presence is what I possess there for me and my Other. Only as such is it objective. Before its expression, it is only subjective (only there for me). This means, Levinas writes, "language makes possible the objectivity of objects." Their presence is linguistic. Such objectivity presupposes the other person to whom I speak. I constitute the linguistic presence of objects in relation to this Other. As Levinas draws the conclusion, "What I communicate therefore is already constituted in function of others. In speaking, I do not transmit to the Other what is objective for me: the objective becomes objective only through communication" (*TI*, 210). Thus, once again we return to the point that objectivity is this linguistic presence. It presupposes the Others to whom it is spoken. It also presupposes the non-identity or "ipseity" of their consciousnesses.

With this, we can understand Levinas's assertion: "if the face-to-face founds language . . . language does not only serve reason, but is reason" (*TI*, 207). The claim is that "reason lives in language," that "reason is defined by signification rather than signification being defined by the impersonal structures of reason" (*TI*, 208). Thus, in direct opposition to Husserl's view that reason is "the internal coherence of an ideal order," Levinas takes "the pluralism of society" as the "condition" of reason. This condition cannot "disappear in the elevation to reason" (ibid.). This is because both language and reason (which are designated by the same word, *logos*, in Greek) involve shared meanings or significations. To signify, however, is to assume plurality. Signification is the way we bridge, without denying, alterity. It involves the self-separation implied by linguistic presence, a separation that gives birth both to objectivity (the world as there for everyone) and reason as something objective and "impersonal." Thus, the impersonal objective relations of formal logic and Husserl's logic of content apply to the linguistic signs we use, but such signs presuppose our acts of signification. As such, their relations are founded on and cannot dispense with, plurality. This means that for Levinas, "it is not the impersonal in me that Reason would establish, but an I myself capable of society" (ibid.). This is the "I" that enters into society by attending to Others and giving reasons for its views. The very impulse to do this presupposes pluralism. As was observed above, to give a reason, that is, to explain why something is one way rather than another, is to assume that both are possible. But it is Others, with their different ways of being and behaving, who present me with such alternatives. My encounter with them thus raises the question of why I should disclose things one way rather than another. In other words, in presenting me with different ways of disclosure, they confront me with my freedom to disclose and, hence, with the question of reason. For Heidegger, as we saw, "freedom is the *Ab-grund* of Dasein."[19] It is an ultimate ground of the question of reason. For Levinas, freedom does have a ground. Not only do Others provide us with the alternatives that form the content of the choices available to us, they also afford us the self-separation that is essential to freedom. Such self-separation both makes possible the objective world and opens us up to the question of why the world is the way it is.

Language and Justice

In the division, "The Other and the Others," Levinas addresses the relation of language to justice. He does so by considering: who is this Other whom I address and who speaks to me? Levinas claims that "the epiphany of the face qua face opens humanity." It "attests the presence of . . . the whole of humanity in the eyes that look at me" (*TI*, 213). The reference here is to "language as the presence of the face." The face attests to humanity by using a language open to all, a language in relation to which all are equal. Here, "language is justice" in Aristotle's sense of justice as equality or fairness.[20] This means that "language as the presence of the face does not invite complicity with the preferred being, the self-sufficient 'I-Thou.'" Rather, "the thou is posited in front of a we" (ibid.). This "we" consists of all the Others of the Other that address me, including myself. There is no preference here. We are all equally obligated when we confront the Other. Thus, between myself and my Other, "equality . . . consists in referring to the *third party* whom . . . the Other already serves." Because of this, my being obligated to the Other occurs in a community of obligation. In Levinas's words, the Other "comes to *join* me. But he joins me to himself for service" (ibid.). The justice, then, that obligates us to treat Others equally, without preference for person or station, comes from the fact that the Other, who "commands me as a Master," is also under a similar command with regard to his Others. As the Other of Others, I myself am a source of obligation. This means that "this command can concern me only inasmuch as I am master myself; consequently this command commands me to command." Here, "the presence of the face, the infinity of the other, is . . . a presence of the third party (that is, of the whole of humanity that looks at us) and a command that commands commanding" (ibid.). I am, thus, not just passively obligated by the command issuing from the face of the Other—the command not to kill and to look after the stranger, the widow, and the orphan. I also, in my "prophetic word" that "responds to the epiphany of the face," actively command these things. My response to the "command that commands commanding" is to demand justice. The role of language here is that of a medium for this community of obligation. In Levinas's words, "the relation with the Other, discourse, . . . is not only the speech by which I divest myself of the possession that encircles me by setting forth an objective and common world, but is also sermon, exhortation, the prophetic word" (ibid.). The prophetic word demands that we realize the justice implicit in language.

With this, we have the answer to a common criticism of Levinas, one that Paul Ricoeur forcefully voices. He too raises the question: Who is this Other whom I address and who speaks to me? Whose face is it? He answers by saying "this face is that of a master of justice, of a master who instructs and who does so only in an ethical mode: this face forbids murder and commands justice." Ricoeur doubts that this instruction can take place in the asymmetrical relation I have to the Other. The difficulty, he writes, is that "the summons to responsibility has opposite it simply the passivity of an 'I' who has been called upon." This "dissymmetry of the face-to-face encounter," if "left uncompensated, . . . would break off the exchange of giving and receiving and would exclude any instruction by the face within the field of solicitude."[21] Does the passivity of the subject allow for such compensation? Does it permit the responding subject "a capacity of discernment and judgment"[22] or does it, rather, render its "interiority sterile"?[23] Without this capacity, he asks, "who will be able to distinguish the master from the executioner, the master who calls for a disciple from the master who requires a slave?"[24] The answer to all these questions is the community obligation that encompasses the self and its Others. "Language as the presence of the face" obligates them equally to respond to those addressing them. All are obligated by the language that they speak to set forth "an objective and common world." Within it, the master's command, which seems to lock me into a passivity, "commands me to command," that is, demand justice for all the Others of my Other, that is, for "the whole of humanity in the eyes that look at me."[25]

Plurality

Levinas's account of justice presupposes plurality. It assumes the otherness of the contending parties. While there is a common genus or concept that unites human beings as a biological species, this is not the case with language. In Levinas's words, "the human community instituted by language, where the interlocutors remain absolutely separated, does not constitute the unity of [a] genus . . . That all men are brothers is not explained by their resemblance, nor by a common cause of which they would be the effect, like metals which refer to the same die that struck them" (*TI*, 214). The implicit reference here is to the section of the Talmud that was cited in the "Introduction." In it the claim is made that whoever saves a life saves a world. This is put in terms of the uniqueness of every human life. According to the passage, "if a man strikes many coins from one mold, they all resemble one another." But God "fashioned every man in the stamp of the first man, and yet not one of them resembles his fellows. Therefore every single person is obliged to say: the world was created for my sake."[26] The point is that every person is unique like Adam. Just as the world was created for Adam's sake, so it is created for every person's sake. The phenomenological significance of this is that the "world" of each person, the world that comes to presence in and through this person, is unique.

If we take this biblical view seriously, then we have to say with Levinas, "Fraternity is radically opposed to the conception of a humanity united by resemblance" (*TI*, 214). In its account of the creation of Adam as the father of humanity, *Genesis* makes all men implicitly brothers. The result, according to Levinas, is a view of humanity and, hence, of language and reason, that is radically different than the Greek view. Being, for the Greeks, is one. Being, in the view that Levinas is advancing, is plural. It is not first a unity that would "afterwards, by breaking up, give place to a diversity, all of whose terms would maintain reciprocal relations among themselves, exhibiting thus the totality from which they proceed" (*TI*, 215). Rather, as created, being is from the start diverse. This holds in particular for human being. It confronts us with a "multiplicity of being which refuses totalization but [which] takes place as fraternity and discourse" (*TI*, 216).

The consequences of the Greek view are apparent in the tradition of German idealism. In Kant's moral "kingdom of ends . . . ," Levinas writes, "multiplicity rests, in fact, only on the hope of happiness" (*TI*, 217). Happiness occurs when we satisfy our inclinations—that is, in enjoyment. Humans are distinct only through this satisfaction. We can, of course, act so as to be worthy of happiness. Yet, Kant insists that faced with the choice between satisfying an inclination and fulfilling our duty, we must, *as free*, choose the latter. Doing so, we become part of the "kingdom of ends," but the price we pay for this membership is the loss of all particularity with regard to our will. This follows for Kant since we can only conceive of this kingdom "if we abstract from the personal differences between rational beings, and also from all the content of their private ends."[27] As free, then, the autonomous self is like everyone else. Only the pure form of its willing—that of the universality of its maxims—remains once it enters this kingdom. There is a certain paradox here. It comes to the fore when we ask: Who is actually willing according to these universal maxims? Whose freedom is Kant actually referring to? In Levinas's words, the difficulty here stems from the "identification of will and reason" (*TI*, 217). I am free only insofar as I follow universal laws given by reason. The alternative, that I follow my inclinations, makes me unfree. As Kant writes of a person who follows his inclinations, his "will does not give itself the law [of its actions], but the object does so in virtue of its relation to the will."[28] His point is that the world in which this person is situated is the ultimate agent. It acts through his desires for the object. Thus, the person is only free insofar as he abstracts from all such inclinations, that is, insofar as he lets reason guide him to follow the universal laws of duty. If he follows his inclinations, he does affirm his individuality, but he also reduces his willing to appetite and is not really free.[29] Hegel, in his political works, follows Kant's lead, but adds that "substantial freedom" is the objectification of the moral universal laws that form the content of the free will in the laws of the state. Politics is the way we work out the nature of this substantial freedom. This is why Levinas writes, "Idealism completely carried out reduces all ethics to politics" (*TI*, 216).

According to Levinas, "This identification of will and reason, which is the ultimate intention of idealism, is opposed by the entire pathetic experience of humanity" (*TI*, 217). Such experience shows that will and reason are not the same. Their identification "cannot serve as the ontological touchstone . . . of society" (*TI*, 218). This is because "the individual and the personal count and act independently of the universal that would mold them [in Kant's and Hegel's accounts]" (ibid). Behind this opposition are two different accounts of freedom. For Levinas as for Hegel and Kant, self-separation is required for freedom. Hegel and Kant see reason as providing this. They take the universal standpoint that reason seems to afford a person as that which allows her to step back from herself and regard herself. The paradox of their account concerns the identity of the person stepping back. This cannot be the embodied individual as defined by his "pathetic experience." But only an embodied individual can actually act. For Levinas, by contrast, self-separation and, hence, freedom occur through the Other. They arise when I respond to the Other's alternative perspective. The distinction of my will from inclination or appetite occurs when I have to explain myself to the Other, that is, present him with my reasons for what I say and do. As for reason, its origin is precisely this need of explaining oneself. The question of reason, the question "why?" originates in the encounter with the Other's alternative perspective. If we accept this account, then we break up the equation of freedom, reason, and universality. We assert with Levinas that particularity (or egotism) must first be there to be called into question. The response to this call is given in language and through the reason that language supports. But this presupposes separation, that is, presupposes the Other as the person to whom one speaks. In fact, without Others, reason cannot begin. It cannot even formulate its initial question, let alone linguistically express it.

10

The Temporality of Finite Freedom

Totality and Infinity, III, C

The Question of Freedom

In this final part of section 3, Levinas returns to the question of the freedom of the embodied will. Such freedom is not equivalent to a universal reason. Rather, given its basis in our embodiment, it must be consistent with our plural condition. As we have seen, the sense of plurality Levinas insists on is the radical one he draws from the Bible according to its Talmudic interpretation. This is a "radical multiplicity, distinct from numerical multiplicity." By this he means a multiplicity that would not be "defenseless against totalization" (*TI*, 220). In a numerical multiplicity, each individual is "one," and as such is just like every other "one." By virtue of a common measure, the individuals forming it can be counted.[1] This presupposes an external viewpoint by which we grasp their commonality. But, for Levinas, what makes human beings uncountable is the absence of this viewpoint. The "total reflection" it would afford is impossible because of the "surplus of the social relation." This surplus comes from the excessive presence of the speaking face, that is, from the fact that it exceeds the intentions that we can form of it. Because of the impossibility of "congruence" between our intentions and this presence, we confront a non-numerical multiplicity. In Levinas's words, we face "an objectivity posited in the impossibility of the total reflection, in the impossibility of conjoining the I and the non-I [the Other] in a whole. This impossibility . . . results from the surplus of the epiphany of the other" (*TI*, 221). The Other, in his ability to add the saying that exceeds the said, exceeds or brings a "surplus" to any concept I might form of him. The experience on which this concept would be based becomes outdated by what the Other adds.[2]

Levinas raises the question of freedom by noting the problem it raises for the ways we bend one another to our will. Given our essentially plural condition as based on the "surplus" of the face, it follows that "war and commerce presuppose the face and the transcendence of being appearing in the face" (*TI*, 222). In particular: "War like peace presupposes beings structured otherwise than as parts of a totality." The presupposition is that of opposition: "War presupposes the transcendence of the antagonist; it is waged against man," in particular, against his plural condition (ibid.). Levinas, we recall, made the same claim in his "Preface." There, he wrote that "war establishes an order from which no one can keep his distance." Its aim is to eliminate exteriority and the Other as other (*TI*, 21). As such, it presupposes the exteriority it seeks to undo. This means that war "aims at a presence that always comes from elsewhere, [it aims at] a being that appears in a face" (*TI*, 222). The problem of freedom arises because the combatants in war are not pure activities, not pure *causa sui* (self-caused beings). If they were, they could not do violence to each other. In Levinas's words, "as pure activities, capable of receiving no action, the terms could undergo no violence" (*TI*, 223). They cannot, however, be pure passivities, since then they could not act on each other. They thus have to be both. But how is this possible? Levinas calls it a "living contradiction." In his words, "Violence bears upon only a being both graspable and escaping every hold. Without this living contradiction in the being that undergoes violence, the deployment of violent force would reduce itself to labor" (ibid.). Thus, I must be able to grasp the Other to whom I mean to do violence. Yet if he is a mere thing, if he does not escape the hold I have on him, then my action on him would be like that on something inanimate, something that I labor on—for example, a tree that I cut down and make into boards. I want, however, to do violence to the Other. I demand that he suffer it as a person. This means that the freedom that marks him as a person must somehow become unfreedom in my hands. It must as freedom, as something escaping every hold, be graspable by me.

Temporality and Finite Freedom

One possible solution to this puzzle is Heidegger's finite freedom—our freedom as "finite Dasein." Our finitude comes from the fact that, as "thrown," we are subject to the limiting conditions of a finite past. Our freedom consists in choosing among the possibilities our past or "having been" offers to us. For Heidegger, we are passive with regard to this past and active with regard to our choices. Levinas sees this as "a singular compound of activity and passivity" (*TI*, 224). Regarding such a compound, we face "the problem of the relation existing in it between the free part,

causa sui, and the non-free part. To say that the free part is impeded
in the non-free part would bring us back indefinitely to the same difficulty: how can the free part, *causa sui*, undergo anything whatever from
the non-free part?" (*TI*, 223). Of particular concern, here, is the fact of
"birth, non-chosen and impossible to choose" that initiates one's thrown
situation. How can we say that we are limited by this *and* transcend our
situation, standing out from it by the choices we make? Moreover, what
allows us to transcend the world of our Others—the "they-world" of their
mutually reinforcing prejudices? How do I grasp the fact that the world
offers possibilities distinct from those *collectively* approved by my Others?

Levinas's answer is couched as a response to a relation Heidegger
draws between finite freedom and our sense of time. Such freedom gives
time its human intelligibility by letting us define it in terms of a finite
stretch. For Heidegger, the finite freedom that flows from my situation
involves a finite past (a distinct "having been") that pertains to me. It also
involves the fact that, as mortal (as a "being towards death"), I have only
a finite time to act. As involving a limited past and future, finite freedom
thus makes time finite and, hence, comprehensible. For Levinas, however, "it is not finite freedom that makes the notion of time intelligible;
it is time that gives meaning to the notion of finite freedom." In his view,
"the whole existence of the mortal being . . . is not being towards death,
but [towards] the 'not yet,' which is a way of being against death." Time
is what "separates a being from its death." Corresponding to this, "freedom itself is but [death's] adjournment by time." It is a "postponement
by virtue of which nothing is definitive yet, nothing consummated" (*TI*,
224). For Levinas, then, time gives meaning to the notion of freedom
since we are free only as long as we have time to act. We use our freedom
to postpone our inevitable death by warding off dangers and providing
for ourselves.

At issue here are all the activities involving labor and the home by
which we attempt to transcend our situation. Since, however, our situation is fundamentally that of "living from," such transcendence can only
assume the quality of a postponement. As such, it can be interrupted by
violence. Houses can be destroyed; the results of labor seized by Others.
The death that they put off can be brought close in conflict. This is what
makes possible war. In Levinas's words, "War can be produced only when
a being postponing its death is exposed to violence" (*TI*, 225). On the
most basic level, we are exposed because we are embodied. Yet, such
exposure is limited by the fact that we use our bodies to postpone our
inevitable deaths. As Levinas expresses this, "my skill postpones the inevitable . . . This skill is inscribed in the very existence of the body . . .
Corporeity is the mode of existence of a being whose presence is post-

poned at the very moment of his presence" (ibid.). This postponement occurs because I am ahead of myself as I engage in my projects. Such projects situate me intentionally at their goal. Even as I reach for a glass of water, I await myself as lifting the glass to my lips. I can be ahead of myself because my body is the instrument of my will. I accomplish my goal by employing it. My bodily "I can" thus serves as a condition for my having projects, my being ahead of myself, and, hence, my having the time that postpones my death. I am both subject to violence and capable of postponing the death that it can bring by virtue of one and the same embodiment.

In asserting the above, Levinas does not mean to limit transcendence to our bodily "I can." The face is part of our embodiment. It manifests, by itself, vulnerability and postponement. Thus, you can postpone something when you absent yourself from it. Postponement, in this sense, is being elsewhere and, hence, avoiding it. Now, the face is vulnerable since, as embodied, it can be struck. Yet, as manifesting alterity, it is elsewhere and, hence, enacts a postponement. It is, of course, precisely this alterity that violence seeks to destroy. "Violence," as Levinas writes, "can only aim at a face." In doing so, it aims at the postponement the face enacts. Such postponement "consists in [its] soliciting a response" (*TI*, 225). As a speaking face, it is always adding to the said, always awaiting a response, always opening up time as a postponement of the end of our relation. The "violence of war" seeks to reduce this to silence, to end the time available. But as long as such violence does not succeed, I have, Levinas writes, a "relation with the other who, as infinity, opens time" (ibid.).

Freedom and the Other

The infinity that "opens time" is the transcendence of the face. My relation to the Other, insofar as it includes the transcendence of the face, is not part of the totality. As such, it opens up the self-separation that makes freedom possible. In Levinas's words, "Freedom . . . can be manifested only outside totality, but this 'outside totality' opens with the transcendence of the face" (*TI*, 225). It is this transcendence that separates me from my situation. It manifests itself in the "saying" that adds to "the said," that is, to the situation into which I have been thrown. For Levinas, "it is therefore not freedom that accounts for the transcendence of the Other, but the transcendence of the Other that accounts for freedom" (ibid.). Thus, my Other presents me with an alternate perspective on the situation confronting us. Embracing it, I separate myself from the self that was defined by this situation. The freedom this separation brings is not abstract, but involves real choice. Thus, in the Other, I encounter the could-be-otherwise of the possibilities that define me. In interpreting differently the situation confronting us, he makes me aware of alternate possibilities for disclosing it and hence of my choices to alter it.

The fact that my freedom is conditioned by the Other gives us yet another perspective to grasp the "living contradiction" of ourselves as "both graspable and escaping every hold," that is, as being free as agents and yet subject in this very agency to violence. Both are possible insofar as the freedom that the transcendence of the Other accounts for can, itself, be undermined by Others. This is particularly true for political freedom. Such freedom requires a public space—that is, a place, accessible to all, for debates about our possibilities for disclosing the world through our collective projects.[3] In the alternatives debated, this public conversation bears the content of our collective freedom to shape our society's course. This implies that the narrowing of the horizons of discourse, either through censorship or social constraints, is an impoverishment of this freedom. The empirical evidence for this view consists in the susceptibility of humanity to tyranny, that is, the ability of states, social constraints, and ideologies to limit human freedom for long periods of time. It also involves the importance tyrannies place on the control of ideas, that is, on the control of the language that serves as their medium. Were liberty innate, the breakup of a tyranny—no matter how long its duration—would necessarily involve the restoration of our "natural" freedom and with this, our ability to immediately recommence the give and take of political and civil society. But this is rarely, if ever, the case. Thus, the freedom that Others afford us is inherently vulnerable. It can always be undermined by undermining our relations to Others. Given this, the "living contradiction" that we are comes from the fact that our ability *to escape every hold* requires Others. Rather than being *causa sui*, we are, as free, dependent on accessing the transcendence of these Others.

The transcendence of the Other is not, per se, an unqualified good. It also makes possible economic exploitation. For Hegel, as we mentioned, the laboring slave recognizes himself in his products and, more generally, in the human world he creates. Because of this, he overcomes the alienation that his slavery imposed upon him. Hegel wrote before the industrial revolution, that is, before mass production and what Marx called the "alienation of labor." The term refers to the selfhood that is recognized in the products of labor. It becomes alienated by the conditions of modern capitalism, which allows these products to become anonymous commodities. Levinas accepts this critique of Hegel. The products of labor, he writes, "take on the anonymity of merchandise, an anonymity into which, as a wage-earner, the worker himself may disappear" (*TI*, 226). More generally, when I make, write, or do something, I issue it "into the unknown." I have control neither of the use Others make of it nor the interpretation they impose (*TI*, 227). In fact, history is just such an external interpretation. What history interprets are the works we leave behind us, our products, our sayings, our deeds. As Levinas observes, "Wills without works constitute no history; there is no purely interior history" (ibid.). Moreover, history waits till their authors have departed to begin its workings. In Levinas's words: "As long as the will, in a being who speaks . . . defends his work against a foreign will, history lacks the distance it lives from. Its reign commences in . . . the world of 'complete works,' the heritage of dead wills" (*TI*, 228). Quite apart from this, the entanglement of humans and their actions is such that I can never claim complete responsibility for what I do. In no case am I entirely "what I want to do" (ibid.). Now, at the root of all these phenomena is the transcendence of the Other. The Other has his own interpretations, his own plans and uses for my deeds and products. Their very alterity implies, in Levinas's words, that "the work is destined to this alien *Sinngebung* [interpretation] from the moment of its origin in me" (*TI*, 227). Thus, we confront once again our plural condition—that is, the fact that each of us exceeds our Others in our interpretation of the world. The transcendence of the Other by which I have my freedom is precisely what allows my works to be alienated from me. The Other's interpretations present me with the alternative choices that make my freedom real. But such interpretations also open up the possibility that my works along with the selfhood that I place in them can be misinterpreted and alienated.

At the basis of the "living contradiction" that we have been commenting on is, of course, our embodiment. It causes us never to see the world from the same physical point of view, never to have exactly the same bodily experiences of the world. It thus stands as a necessary condition for the plurality of interpretations offered by our Others. This same embodiment, however, makes our embodied wills subject to Others and, hence, to their violence. This holds with regard to the works that result from the embodied will. The Other can undo my willing by destroying or making impossible the works in which it manifests itself. In Levinas's words, "The part of eternal truth that materialism involves lies in the fact that the human will can be laid hold of in its works" (*TI*, 229). On an even more basic level, my having a body as an instrument of my will is what allows this will to be attacked through this body. It allows me to be treated as a passive thing. As Levinas writes, "the body in its very activity, in its for-itself, inverts into a thing to be treated as a thing." As he quotes Molière in *Le médecin malgré lui*, "'I am any thing you like,' says Sganarelle, under the blows" (ibid.).[4] This does not mean that the will *itself* becomes a thing. As embodied, the will "is affected as a thing by things." Yet as willing, it is ahead of itself and "gives itself a reprieve and postpones the contact." Here, the living contradiction is that of the "corporality of the will." It is that of a will that, as embodied, can accomplish its purposes and yet, as embodied, can also be "coerced and enslaved as a will, becoming a servile soul" (ibid.). Thus, as embodied, "the will . . . moves between its betrayal and its fidelity which, simultaneously, describe the very originality of its power" (*TI*, 231).

The Ambiguity of Death

For Levinas, the "living contradiction" that we are as embodied embraces our mortality. Our embodied temporality is such that we are able both "to be for death and still have time to be against death" (*TI*, 235). Our being alive is both a being for death and a postponing it. In presenting this position, Levinas is at pains to distinguish it from Heidegger's. Heidegger calls death our "ownmost potentiality of being." It is one that annuls the whole of our being-in-the-world. In Heidegger's words, it is "the possibility of no-longer being able to be there" at all. Thus, in death, all of Dasein's relations "to any other Dasein are extinguished." As concerning me alone, it is my "non-relational possibility," one that is "not to be outstripped" since there is nothing beyond it.[5] According to Heidegger, it is death, rather than the Other, that makes me face my freedom. The very isolation it involves awakes me to the fact that I have take responsibility for the choices shaping my life.

To break up this isolating interpretation of death, Levinas begins by noting that death is usually "interpreted either as a passage to nothingness or as a passage to another existence" (*TI*, 232). We take it either as annihilation or our entrance into the afterlife, situating death "either in nothingness or in being" (*TI*, 233). There is, however, a third possibility, one where "my relation with my own death places me before a category that does not enter into either term of this alternative" (ibid.). This category appears once we realize that the terms "nothingness" and "being" implicitly take death as something comprehensible. In fact, however, I cannot know anything about my death. In Levinas's words, "The unforeseeable character of death is due to the fact that it does not lie within any horizon. It is not open to grasp" (*TI*, 233). Of course, I can witness the death of Others. In fact, as Levinas notes, one of the alternatives, the "identifying of death with nothingness," "befits the death of the other in murder." Yet, even here, death escapes us. It is as ungraspable as the face. As Levinas continues: "But at the same time this nothingness presents itself there as a sort of impossibility. For the Other cannot present himself as Other outside of my conscience, and his face expresses my moral impossibility of annihilating" him (*TI*, 232). The murder that would manifest his death leaves me with a thing rather than a person.

How, then, is death grasped? What is the horizon that situates it? According to Levinas, my relation to my own death confronts me with neither nothingness nor being, but rather with "the fear I can have for my own being" (*TI*, 233). Such fear is not the isolating anxiety that Heidegger speaks of. Rather, "a social conjuncture is maintained in this menace. It does not sink into the anxiety that would transform it into a 'nihilation of nothingness.' In the being for death of fear I am not faced with nothingness, but faced with what is against me, as though murder . . . were inseparable from the essence of death, as though the approach of death remained one of the modalities of the relation with the Other" (*TI*, 234). Levinas's point is that the very unknowability of death associates it with the transcendence of the Other. It is my relations with the Other that give death a horizon. Within it, the Other does not just appear as a threat, but also as a source of aid. In Levinas's words: "The solitude of death does not make the Other vanish, but remains in a consciousness of hostility, and consequently still renders possible an appeal to the Other, to his friendship and his medication. The doctor is an a priori principle of human mortality. Death approaches in the fear of someone, and hopes in someone" (ibid.).

For Heidegger, facing death is facing the "nihilation of nothingness." It is ultimately isolating. For Levinas, the very unknowability of death confronts us with neither being nor nothingness, but with alterity. This alterity can have a threatening form. In his words, "the fear for my being which is my relation with death is not the fear of nothingness, but the fear of violence—and thus it extends into fear of the Other, of the absolutely unforeseeable" (*TI*, 235). But precisely because it involves the Other, it also involves the possibility of transcendence, of postponement. Such postponement can take the form of an appeal to the Other or, alternately, of preparing a defense. It can also involve "the founding of institutions in which the will ensures a meaningful, but impersonal world beyond death" (*TI*, 236). In other words, rather than thrusting me into "absurdity," my relation to death leads me to make provisions for it.

The assumption that death confronts us with either being (in the form of an afterlife) or the "nihilation of nothingness" arises, for Levinas, from an abstraction. In the first alternative, we consider ourselves a for-itself in the form of a self-caused cause. In the second, we are taken as in-itself, that is, something merely physical. Since the former cannot die, death appears as a translation to a new life. A physical thing can resolve itself into its elements and, in this sense, can "die." But, here, we beg the question whether it was, as merely physical, ever alive. What both abstractions ignore, according to Levinas, is the fact of mortality. "Mortality is the concrete and primary phenomenon" (*TI*, 235). It designates us as *both physical and psychical* and, hence, as the living contradiction that is the embodied will. As both, we are subject to death and act to postpone it. By focusing on this concrete phenomenon, Levinas avoids the critique that Derrida directs against Heidegger's account of death. Derrida attacks Heidegger's definition of death as the possibility of an impossibility—the possibility of "the impossibility of any existence at all." As Derrida notes, this impossibility, as all-embracing, includes "the impossibility of appearing as such." As such, it includes the impossibility of death's appearing. Yet, if death cannot appear, how can we authentically confront it? If we cannot, "then," as Derrida concludes, "man, or man as Dasein, never has a relation to death as such." We cannot even talk here of anticipating death, given that we have no idea what to expect from it.[6] By locating death with the horizon of our relations to the Other and, hence, within the ambiguity of our embodied existence, Levinas shows how we give it a human content.

Violence and Time

To emphasize the vulnerability of the embodied will, Levinas quotes Sganarelle's willingness to be "anything you like" as he is being beaten (*TI*, 229). In spite of this, the will still has resources even under coercion. It can be "coerced and enslaved as a will." Yet, as conscious, it is never really reducible to a mere thing. In fact, "the will combines a contradiction: an immunity from every exterior attack to the point of positing itself as uncreated and immortal . . . and the permanent fallibility of this inviolable sovereignty" (*TI*, 237). The immunity comes from the temporal extension of consciousness. According to Levinas: "To be conscious is to have time—not to overflow the present by anticipating and hastening the future, but to have a distance with regard to the present: to relate oneself to being as to a being to come, to maintain a distance with regard to being even while already coming under its grip" (ibid.). Here, freedom is thought in terms of self-separation. I am free insofar as I am distinct from the being that grips me. It is present, but I am ahead of it. I am "to come" (*a-venir*). Grasping my present situation from the perspective of already having gone through it, I can see that I have been subject to the "techniques of seduction, propaganda, and torture" (ibid.). For Levinas, then, to will is to have a relation to the future. It is to choose the future where what one wills is accomplished. The freedom of the will thus depends on our holding open this future. This, of course, is impossible if we take the future as determined by the past. But, as free, a person's "nature" is not just determined by his birth and given situation. As free, "the being defined by its birth can . . . take up a position with regard to its nature." It is not totally defined by it. It can judge it, partially reject it. As Levinas continues, "it disposes of a background and, in this sense, is not completely born." It still has a future of coming to be (*TI*, 238).

Suffering attacks our ability to be ahead of ourselves. In physical suffering, "at the limit of consciousness," "we find ourselves backed up to being." We are reduced further and further into the present; our ability to separate ourselves from ourselves by maintaining a distance from it progressively diminishes. Here, "the acuity of suffering lies in the impossibility of fleeing it, [in the impossibility] of being protected in oneself from oneself" (*TI*, 238). This being protected in oneself is one's ability to be ahead of oneself, that is, stand in the future as opposed to the present. The self one is protected from is the self that is in the present and, hence, vulnerable to the present pain.

One way to understand the effect of suffering is in terms of the two main elements that characterize the traumatic experience: extreme bodily affect and lack of sense. For both Heidegger and Husserl, sense involves futurity. For Heidegger, I make sense out of my world through pragmatic disclosure. Such disclosure shows the "Wozu" or purpose of the objects that surround me. It thus involves the futurity of the goals of the projects that shape this disclosure. For Husserl, futurity is implicit in our sense-making on an even more basic level. We grasp the basic perceptual sense of objects when we run through a series of experiences— those, say, forming patterns of perspectival appearing—and interpret them as experiences *of* perceptual objects. We do this even though we actually see only a small fraction of such patterns. What occurs is that we project ourselves forward and anticipate the patterns that *will fulfill* the interpretations we initially form.[7] Now, it is just such projection that suffering hinders. It nails one to the present. In extreme cases, one is reduced to the bodily affect, that is, the pain that illness, injury, or the malignant Other imposes on one. The result is trauma, understood as the experience of the affect without any futurity and, hence, without any ability to make sense of it.

This being nailed to the present is never complete. Were it total, we would not be conscious. This implies that "as consciousness, the pain is always yet to come" (*TI*, 238). For Husserl, this holds because consciousness involves intentionality, and intentionality involves futurity.[8] I am conscious insofar as I grasp objects, things, and events in the world. But this means intending what is coming by anticipatively interpreting it as the oncoming of things, events, and so on. Such intending, in other words, is our projecting ourselves forward and anticipating the experience that we interpret as presenting us with things, events, and so on. Given that suffering does involve consciousness, this means that "suffering remains ambiguous." We suffer and we witness this turning of ourselves into a thing defined as that which has no inner distance, no being-ahead-of-itself. Because of this, "we are at the same time a thing and at a distance from our abdication" (ibid.). Those who make us suffer know this. In Levinas's words: "To inflict suffering is not to reduce the Other to the rank of object, but on the contrary is to maintain him superbly in his subjectivity. In suffering the subject must know his reification, but in order to do so he must precisely remain a subject. Hatred wills both things" (*TI*, 239). This is not illogical. It simply takes cognizance of the fact that "the will combines a contradiction" (*TI*, 237) since it is both free and liable to coercion, both ahead of itself and bodily present.

Excursus: The Double Causality of the Embodied Will

One way of expressing this "contradiction" is in terms of the two types of causality. There is, first, the natural causality of bodies where the past determines the present, which determines the future. It can be represented by a line.

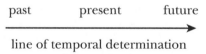

past   present   future

line of temporal determination

Then there is the causality of the will taken simply as our conscious intent. Here, the goal determines the past insofar as it determines how we interpret what it offers as material for accomplishing our goal. This interpreted past determines the present, since it determines our present use of this material. Suppose, for example, that you decide to run in a marathon race. Your running this race exists as a future whose determining presence is that of a goal. The goal determines the past since it makes you view it in terms of the resources you bring to accomplish this goal. This determines your present activity—that is, how long you are in training. Here, the line of determination proceeds from the future through the past to the present.

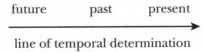

future   past   present

line of temporal determination

Now, to speak of the *embodied* will, we have to combine *both* forms of causality. This can be represented by a diagram where we bend the line of temporal determination into a circle:

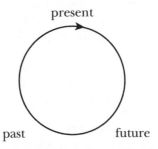

The circle points to two ways of viewing the functioning of our will. In the first, which emphasizes its freedom, we start out with the future and go to the past and then to the present. We assert that the future determines the way the past determines the present. Here, the goal makes the past into a resource for the process of its own realization. The goal thus determines the past in the latter's determination of the present by structuring it as a potential for some particular realization. In the second, which emphasizes our susceptibility to coercion, we start out with the past, which determines the present, which determines the future. This is the causality of our bodily agency with regard to the things it deals with. We employ natural causality to accomplish our will. Thus, the body in the movement of its limbs through its muscles and tendons follows this causality. Now, the "living contradiction" of our embodied will employs both forms of causality. The "contradiction" is, therefore, between two different lines of temporal determination: *past, present, future* and *future, present, past*. It disappears when we join the two in a circle and take this circle as the ontological form of the embodied will.

There is a certain intertwining that also can be represented by the circle. By virtue of my body, I am in the world. As such, I employ the causality of the world. But by virtue of my being ahead of myself, the world is in me. It is in me as a future that I envisage and attempt to bring about. It is also in me perceptually insofar as consciousness involves intentionality and intentionality involves futurity.[9] To understand the embodied will, both views have to be maintained. I have to say that I am bodily in the world that is consciously in me.

Dying for Others: The Truth of the Will

Given the duality of the embodied will, the ultimate resistance to coercion is what Levinas calls "patience." This involves a "disengagement within engagement." In extreme suffering, we find ourselves "backed up to being," almost nailed to the present (*TI*, 238). Yet, in the very limitation of the future that suffering imposes, the Other intervenes as that for whom I die. He becomes my future.[10] He gives me the temporal distance from myself that makes patience and the enduring of suffering possible. As Levinas remarks, when I suffer for Others, there is a kind of inversion. It is one where "the will breaks through the crust of its egotism and, as it were, displaces its center of gravity outside of itself." In its passivity, the will remains patient since it realizes not just that it "can die as a result of someone." It also sees that it can die "for someone." Hence, the resistance fighters who died at the hands of the Nazis rather than revealing the names of their compatriots died for them. According to Levinas, when we do die for someone, we "will as Desire and Goodness limited by nothing" (*TI*, 239). In these extreme situations, we become "transported to a life . . . for someone," a life where "death no longer touches the will" (*TI*, 240). Here, "in the midst of torture, understanding the reasons for the torture reestablishes the famous inward freedom" (*TI*, 241).

    The question that arises is why, given our natural egotism, would we die for Others? What is the "truth of the will" that exercises such patience? Objectively, the reasons for doing this "appear only to the beneficiaries." But there may be none. History, after all, is written by the victors. It is in this context that Levinas raises the issue of the "apology" for our "inner life." This inner life, he insists, is "not an epiphenomenon and an appearance" (*TI*, 240). It is not something, like the rainbow, which appears but has no causal efficacy. As active, it can present an apology. The term "apology" appears in Plato's *Apology*. In Greek, it signifies the defense statement of the accused as he faces judgment. On what grounds, then, does the will exercise patience? What is the judgment our inner life appeals to? Levinas, having asserted that understanding the reasons for torture reestablishes our inward freedom, goes on to add, "but these reasons themselves appear only to the beneficiaries of historical evolution and institutions" (*TI*, 241). Does this mean that the ultimate judgment appealed to is that of these institutional beneficiaries?

This seems to be true insofar as the sacrifice can lead to changes on the institutional level. As Levinas notes, "freedom . . . takes refuge from its own perfidy in institutions" (*TI*, 241). It fashions institutions that can protect the will from the assaults it is subject to as an embodied will. These institutions—such as the legislative assembly that passes laws, the judiciary that interprets them, and the police that enforce them—are fashioned to drive "violence and murder from the world" (*TI*, 242). They enact a postponement. They do so in the same way that "the animal fabricating tools frees itself from its animal condition." The human animal does this "when instead of going of itself to its goal as an inviolable will, it fabricates tools and fixes the powers of its future action in transmissible and receivable things" (*TI*, 241). The tools in this case are the universal laws of the state and the institutions that sustain them. Are these the ultimate references of the apology of the person, who as a matter of conscience, undergoes torture? Is the objective judgment he appeals to that which is "pronounced by the existence of rational institutions"? Does the apology amount to "the submission of the subjective will to the universal laws which reduce the will to an objective signification"? (*TI*, 242). Is this the "truth of the will"?

Levinas doubts that this is the whole story. He objects that "the possibility of seeing itself from outside [that is, seeing the objective historical signification of my act] does not harbor truth . . . if I pay for it the price of my depersonalization" (*TI*, 243). An apology is personal. But this means that "judgment must be borne upon a will that could defend itself during the adjudication." This is a will that "could be present at the trial and does not disappear into the totality of a coherent discourse" (ibid.). The same objection applies when we say that the appeal is to history. Once again, the totality seems to swallow up the particularity required by the apology. In Levinas's words: "The judgment of history is set forth in the visible. Historical events are the visible par excellence; their truth is produced in evidence. The visible forms, or tends to form, a totality." The totality is that given by the encompassing view that history demands. Such a view "excludes the apology, which undoes the totality in inserting into it, at each instant, the unsurpassable, unencompassable present of its very subjectivity" (ibid.). This is the subjectivity that breaks up the totality through its excessive presence. The breakup occurs through the presence of a surplus, of something added beyond the already established totality.

What is this addition? It is not something that remains on the invisible, noumenal plane, that is, that of the Kantian "kingdom of ends." As Levinas observes, "The invisible must manifest itself if history is to lose its right to the last word" (*TI*, 243). The surplus is, in fact, the goodness that is produced by patience. It is manifested in the lives that have *not* been betrayed. Here, "the manifestation of the invisible . . . is produced in the goodness reserved to subjectivity." This means that it "is subject not simply to the truth of judgment, but to the sources of this truth," namely, those Others to whom one remained faithful (ibid.). These Others are the sources of the truth of judgment insofar as fidelity is essential to the truth. As we saw, the inquiry into truth presupposes both generosity and receptivity in our relations with Others. On one level, then, the apology is to these Others. Such Others, however, may never know of one's sacrifice. One cannot know if someone else might not betray them. Equally, one is ignorant of the outcome of the struggle and, hence, of the history that will be written by the victors. With this, we come to "the idea of a judgment of God" (*TI*, 244). It "represents the limit idea of a judgment that . . . takes into account . . . the essential offence to a singularity" that a universal judgment involves. This judgment of God "does not silence by its majesty the voice and the revolt of the apology." Rather, God is taken as seeing "the invisible without [himself] being seen." He, himself, in his alterity, is manifested in the alterity of Others.[11] The appeal to his judgment is not really separate from the appeal to the judgment of those whom one will not betray. Rather, as Levinas writes, "the will is under the judgment of God when its fear of death is inverted into fear of committing murder" (ibid.). Thus, the members of the French Resistance who kept silent under torture had their fear of death inverted into the fear of betraying their comrades and, hence, of indirectly committing murder. The temporal distance that allowed them to separate themselves from themselves was that of the Other. Fear for the Other's future supported their patience.

Being an Individual

I asked above: why, given their natural egotism, do we see people sacrificing themselves for Others? To answer this, we must first ask: what remains of the I or self once it gives up its egotism for the sake of the Other? Levinas's answer involves the nature of the judgment we appeal to. He writes, "Judgment is pronounced upon me in the measure that it summons me to respond" (*TI*, 244). The judgment of a universal law, for example, touches me only insofar as I come under its purview. I am judged as a thief, as a careless driver, and so on. The point of contact is the category of the offense. It is in terms of this category that I am summoned to respond. I respond as a supposed member of the category. When, however, I am summoned to respond to the particular demand of a specific person in need, I am called to respond as this person now—that is, as myself. My response thus confirms my uniqueness or individuality. Viewed in this light, self-sacrifice is not self-abandonment, but rather an affirmation of my uniqueness. As we have seen, this uniqueness begins with my separation and enjoyment. It is confirmed in my responding to the Other. In Levinas's words: "The I, which we have seen arise in enjoyment as a separated being having apart, in itself, the center around which its existence gravitates, is confirmed in its singularity by purging itself of this gravitation" (ibid.). "Goodness" denotes this "incessant effort to purge itself" (*TI*, 245). Thus, Levinas's answer is that one sacrifices oneself for Others both for "goodness" and for the personal I that is identified in responding to them. The doctrine here is that "the I is a privilege and an election." This signifies, for Levinas, that "the accomplishing of the I qua I and morality constitute one sole and same process in being." I am elected or chosen in the demands I encounter "of serving the poor, the stranger, the widow, and the orphan." Such demands "converge at one point of the universe"—this being myself. This holds, not just for me but for everyone. "Thus, only through morality are I and the others produced in the universe" (*TI*, 245).

With this, we have Levinas's alternative to Heidegger's and Nietzsche's accounts of individuality. For Heidegger, being an individual means resolutely accomplishing your being, this by seeing and acting on the possibilities present in your situation. These possibilities are present in what the past has given you. For Levinas, by contrast, individuality is a result of your acting according to the irreplaceable responsibility that Others summon you to. This responding is morality. This is the direct opposite of Nietzsche's position, which takes being an individual not as being moral, but rather as having the courage to go beyond good and evil. Such categories are simply social norms imposed on us by the many—the "they-world" in Heidegger's terms. For Nietzsche, I am an individual when I can will beyond them. Individuality is a function of transcending the social categories of good or evil by virtue of the affirmation of the will as will, the will that does not need such categories to justify itself. In Levinas's alternative vision, individuality is a matter of an individual response to an individual summons. The transcendence of the categories imposed on us by the many is in the individuality of our response. For Levinas, then, "to place oneself under the judgment of God is to exalt the subjectivity, called to moral overstepping beyond laws" (*TI*, 246). This moral overstepping consists in goodness. "Goodness," he writes, "consists in taking up a position in being such that the Other counts more than myself." Doing so, I make my "apology." I respond to the Other (*TI*, 247).

According to Levinas, this responding *to* the Other can even take on the form of responding *for* the Other, that is, taking responsibility—and, hence, making an apology—*for* the Other's actions. As Levinas puts this in *Ethics and Infinity*, "I am 'subject' essentially in this sense . . . I am responsible for a total responsibility which answers for all the Others and for all in the Others, even for their responsibility."[12] Here, "the more I am just, the more guilty I am" (*TI*, 244). This is a responsibility that transcends the universal categories of the moral laws. Normally, I am responsible only for my actions, which are judged according to such laws. For Levinas, however, the apology through which I answer for my actions is not thought in terms of the "submission of the subjective will to the universal laws which reduce the will to an objective signification" (*TI*, 242). It is through a responsibility that uniquely identifies me as "just." In taking responsibility for the Other's responsibility, I engage myself to fulfill his responsibilities, that is, to undo the harm that his actions have caused. Aid workers who work with war victims manifest this responsibility. As do those who compensate for the political and social deficits of different communities. In their engaging in this unending obligation, they are actually affirming the radical, non-numerical individuality of their moral selfhood.

Beyond the Face: The Analytic of the Erotic

Totality and Infinity, IV, A–G

Recapitulation

Levinas agrees with Heidegger that "fundamental ontology [the study of being qua being] . . . must be sought in the existential analytic of Dasein" (*SZ*, 13). What makes his existential analytic so different from Heidegger's is the fact that its subject is embodied Dasein. Nowhere is this clearer than in part 4 of *Totality and Infinity*, where he analyzes sexuality and the parent-child relation. Levinas remarks, "Dasein in Heidegger is never hungry" (*TI*, 134). He or she also does not have sex or children. Embodied Dasein, however, is characterized by such features. Only through sex can it reproduce itself; only by reproducing itself can it continue to be—that is, overcome death by continuing itself through its offspring. When such facts are taken up in an existential analytic, we face the issue of how they affect our disclosure of being. What, in fact, is the sense of being that appears through these features of our embodied humanity? A similar set of questions can be raised with regard to time. One of the goals of Heidegger's analytic is to exhibit "temporality as the meaning of the being that we call Dasein." This involves "the repeated interpretation . . . of the structures of Dasein . . . as modes of temporality" (*SZ*, 17). Such modes serve "as the horizon for all understanding of being and for any way of interpreting it" (ibid.). Here, we have to ask how our embodiment, in determining our temporality, sets this horizon. How does the fact that Dasein exists generationally affect the meaning of being?[1]

Before Levinas takes up these issues, he recapitulates the ontology he has already developed on the basis of our embodiment. His summary consists of four basic points. The first is that, if we begin with Dasein, alterity is prior to identity. It is not the case that, in their face-to-face relation, "the alterity of B with respect to A results simply from the identity of B being distinct from the identity of A" (*TI*, 251, my translation).

Rather, as Levinas writes, "the alterity of the other does not result from its identity, but constitutes it: the other is the Other" (ibid.). Thus, it is in relation to the Other that you have your distinct identity. This identity is a result of your acting according to the irreplaceable responsibility that the Other summons you to. For Levinas, such responding is morality. As he expresses this, "the accomplishing of the I qua I and morality constitute one sole and same process in being" (*TI*, 245). If we translate this into our understanding of being, then the priority of alterity over identity signifies that difference is prior to identity. This recalls the position that Derrida advances in *Speech and Phenomena*, where he asserts that "différance," understood as "the operation of differing," precedes and, indeed, makes possible every identity.[2] This "différance," Derrida writes, "is always older than presence and procures for it its openness."[3] In Levinas's view, the openness of presence (and, hence, of being as presence) is its transcendence. It is the result of our relation to the Other, a relation that always enriches presence on the basis of the Other's perspectives (*TI*, 193).

The extension of this position to the sense of being in general implies that every identity can be deconstructed into an alterity that makes it possible. This ontological principle recalls the biblical account of the origin of the world, where God creates by dividing (light from dark, day from night, waters above from waters below, land from water, living from nonliving, Eve from Adam, and so on). The result of each division is an identity, which is called "good."[4] Levinas and Derrida were friends, and both were Jewish by birth. It may have been that Derrida, like Levinas, was influenced by this account. Here, of course, caution is in order, given Derrida's claim that he "rightly passes for an atheist."[5] What one can say is that when Levinas writes, "The other is the Other," he means that this Other is prior to and constitutive of human identity. This affects how we understand the "primordial multiplicity" of human beings. Such multiplicity, he writes, "is produced in multiple singularities and not in a being exterior to this number, who would count the multiples" (*TI*, 251). It is not produced by someone who counts—that is, who has a given conception of the human as the unit for his counting. There is no unit here. Humans are not present as replications. Their multiple presence is that of multiple singularities. In other words, there is multiplicity only insofar as there are multiple individuals whose uniqueness is given by the Others they respond to.

Levinas's second point concerns language. The assertion that human beings are not, primordially, countable units by a being "exterior" to them corresponds to Levinas's insistence on the "impossibility of the exterior point of view" regarding a face-to-face relation. Given that language itself is based on this relation, the external, impersonal perspective also fails to capture it. This signifies that "language is not added to the impersonal thought dominating" the speakers (*TI*, 251). It is not an external addition to an impersonal rational order. The relation of language to such thought is, in fact, the reverse: "impersonal thought is produced in the movement that proceeds from the same to the other, and consequently in *inter*personal . . . language" (*TI*, 251–52, my italics). This is the language of the first and second persons—the *I* and the *you* who face each other. It is not that of the impersonal third person—the external *he, she, it*, or *they*. There is, here, an implicit critique of analytic philosophy. In making its "linguistic turn" from subjectivity to language, such philosophy privileges the third person; it sees in its very impersonality a non-subjective basis for its objective analyses. In this, it is the heir of the Enlightenment rationality that Leibniz exemplified in his conception of an impersonal *mathesis universalis*. For Levinas, by contrast, "the interlocutors as singularities, irreducible to the concepts they constitute in communicating their world . . . preside over communication" (*TI*, 252). It is they that ground the commonality of the conceptual order. This involves "the one giving the world, his possession, to the other" by communicating it. It also involves "apology," that is, "the one justifying himself in his freedom before the other" (ibid.). At work here is the priority of difference over identity. In language, this manifests itself in the priority of the interpersonal over the impersonal. At its basis are individuals as non-numerical singularities."Reason," Levinas writes, "presupposes these singularities or particularities, not as individuals . . . divesting themselves of their particularity so as to find themselves as identical, but precisely as interlocutors, irreplaceable beings, unique in their genus, faces." Reason does not create "the relations between me and the other." The reverse is the case: "the Other's teaching me creates reason" (ibid.).

This brings us to the third of Levinas's points: which is that of the priority of intersubjectivity to reason. The view that reason is prior is advanced by both Kant and Hegel. Hegel asserts that the universal reason that the Kantian subject employs to test the moral maxims forms the content of the "substantial freedom" that is embodied in the universal laws of the state. Thus, reason convinces me that I cannot universalize theft and, therefore, persuades me that theft is immoral. The state embodies this rational principle in its universal laws against theft. The relation between the citizens is "rational" in this sense. The difficulty for Levinas is that there is no "face-to-face," no individuality in this view. What we confront here is "the inhumanity of a humanity where the self has its consciousness outside of itself" in a universal reason. Such an impersonal reason does not convince me of my inhumanity when I violate its strictures. It does not persuade me personally that theft is immoral. It is the Other, to whom I have to respond, who does this. As we have seen, for Levinas, reason grows out of this response. Its basis is the "Other's teaching me" by pointing out objections, by calling me into question. Here, "apology . . . is the primordial phenomenon of reason" (*TI*, 252). It is my having to answer to and explain myself to the Other. Reason, so grounded, does not deny individuality. It flows from "personal discourse." By contrast, for Kant and Hegel, reason does deny individuality. Individuality is a function of my "animal partiality," that is, my subjective desires and inclinations. I abstract from these in following the universal rules of reason. The question that Levinas raises is whether such universalization is possible for individuals defined by such partiality. He asks: "if the partiality of the individual, understood as the very principle of his individuation, is a principle of incoherence, by what magic would the simple addition of incoherencies produce a coherent impersonal discourse, and not the disordered din of the crowd?" (*TI*, 253). In other words, if our individuality were really founded in "animal partiality," how could we ask: "What would happen if everybody performed a specific act, that is, made a false promise?" Wouldn't the universalization invoked here be "an addition of incoherencies"? In point of fact, "my individuality is . . . quite different from this animal partiality." Individuality and reason both have the same root. This "is apology, that is, personal discourse, from me to the others" (ibid.).

Levinas makes the same point with regard to freedom: I achieve not just my individuality but also my personal freedom through responding to the Other. He writes, "the freedom of the I is neither the arbitrariness of an isolated being nor the conformity of an isolated being with a rational and universal law incumbent upon all" (*TI*, 252). Freedom as such arbitrariness is animal desire. As the bearer of such desire, I am an individual, according to Kant. The content of my freedom, however, is simply the immediate object of my appetite. At this point, rather than being a willing agent, the world wills through me. In Kant's words, as animal desire, my "will does not give itself the law [of its actions], but the object does so in virtue of its relation to the will."[6] Thus, the result of this position is an individuality, based on "animal partiality," that is not really free. The alternative to this is Kantian freedom, taken as the "conformity of an isolated being with a rational [and universal] law." Here, I am free only to the point that I abstract myself from my circumstances, that is, follow the categorical imperative and act such that the maxim of my will could be taken as a universal law. Otherwise, my will is bound by the desires that tie it to its particular situation. For Kant, then, the thought of my freedom abstracts from my individuality. As he expresses this, freedom, as conformity to universal law, demands that "we abstract from the personal differences between rational beings, and also from all the content of their private ends."[7] Without these, however, we have no distinct agents. The result is a freedom that is not really individual. How, then, do we combine individuality with freedom without reducing freedom to mere animal desire? For Levinas, the individuality consonant with non-arbitrary freedom is given to me by the Other. He writes, "my arbitrary freedom reads its shame in the eyes that look at me" (*TI*, 252). What prevents my freedom from being arbitrary is not the universality of reason that Kant and Hegel invoke. It is the Other calling me into question and my having to respond to him. This is not a limitation of my freedom. It is not a reduction of it to a Heideggerian "finite freedom." It is, rather, the way it achieves the individuality of agency. The Other who makes me an individual in calling me to respond to him "invests" my freedom. He calls upon it to transform itself from egotism to goodness.

Erotic Alterity: The Feminine

Heidegger in his description of "being with" (*Mitsein*) Others never mentions our erotic attachments. For Levinas, however, a "phenomenology of Eros" is an essential part of his existential analytic. He begins his descriptions by observing that the erotic is "the equivocal par excellence" (*TI*, 255). It involves both the otherness of the Other and the Other as an object of need, of appetite. In his words, "Love remains a relation with the Other that turns into need, and this need still presupposes the total, transcendent exteriority of the Other, of the beloved" (*TI*, 254). What we experience in love is "the possibility of the Other appearing as an object of a need while retaining his alterity." We experience "this simultaneity of need and desire, of concupiscence and transcendence" (*TI*, 255). Given this dual nature, love cannot be interpreted as mere sensuous appetite. Equally, it cannot be just "a desire for the transcendent." It has to involve both.[8]

This, according to Levinas, is the pathos of love. We seek the Other through his or her body. We expose this body in erotic nudity as if we were uncovering the Other, but the Other still escapes us. In such nudity, as he writes, "the essentially hidden throws itself towards the light without becoming signification. Not nothingness—but what is not yet." The "not yet" refers to the fact that the Other, in spite of our "profaning" the Other's nudity, is still beyond us (*TI*, 257). As Levinas puts this, "'Being not yet' . . . refers to a modesty that [erotic love] has profaned without overcoming. The secret appears without appearing" (*TI*, 257). Thus, in erotic love, you want the Other in and through the Other's flesh.

The "secret" that is the Other appears in the Other's flesh without appearing. It constantly eludes you. This modesty, this refusal to exhibit itself, is profaned again and again in one's attempts to get at the Other through bodily passion. Yet, the modesty remains. This is love's pathos. In Levinas's words: "modesty, insurmountable in love, constitutes its pathos" (ibid.).

One of the expressions of this "pathos" of love is the caress. The caress does not grasp. It does not seize on anything. It solicits "what slips away as though it were not yet" (*TI*, 257–58). Rather than grasping, "it searches, it forages. It is not an intentionality of disclosure but of search; a movement unto the invisible" (*TI*, 258). It is, in fact, a physical expression of metaphysical desire. The body of the Other is present to me, lies exposed to my caress. The embodied Other is always just ahead of this. With the caress, I try to expose the Other, to profane or exhibit the essentially hidden, but always without success. This is why the caress is more of a searching than a grasping. Its searching is response to the hiddenness of the Other. For Levinas, "The profanation which insinuates itself in caressing responds adequately to the originality of this dimension of absence" (ibid.).

Levinas distinguishes the not-yet of such absence from the Heideggerian not-yet. It is not the not-yet of "the possible, which would be open to anticipation" (*TI*, 258). Thus, it is not the not-yet that "a project maintains" as a goal that can be accomplished, disclosed and, hence, brought to the light. Rather, "the caress does not act, does not grasp possibles" (*TI*, 259). This is because, "what the caress seeks is not situated in a perspective and in the light of the graspable." The caress, in other words, expresses a movement that is fundamentally different from Heideggerian disclosure. It exhibits neither the "what is it for" (*Wozu*) nor the goal of pragmatic action. Equally alien to it is the bare presence (*Vorhandensein*) that appears when a tool breaks down. In its seeking the Other in and through the flesh, "the caress," Levinas writes, "aims at the tender . . . The tender designates a *way*, the way of remaining in the no man's land between being and not-yet-being" (*TI*, 259). In "being" is the Other's body; in "not-yet-being" is the embodied Other. In seeking the one through the other, the caress uncovers "the essential frailty of the Beloved produced as vulnerable and as mortal." As such, "it is compassion for the passivity, the suffering, the evanescence of the tender" (ibid.). Flesh appears as the Beloved's exposure to harm, as his or her nudity before death.[9]

All of this is excellent phenomenological description. It is, however, one-sided insofar as it is limited to the male perspective. Thus, Levinas takes the Other that is sought through the flesh as "the feminine." For example, having stated that "the desire that animates [the caress] is reborn in its satisfaction," and is "fed somehow by the *not yet*," he takes this desire as "bringing us back to the virginity, forever inviolate, of the feminine." He adds, "The beloved, at once graspable but intact in her nudity . . . abides in virginity. The feminine essentially violable and inviolable, the 'eternal feminine,' is the virgin of an incessant recommencement of virginity, the untouchable in the very contact of voluptuosity, future in the present" (*TI*, 258).

The general point he is making is that the body of the Other can be penetrated, can lose its virginity. But the embodied Other, as other, is always future, always is ahead of the lover. In its essential status as a not-yet, the Other's "virginity" is recommenced as it continually escapes the lover's grasp. Thus, in aiming at the tender by oscillating between the body of the Other and the Other as embodied, the lover experiences "an incessant recommencement of virginity." The problem with this is not the point itself, which holds both for men and women since either can be the Other. It is with Levinas's descriptions, which take the female (as opposed to the male) body as the object of the caress. Levinas, accordingly, associates inviolability with *feminine* virginity. He understands the escape of the Other that constitutes the pathos of love as the "recommencement of [this] virginity." Similarly, the erotic nudity which manifests the Other as other in the flesh, the nudity that is the object of the caress, is taken as *feminine* nudity. The inability of the caress to grasp its object thus signifies that "the virgin remains ungraspable . . . withdrawing into her future, beyond every possible promised to anticipation" (ibid.). In the beloved, we confront "the night of the hidden, the clandestine, the mysterious, land of the virgin, simultaneously uncovered by *Eros* and refusing *Eros*" (*TI*, 259).

With this, all the shortcomings of erotic love with regard to ethics become shortcomings of the feminine. Thus, the fact that lovers seal themselves off from society, forming between themselves a closed couple, is ascribed to the feminine. This allows Levinas to write, "The relationship established between lovers . . . is the very contrary of the social relation. . . . The feminine is the other refractory to society, member of a dual society, an intimate society, a society without language" (*TI*, 264–65). It also allows him to contrast the ethical and the corresponding signifying character of the masculine face with the non-signifying character of the erotic taken as "the feminine." With this, he falls into the stereotype: the ethical relation is masculine, the loving, emotional relation is feminine. He writes, for example: "In the face, the Other expresses his eminence, the dimension of height and divinity from which he descends. . . . The frailty of femininity involves pity for what, in a sense, is not yet, [it invites] disrespect for what exhibits itself in immodesty and is not discovered despite the exhibition" (*TI*, 262).[10]

The obvious rejoinder to this is that women also have a face. For Levinas, however, this is the "beautiful face." It is the face that makes you see the Other *in* it, even though you know that the Other is *beyond* it. It thus exemplifies the equivocation of the erotic. As Levinas expresses this: "Equivocation constitutes the epiphany of the feminine. . . . The face . . . in its feminine epiphany dissimulates allusions, innuendos. It laughs under the cloak of its own expression, without leading to any specific meaning" (*TI*, 264). His point is that the beautiful face does not signify. It simply is. One looks at it, not through it. One grasps the Other as flesh and grasps flesh as the Other in the beautiful feminine face. In gazing at it, one mistakenly sees the Other in the expressions, gestures, modulations of voice, and so on that constitute the face's beauty. Such a face does not call one into question. Its little phrases and raillery do not signify. Because of this, from the ethical perspective, its beauty appears as a disfigurement. In Levinas's words: "In this inversion of the face in femininity, in this disfigurement that refers to the face, non-signifyingness abides in the signifyingness of the face. This presence of non-signifyingness in the signifyingness of the face . . .—where the chastity and decency of the face abides at the limit of the obscene still repelled but already close at hand and promising—is the primordial event of feminine beauty" (*TI*, 263). Such statements, needless to say, are highly questionable. They prompt one to ask: Does the fact that a woman has a beautiful face mean that the decency of her face abides next to the obscene? What about the male face seen from the feminine perspective? Why couldn't we make the same assertions about it? Do men have no erotic attraction for women?[11]

If we eliminate the male bias in Levinas's account, the point still remains that the erotic relation differs from the ethical insofar as the erotic is "the equivocal par excellence" (*TI*, 255). Alterity and flesh, desire and need equivocate in the erotic, but not in the ethical relation. In the ethical relation, the Other is other; in the erotic, "the other is me and separated from me" (*TI*, 265). He is me because of "the identity of the feeling" that we both experience. As Levinas describes this: "The non-sociality of voluptuosity is, positively, the community of the sentient and sensed: the other is not only a sensed [entity], but in [it] the sensed is affirmed as sentient, as though one and the same sentiment were substantially common to me and to the other." This is not a community like that of two people observing the same external object—for example, a landscape. It is not a sharing of a common language or having a common idea. "Nor is the community due to an analogy of feeling; it is due to an identity of feeling" (ibid.). This identity prompts us to experience the Other's body as our own.

To see what Levinas is getting at, we can turn to an observation Husserl makes with regard to how we recognize our body as our own. Behind this recognition is the fact that, when we touch ourselves, we feel both the flesh that we touch and the flesh, that is, the touching hand, that is touching ourselves. We do not experience this "double sensation" when we touch other objects. Touching them, we feel sensations in the touching hand, but not in the object touched. Having no sensation of *its* being touched, we cannot immediately affirm it as sentient.[12] With the other as an erotic partner, however, "the sensed," as we cited Levinas, "is affirmed as sentient." The intermingling of pleasures is such that I feel the Other's pleasure as my own. Doing so, the distinction that allows me to recognize my body as my own breaks down. My affirming the sensed as sentient is, in passion, my affirming my partner as part of my bodily identity.

This affirmation does not undo the equivocation of the erotic relation. In spite of this feeling of identity, I do not desire my own body, I desire the Other's body. This is why Levinas asserts: "In voluptuosity, the other is me and separated from me. The separation of the Other in the midst of this community of feeling constitutes the acuity of voluptuosity" (*TI*, 265). Desire is desire for what I do not possess. In the erotic, this is a desire for what is me and yet is not me, is my flesh, and yet is beyond this. Now, from Levinas's perspective, the true satisfaction of this desire is the child. The child is and is not me. In his words, "the I is, in the child, an other." My child "is not only mine . . . he *is* me" (*TI*, 267). Because of this, the voluptuosity of the erotic goes beyond itself. It implicitly contains the relation to the child. As Levinas expresses this: "Already the relation with the child . . . takes form in voluptuosity, to be accomplished in the child himself" (*TI*, 266).

Fecundity as an Ontological Category

We asked at the beginning of this chapter: how does the fact that Dasein exists generationally affect the meaning of being? Levinas's account of fecundity presents his answer. Its key point is that "fecundity is to be set up as an ontological category." According to it, "being is no longer Eleatic unity" (*TI*, 277). Rather, with the fact of reproduction, "being is produced as multiple . . . this is its ultimate structure." In other words, through fecundity, considered as "a new ontological principle" (*TI*, 276), we "leave the philosophy of Parmenidean being" (*TI*, 269).[13]

Because Parmenides's conception of being forms the essential reference point to Levinas's ontological principle, let us take a moment to review its main points.[14] The first is the necessity of being. According to Parmenides, "it is impossible that it not be." Being *means* to be and vice versa. Given this, we cannot say that non-being *is*. The assertion "that not-being is and that it necessarily is" Parmenides calls "impossible." How would you recognize or posit non-being? How would you speak of it? The claim here is that "thinking and being have the same object"—namely, "what is." In other words, one cannot think "what is not" because there is no object for one's thought. Given the necessity of being, we also have its eternity. Being cannot come to be, for if it did, it would come from nothing. But this would mean that nothing is actually something—that is, a source of being. This, however, is ruled out since "it is impossible to think or to say that not-being is." Furthermore, given the lack of determinacy in non-being, how could one say, for example, that being came to be "later rather than earlier"? Lacking all determination, how could non-being determine what comes to be? In fact, since it does not exist, how could it act? The same arguments show that being cannot be destroyed. Nothingness cannot destroy it. The non-being of nothingness precludes its agency. Given this, the destruction of being would have to be by being. But this means that being would have to both precede and follow this supposed destruction. Furthermore, since being qua being is not diverse, being is not divisible. Everything is "full of being." In fact, since everything is and nothing is not, being is continuous and unlimited. Unlimited, it is unmoved; for where would it move to? Not into the nothing, since this does not exist. Incapable of motion or becoming other than itself—which would signify its destruction—being is thus unchanged. Being is, and continuously remains, being.

Levinas's account of being is the opposite of this. His attempt to think "otherwise than being" is an attempt to escape the series of tautologies by which Parmenides constructs his account of being. Such tautologies come down to the fact that being is. As such, it is not other than itself, but is inherently one. For Levinas, by contrast, being is plural. This is because our privileged access to it, our own humanity, is plural. This access arises with our coming to be. It involves the relation of one human being (the female) to another (the male), the result being the engenderment of another human being (the child). From the perspective of our fecundity, then, "being is produced as multiple and as split into same and other; this is its ultimate structure. It is society" (*TI*, 269).

Fecundity, considered as an ontological (as opposed to a merely biological) principle, is my relation to the future that my child embodies. This relation is "irreducible to the power over possibles" (*TI*, 269).

Levinas is referring to the Heideggerian project, where I employ power to actualize one of the possibilities I find in myself. In my relation to this possibility, I am ahead of myself. It represents what I will do or be and, hence, presents my future to me. According to Levinas, I am ahead of myself, that is, I have a future, in a very different way in my child. The Heideggerian "project . . . emanates from the solitary head." It expresses my possibility. By contrast, "the encounter with the Other as feminine is required in order that the future of the child come to pass from beyond the possible, beyond projects" (*TI*, 267). As Levinas notes, this relation resembles that ascribed to the "idea of infinity." Like Descartes's conception of God, the future of the child could not have come from himself. It exceeds his "power over the possibles." To engender a child, the self requires the Other. As requiring both, the future the child embodies is "both my own and non-mine, a possibility of myself but also a possibility of the other." As such, it "does not enter into the logical essence of the possible" (ibid.). This essence requires unity. A possible would be impossible if it could not be instantiated in reality, that is, if it were incapable of forming a unitary being. In fecundity, however, we face "a duality of the Identical" (*TI*, 268). We have otherness as prior to identity. This alterity, which is composed of myself and the Other—myself and my Beloved— cannot be composed into a unity; neither can the alterity that links the parent to the child.

The future opened up by such alterity is that of "infinite being," whose infinity consists in its continually beginning again. Embodied by the child, it continues in the child's child and so on, down through succeeding generations. This "infinite being" is not the unbounded being of Parmenides—the being that could only be limited by more being. It is, rather, "ever recommencing being." It is being "produced in the guise of fecundity" (*TI*, 268). The contrast is equally stark with Heidegger. For Heidegger, I define myself through my projects as a self that has accomplished various things. The I is reiterated as the performer of these projects. In fecundity, however, "the tedium of this repetition ceases; the I is other and young." This signifies that "fecundity continues history without producing old age." It "does not bring an eternal life to an aging subject. It is *better*" than this, as it involves "the inexhaustible youths of the child." Through these, infinite being "is produced in the mode of an I that is always at the origin" (ibid.). It involves what Hannah Arendt called the miracle of "natality"—that is, the fact that the world is born anew in each child. The child's birth is the recommencement of the world's presence.[15]

The fact that "infinite being" is "produced as fecundity indicates," for Levinas, "the vanity of pantheism." God is not present in everything. He is not to be thought in terms of Parmenidean being. Rather, the ultimate structure of being is "multiple." It is "split into the same and the other." Because of this split, it involves a multiple transcendence. Transcendence does not aim at an immobile, unchanging being that is outside of time. It does not demand a perspective where motion and, hence, time appear as illusionary. Rather, "transcendence is time and goes unto the Other" in the form of the child (*TI*, 269). This other, however, does not stop the process. He continues it. In his own erotic desire for the Other, he also produces a child. Thus, "transcendence transcends toward him who transcends." What we have is "fecundity engendering fecundity." What generates the different, transcendent temporalizations is the erotic desire for the Other (*TI*, 269). This erotic desire produces both "the independence of separate being and its transcendence" (ibid.). It produces being as plural. Its meaning, in other words, involves something more than Heidegger's three temporal ecstasies—the future, the past, and the present—that define Dasein as a given finite totality. It involves the temporality of new generations, new temporal centers that are successively linked. In Levinas's words: "Being is here produced not as the definitiveness of a totality, but as an incessant recommencement, and consequently as infinite" (*TI*, 270).[16]

The moral aspect of this comes from the fact that the transcendence implicit in fecundity is not that of an impersonal, immobile Parmenidean being. It involves the "for the Other" of family relations and, hence, "the goodness [that is the] correlative of the face." As Levinas puts this, "Fecundity engendering fecundity accomplishes goodness" (*TI*, 269). It does this by engendering individuals that can be morally good. In it, "the Desire that is the independence of the separated being and its transcendence is accomplished." This metaphysical desire, which relates one individual to another, is goodness. The fecundity that generates it is "the goodness of goodness." It is what implants in being the *moral* transcendence, the being for the Other that is goodness. For Levinas, then, fecundity is the biblical analogue to the Good that Plato situated at the top of his divided line. This Good, however, is not thought of in terms of the persistence of forms that are inherently timeless and self-identical. Its root is "the conception of the child" and all the moral possibilities "the future of the child" involves (ibid.).

The Erotic Subject

Levinas now turns to examine more closely the subjectivity that is present in Eros. His aim is to distinguish it from Heidegger's Dasein. The voluptuosity that constitutes this subjectivity is marked by "the coinciding of the lover and the beloved." As we have seen, this coincidence is a matter of "the community of the sentient and sensed," one where "the other is not only sensed," but "affirmed as sentient" (*TI*, 265). In the passion of voluptuosity, I sense the Other's body, not simply as an object of my sensation. I sense it as sentient. The result is the identification of the Other's body as my own. In spite of this, however, the embodied Other remains other. The caress continues to search for the Other. The result is that "voluptuosity . . . is charged by [the] duality" of the lover and the beloved; "it is simultaneously fusion and distinction" (*TI*, 270). The relation between lovers is not that of Hegelian recognition. "To love to be loved" is not a desire to be desired by the Other. Its aim is not the testimony of the Other's recognition.[17] Rather than being an identity that affirms itself by enforcing the Other's recognition, the subject itself is transformed by voluptuosity. As Levinas expresses this: "Voluptuosity transfigures the subject himself, who henceforth owes his identity not to his initiative of power, but to the passivity of the love received." In this passivity, "he finds himself again as the self . . . of an other and not just as the self of himself." He is the Other in the "fusion" of voluptuosity. Given the Other's unbridgeable alterity, he is simultaneously *not* the Other, but rather "the self of himself." In the passion of love, "the relationship with the carnal . . . makes this [dual] self arise incessantly" (ibid.).

Given that this dual self's identity involves "the passivity of the love received," its arising is the opposite of the self-positing by which the "virile and heroic I" establishes itself (*TI*, 270). The heroic I establishes itself through acting. It posits itself as the actor who, through his action, has accomplished things. As Levinas observes, "the freedom of the subject that posits itself . . . implies responsibility" (*TI*, 271). The self that engages in its projects commits itself to their fulfillment. It responds to itself by keeping the commitments it makes to itself. Freely binding itself to its word, it pursues its goal and, hence, maintains its identity (as the self that gave its word) across the time that separates the commitment and its fulfillment. Here, as Levinas writes, "The coinciding of freedom with responsibility constitutes the I, doubled with itself, encumbered with itself." By contrast, "Eros delivers from this encumberment." It does not weigh us down with the commitments we make. It does not encumber our identity with all our accomplishments. Rather, "it goes toward a future which is not yet and which . . . I will be." The reference here is to the "future of the child." In such a future, the I does not return to itself as the one who, through his accomplishments, has realized the future he projected. Equally, the future of the child is not a projection of our past experience. It is neither an anticipation based on what we have already experienced nor an

intentionality formed on this basis. It consists, rather, "in transcending
[the past] absolutely in fecundity" (ibid.).

This "transcendence of fecundity" can best be understood by returning to Levinas's description of the constitution of erotic subjectivity.
In his words: "the erotic subjectivity is constituted in the common act of
the sensing and the sensed as the self of an other, and accordingly is constituted within a relation with the other, within a relation with the face"
(*TI*, 271). So constituted, such subjectivity is inherently equivocal. On the
one hand, in the community of the sensing and the sensed, "the other
presents himself as lived by myself." On the other hand, the relation
with the face marks the Other as irretrievably other. As combining both,
"erotic love oscillates between being beyond desire and being beneath
need." It involves both carnal and metaphysical desire in an unstable
equilibrium. In the fusion and distinction that constitute it, the erotic
subject exhibits an intentionality, a drive beyond itself. As embodying
the union and non-union of lover and beloved, it points to the child who
is and is not the parent. In Levinas's words, "This unparalleled relation
between two substances, where a beyond substances is exhibited, is resolved in paternity" (ibid.). The unity that is and is not the erotic subject
becomes concrete in the child.

The "transcendence of fecundity" and "erotic subjectivity" are,
here, mutually defining terms. Levinas's transformation of the concept
of subjectivity also changes our conception of transcendence, and vice
versa. Both involve a reworking of what we mean by the future. For Heidegger, subjectivity designates the temporal structure of Dasein. Its primary element is the future, understood as the "ahead of itself" that is
formed when Dasein projects one of its possibilities, choosing to actualize it. When we transform what we mean by the future, we necessarily
transform the temporal structure of subjectivity. As Levinas expresses
this: "In fecundity, subjectivity no longer has the same meaning." This is
because "the inevitable reference of the erotic to the future in fecundity
reveals a radically different structure: the subject is not only all that he will
do" (*TI*, 272). His future does not simply involve his accomplishments.
It involves the child. Through the child "he will be other than himself
while remaining himself." Needless to say, this "structure of the identity
of subjectivity . . . takes us outside of the categories of classical logic."
Subjectivity, here, does not involve some transcendent I that speaks "in
the depth of the I and guides it." It also does not signify an impersonal
force beyond the I that secretly shapes it—for example "Hegel's universal, Durkheim's social, the statistical laws that govern our freedom,
Freud's unconscious, the existential that sustains the existentiel in Heidegger," and so on. All these alternatives involve "the presence behind

the I of a foreign principle." The logical alternative is the assertion of the I as an absolute origin. As Levinas remarks, this is exemplified by Paul Valéry's M. Teste. In Valéry's *An Evening with M. Teste,* Teste "wishes to be *nothing but myself* at the absolute origin of all initiatives" (ibid.).[18] By contrast, erotic subjectivity is neither subject to "a foreign principle" nor is it an absolute origin. Rather, it is "as itself . . . liberated of its identity." This is because it is transformed through its relation to the Other (the "feminine"). In Levinas's words: "It is precisely as itself that the I is, in the relation with the Other in femininity, liberated of its identity, that it can be other on the basis of self as origin" (ibid.). This liberation comes from the child. In the child, it can both be other than itself and, as such, be an origin. That this origin can engender a new origin that has the same engendering capability means that this relation of otherness and identity that defines parenthood can extend through the generations. As a consequence, we can say that "in the I," understood as erotic subjectivity, "being can be produced as infinitely recommencing, that is, properly speaking, as infinite." Involving otherness and identity, this infinity is shot through with transcendence. Multiplicity, in the sense of a plurality of unique singularities, is inherent in it. For Levinas, then, "fecundity evinces a unity that is not opposed to [this] multiplicity, but, in the precise sense of the term, engenders it" (*TI,* 273).

Transcendence and Fecundity

In a section of the *Talmud* advising judges how to caution witnesses in capital cases, the *Mishnah* notes that "capital cases are not like monetary cases."[19] Giving false witness in the latter can result in a financial loss for the defendant, which can be made good by "monetary restitution." But, "in capital cases [the person giving false witness] is held responsible for [the accused's] blood and the blood of his descendants until the end of time."[20] If we take this seriously, then we have to say that the "I" of the accused is more than the "I" of a solitary individual. It includes his descendants. Levinas expresses a similar conclusion when he writes of the parent, "In this 'I am,' being is no longer Eleatic unity. In [this I's] existing itself there is a multiplicity and a transcendence" (*TI,* 277). The I in its existing transcends itself in the child. If we stay with the classical conception, then, as Levinas writes, "the idea of transcendence is self-contradictory" (*TI,* 274). This is because the subject cannot really transcend himself. If transcendence touched its identity, "we would witness the death of its substance." Were we to insist that substance can continue after its annihilation, that is, transcend itself, then this "would shake the foundations of our logic." This is because "our logic rests on the indissoluble bond between the One and Being . . . Being qua being is for us monadic." Thus, we always see "existing in an existent," which is understood as a unitary substance. This means that "pluralism appears . . . only as a plurality of subjects that exist. Never has it appeared in the existing of those existents" (ibid.). The claim, however, that I am my child and, through him, am the totality of my descendants breaks with this logic. The logic that "privileges" unity can understand transcendence only as change. It takes such change as a change of something. The latter is the subject of change. It is the unchanging being (the substantial identity) that underlies the change of its attributes. Given the identification of being with this unchanging subject, its change would be its annihilation pure and simple. It would be its transcendence of its being. For Parmenides, the father of this logic, this, however, is unthinkable. To assert that "transcendence . . . is situated outside of the event of being" is to claim that it is impossible (ibid.).

Heidegger's solution to this impasse, Levinas writes, is to articulate the concept of "existing as time rather than congealing it in the permanence of the stable" underlying subject of change. As part of this, he engages in "the rehabilitation of the possible" (*TI*, 275). The possible is our being ahead of ourselves, that is, our futurity, as we project it forward as a goal of our project. Here, "the projection of the future transcends . . . by the very existing of being." Dasein exists as ahead of himself. His existing is his temporal distension. In Heidegger's terms, "openness upon the future, 'being for death': these are ways of expressing an existing not in conformity with the logic of unity." The difficulty is that, in speaking of the actualization of the possible, "the possible is immediately inverted into Power and Domination. In the new that springs from it, the subject recognizes himself" as the accomplisher of the possibility projected forward as a goal. Since this was his own possibility coming from his own "thrown" situation, "he finds himself again in it, masters it. His freedom writes his history which is one; his projects delineate a fate of which he is master and slave" (ibid.). The claim, then, is that this strategy never really escapes the logic that equates being and unity. Dasein is "master" insofar as he chooses and accomplishes his projects. He is a "slave" to them insofar as the "history" that he writes through these projects "is one." It is the history of himself as their unitary accomplisher. As "resolute," he chooses to be one thing rather than another. Consistent with this goal, his projects must be compatible. They must be capable of forming a unitary history.

A similar failure to escape Parmenides's logic also appears in Heidegger's "late philosophy." In Heidegger's essay, *De l'essence de la vérité*, "power," Levinas writes, "is at the same time impotence" (*TI*, 276). This can be explained by briefly summarizing this essay. It is distinguished from *Being and Time* by looking beyond the projective activity of Dasein for the source of the meaning of being. Rather than being its origin, this activity is now considered to be guided by such meaning. The meaning of being is taken as determined by a standard of the real that being itself provides. Each epoch is marked by a different standard, a different revelation of what constitutes the being of beings. Humans manifest their impotence in their "wandering," their "errance" from one standard to the next. When a standard breaks down, they "stand out" from it. No longer accepting it as sufficient, they then "stand open" for a new standard. They, however, do not create this revelation of being. They accept it and, holding fast to it, "in-sist" on it, that is, "stand in" it. This insistence persists until the standard proves inadequate and the cycle begins again.[21] Now, according to Levinas, this account still privileges power and disclosure. He writes, "In Heidegger, the human being apprehended as power remains, in reality, truth and light. Heidegger hence disposes of no notion to describe the relation with mystery, already implied in the finitude of Dasein" (*TI*, 276–77). His point is that the relation to being continues to be that of disclosure. As such, it presupposes our power to accomplish our projects and, hence, our standing under the necessity of being their unitary accomplisher. The fact that we have to wait for a revelation of being in order to form the preliminary understanding of being that guides our projects does not change the basic framework of his account. As Levinas writes: "If power is at the same time impotence, it is by reference to power"—that is, to our "I can" and its necessities—"that this impotence is described" (*TI*, 276).

For Levinas, by contrast, "the relation with mystery" implicit in the finitude of Dasein does *not* involve the passive reception of a standard of disclosure. The "notion of being founding transcendence" is not given by the ontological difference between being and beings—that is, by the fact that being itself transcends all the standards by which it allows us to disclose beings. More generally, transcendence is not a matter of "consciousness and power." It cannot be understood in terms of "a subject of knowings and powers." To solve the "problem . . . of maintaining the I in the transcendence with which it hitherto seemed incompatible," we must, rather, turn to the "erotic relation" (*TI*, 276). This is not to be taken as "a psychological curiosity" or "relegated to the biological." It is, rather, "a new ontological principle." Understood ontologically, "the erotic, analyzed as fecundity, breaks up reality into relations irreducible to the relations of genus and species, part and whole, action and passion, truth and error." All of these presuppose the equation of being and unity. The genus expresses the unity of the species under it, the whole the unity of the parts. Action and passion are unified in the sense that each implies the other since to act implies something receiving this action, and vice versa. Similarly, truth is the unity that statements aim at it. They are true when they hit the mark, false when they go astray. Sexuality, however, resists such analysis. As Levinas writes, "in sexuality, the subject enters into relation with what is absolutely other, with an alterity of a type unforeseeable in formal logic" (ibid.). It is unforeseeable because sexuality implies that plurality, rather than unity, is at the basis of being. It takes existing as multiple before it is one. As Levinas expresses its ontological sense: "Sexuality is in us neither knowledge nor power, but the very plurality of our existing." It is not external to the erotic subject. Rather, the erotic relation must be analyzed as characterizing "the very ipseity of the I, the very subjectivity of the subject" (*TI*, 277).

For Levinas, then, the solution to the problem of transcendence comes when we set up "fecundity . . . as an ontological principle" (*TI*, 277). This principle allows us to see the "return of the I to itself" in terms of the child. As he observes, the son is not my work. He is not a "poem" that I wrote, not an "object" that I make. Equally, he is not "my property." The categories of knowledge and power do not apply to our relationship. What we confront in parenthood ("paternity") is "a relation with a stranger who, while being Other, . . . is me, a relation of the I with a self which yet is not me." The relation with a self that *is* and *is not* me is unthinkable in Parmenidean terms, which are those of unity. Thus, "in this 'I am'" that expresses my paternity, "being is no longer Eleatic unity." Similarly, existing is no longer a function of a *unitary* existent. Rather, "in existing itself there is a multiplicity and a transcendence." I am, in my paternity, more than myself. In it, I transcend myself without losing my substance. As Levinas states the conclusion, "In this transcendence, the I is not swept away [as in death], since the son is not me; and yet I am my son. The fecundity of the I is its very transcendence" (ibid.). The point is that when we take fecundity as an ontological principle, we transform the very notion of existence. Its standing out—its ek-sistence—implies more than itself. Here "being is produced as multiple." In the "I am," being's "ultimate structure . . . is society" (*TI*, 269).

Filiality and Fraternity

This ontological reversal of the Parmenidean position is crucial for understanding the move Levinas makes from paternity to fraternity. He begins by asserting that "the I breaks free from itself in paternity without thereby ceasing to be an I, for the I is its son." The "I," in other words, includes both. Given this, we can say that "the father does not simply cause the son" (*TI*, 278). The identity between them prevents this. This identity, however, is not a substantial identity. The I's of the parent and the child do not merge. As Levinas writes: "To be one's son means to be 'I' in one's son, to be substantially in him, yet without being maintained there in identity" (*TI*, 278–79). This is because there is a crucial asymmetry between them: while the parent is his child, we cannot say that the child is his parent. The death of a person before paternity is the death of his successive generations. The reverse, however, is not the case. The child's death does not affect the generations that preceded him. Because of this asymmetry, we can say that "the son resumes the unicity of the father and yet remains exterior to the father" (*TI*, 279). This resumption of unicity is not through causality, but rather through "election." This does not mean that he is the *only* son; he is not unique "by number." Rather, "each son of the father is the unique son, the chosen son." Each is unique by virtue of the "paternal Eros" that "first invests the unicity of the son." As we saw, this Eros, stemming as it does from the "fusion" and the "distinction" of lover and the beloved, already instantiates the relation of identity and difference that becomes concrete in the parent-child relation. The intentionality that springs from this Eros in its voluptuosity is what "elects" the child.

According to Levinas, this election, rather than being a matter of causality, is a type of creation. He writes: "creation, [understood] as a relation of transcendence, of union and fecundity, conditions the positing of a unique being, and his ipseity qua elected." Such creation, he remarks, does not contradict the freedom of the creature. The thought that it does occurs "only when creation is confused with causality" (*TI*, 279). According to the principle of causality, every element in the effect can be traced back to its cause. Nothing comes to be from nothing. Its origin is always some action or feature of the cause. Causality, then, collapses the effect into the cause. By contrast, the relation of the union and fecundity of the parents is "a relation of transcendence." The beloved transcends the lover and the child transcends them both. Such transcendence involves the non-numerical singularity of each. Lacking any common measure that could bridge their alterity, each is unique. In particular, the uniqueness of each child produced by the "union and fecundity" of the parents is a function of such singularity. As non-numerically one, it can only be related to as transcendent. Now, to call its engenderment "creation" is to recall that creation *ex nihilo* involves transcendence. According to Levinas "the separated and created being is . . . not simply issued forth from the father, but is absolutely other than him" (*TI*, 63). As such, it involves the self-limitation of the creator. In Levinas's words, "the paradox of creation" is that of "an Infinity admitting a being outside of itself which it does not encompass" (*TI*, 103). Here, the dependence of the creature on the creator does not contradict the creature's alterity. Similarly, the erotic love that issues in the unique child does not encompass or absorb it. Such love intends the child as unique, that is, as transcendent to itself. Filiality, in other words, inherently involves transcendence. It is this that links it to creation. As Levinas expresses this relation: "Filiality itself can not appear as essential to the destiny of the I unless man retains this memory of the creation *ex nihilo*, without which the son is not a true other" (*TI*, 63).

The move to fraternity comes from the fact that all children are elected as unique in the erotic love that engenders them. Each is a non-numerical singular. Each can, like Adam, say that the world was created for my sake since each uniquely brings it to presence. Such uniqueness means that each maintains a relation of alterity with regard to the other children. Their relation, in other words, involves the face-to-face. In Levinas's words, "The election of the I, it's very ipseity, . . . does not place it among the other chosen ones, but rather in face of them" (*TI*, 279). The uniqueness of the I means that "no one can be substituted for the I to measure the extent of its responsibilities." Its very uniqueness makes it uniquely responsible. Equal to all others in having been elected, it is subordinate to them in the uniqueness of the responsibility that the face-to-face relation imposes on it.[22] The face-to-face, here, is both a result of its elected uniqueness and a moral determination of it. As unique, the I cannot evade its responsibilities. No one else can substitute for it. Responding as a unique individual to the appeal of the Other, it achieves its moral unicity.

This combination of equality and subordination is the origin of fraternity. As Levinas defines it, "fraternity is the very relation with the face in which, at the same time, my election and equality, that is, the mastery exercised over me by the other, are accomplished" (*TI*, 279). It is, in other words, a relation involving the equality and the solidarity of our being for one another. Through it, the erotic is opened to social life. Such life is not posterior to the family. It is not as if family relations form a private sphere that is essentially distinct from the public realm of social solidarity. As involving the face-to-face relation, fraternity begins with the family, but the same relation extends fraternity beyond it. For Levinas "the relation with the face in fraternity, where, in his turn, the Other appears in solidarity with all the others, constitutes the social order" (*TI*, 280). This order is not apart from the family. Rather, "the reference of every dialogue to the third party, by which the We . . . encompasses the face-to-face opposition, opens the erotic upon a social life." No longer "an intimate society, a society without language," the family through its moral relations becomes "all signifyingness and decency." As a result, the social order "encompasses the structure of the family itself" (ibid.).

Ontologically, this social order is implicit in each I. The future that the child represents involves fraternity and hence Others. It thus involves the future's inherent openness. This can be put in terms of Levinas's claim that "the [parental] I, liberated from its very identity in its fecundity, cannot maintain its separation with regard to this future if it is bound to its future in its *unique* child" (*TI*, 279). Were the parental I bound to the future of a single unique child, the child's future would also be the parent's future. This would hold through the generations if each child had only a single child. What ensures separation is the fact that "the unique child . . . is unique and non-unique." It "exists at the same time as unique in the world and as brother among brothers" (ibid.). The parent's future is thus split among multiple descendants. The fact that each is unique means that each brings to its Others a different perspective, a different way of intending the future. Each can call the Other's intentions into question. The future each intends is, thus, opened by its Others. As such, the parent's future, as present in the "future of the child," is itself opened up. In the openness that grounds its separation, this future is, like the child's being, grounded in plurality.

Time's Pardon

Hannah Arendt remarks that "forgiving . . . serves to undo the deeds of the past, whose 'sins' hang like Damocles' sword over every new generation." Forgiveness is necessary so that we can begin again. In her words, "without being forgiven, released from the consequences of what we have done, our capacity to act would, as it were, be confined to one single deed from which we could never recover."[23] We would continuously be entangled in the consequences of our actions. Such forgiveness, like the new that it permits, is, she writes, a "miracle." Rather than being a natural result of the past, it undoes its consequences.[24] How are we to understand this miracle? If we abstract from its religious connotations, what makes forgiveness possible? Arendt points to two factors. The first is our human plurality. Referring, like Levinas, to the biblical account of creation, she remarks that humans are not "endlessly reproducible repetitions of the same model, whose essence or nature [is] the same for all." Our condition is rather that of "plurality." By this she means that "we are all the same, that is human, in such a way that nobody is ever the same as anyone else who ever lived, lives, or will live."[25] Given this uniqueness, we have the capacity for "action," defined as the ability to bring about something that is unique and, hence, new. This capacity to produce the new is manifested by each generation, in fact, by each child, who brings the world uniquely to presence in his particular consciousness. With this, we have the second factor in forgiveness, which is the fact of birth—human natality. In Arendt's words: "The miracle that saves the world, the realm of human affairs, from its normal, 'natural' ruin is ultimately the fact of natality, in which the faculty of action [to produce the new] is ontologically rooted. It is, in other words, the birth of new men and the new beginning, the action they are capable of by virtue of being born."[26] Her point is that the miracle of forgiveness originally occurs in natality. The child, by virtue of his uniqueness, can start afresh. He is, as it were, pardoned by being born.

In the final part of section 4, Levinas presents the existential basis for this view. Again, the initial contrast is with Parmenides. For Parmenides, being is unlimited. It exists without limits in the sense that it can only be limited by itself. It is, in other words, one and continuous. For Levinas, however, "to exist without limits" means to exist "in the form of an origin, a commencement, that is, [to exist] again, [to exist] as an existent." This existent, which takes the form of an origin, is the child. With the child, the world commences anew. "To be infinitely—infiniation" thus signifies unending generational succession (*TI*, 281). As such, it involves the discontinuity that separates the child from the parent. By contrast, in its sheer undifferentiated continuity, Parmenidean being exhibits the "absolute indetermination of the there is, an existing without existents." To break it up, we need "a subject of what can happen, an origin and commencement." We require an "existent . . . that can, while remaining bound to being, take its distances with regard to being" by standing out from it and acting as origin. The requirement, in other words, is for "an elementary gesture of the being that refuses totalization." On one level, this gesture is that of the face. As Levinas writes: "The face arrests totalization" (ibid.). It does so because of the uniqueness of those involved in the face-to-face relation, a uniqueness that is not encompassed by any totality, by any overriding "essence" of man. On another level, the gesture involves the discontinuity of the generational chain. This is because a generation can be trapped by the consequences of its decisions. Keeping its promises to itself, it binds itself to pursue a particular path, which, with the entanglements of history, can become its fate. The same holds for an individual, whose actions can also trap it. For Levinas, this means that "without multiplicity and discontinuity—without fecundity—the I would remain a subject in which every adventure would revert into the adventure of a fate" (*TI*, 282). We escape this through "paternity" understood as "the way of being other while being oneself." This makes the

"I" a "drama in several acts," each act being a new generation. Thus, for Levinas: "A being capable of another fate than its own is a fecund being." By virtue of its fecundity, "the I, across the definitiveness of an inevitable death, prolongs itself in the other, time triumphs over old age and fate by its discontinuity" (ibid.).

Each new generation can thus be understood as renewing the face-to-face relation. This is why Levinas argued that filiality involves fraternity. As we cited him, the child is born not just among others, but "in face of them" (*TI*, 279). The result is the recommencement of the ontological relation that "arrests totalization." Levinas's present focus, however, is not on being, but rather on history. His point is that time is itself made discontinuous by fecundity. In other words, just as the parent *is* and *is not* the child, so the past of the preceding generation *is and is not* that of the succeeding generation. With this, we have the breakup of the causality of time—the causality that makes the present the natural result of the past. Rather than being trapped by entanglements of past decisions, the new generation can begin again. As Levinas puts this: "The discontinuous time of fecundity makes possible an absolute youth and recommencement" (*TI*, 282). The "relation with recommenced past" that the succeeding generation takes up is, as a consequence, "a free return to that past." This involves a "free interpretation and free choice" with regard to it "in an existence [considered] as entirely pardoned." For Levinas, then, fecundity makes "pardon" to be "the very work of time" (ibid.). By virtue of it, the present generation can take up the past of the previous one, since *it is the past* of this generation. Since, however, it also *is not this past*, the deeds it recalls are not its own. The discontinuity between itself and the previous generation thus means that it does not bear the guilt for them. In fact, its "interpretation" and "choice" with regard to them is "free." It is itself pardoned by time's discontinuity.

Levinas's solution for the "miracle" of forgiveness thus involves understanding natality as bringing about the discontinuity of time. In Arendt's terms, this miracle is that of breaking out of the natural temporal series of causes and effects. The conception of such a series, Levinas suggests, is ultimately Parmenidean. It "expresses the unintelligible dispersion of the unity of being, wholly contained in the first cause, in an apparent and phantasmal series of causes and effects," none of which adds anything new to this unity. By virtue of fecundity, time, however, no longer expresses this series. Rather, "time adds something new to being, something absolutely new . . . The profound work of time delivers [us] from this past in a subject that breaks with his father" (*TI*, 283). *Being* his father, the subject relates to the past of his father's generation. *Not being* his father, he can break with this past—that is, interpret it differently or, in fact, choose not to continue it.

With this, we have the solution to "the paradox of pardon." The paradox arises because to pardon is not to forget. As Levinas writes, "forgetting . . . does not concern the reality of the act" (*TI*, 283). It involves only its memory. Erasing this, it "nullifies the relations with the past." At this point, however, there is nothing to forgive. All we have is the innocence of oblivion. Yet, "the pardoned being is not the innocent being." It is precisely as guilty that he must be pardoned. The paradox, then, is that this guilt must be preserved and yet be removed. Levinas solves it by shifting its reference. He writes: "The paradox of the pardon of fault refers to pardon as constitutive of time itself." This is because "the paradox of pardon lies in its retroaction . . . it represents an inversion of the natural order of things, the reversibility of time" (ibid.). The natural order goes from the past to the present to the future, the events of each later time being seen as consequences of the earlier. In pardoning someone, however, I act in the present on the reality of the past. In the present, I treat the past fault as if it had not happened. In Levinas's words: "Pardon refers to the instant elapsed; it permits the [pardoned] subject who had committed himself in a past instant to be as though that instant had not passed on, [it permits him] to be as though he had not committed himself" (ibid.). In other words, pardoning, I nullify not the memory but the *reality* of the past instant. This reality is its *effect* on the present. Pardoning, I choose to nullify this effect. Inter-generationally, what allows this is the discontinuity of time. As we said, the child can choose not to take up the conflicts of the succeeding generation. He can reinterpret the causes of such conflicts. The very possibility of his doing so does not involve his forgetting them. As constituted by pardon, time involves both "a rupture of continuity and a continuation across this rupture." It involves both the rupture of annulling the guilt and the continuity of preserving it in memory. Both are possible in the temporality constituted by fecundity. Fecundity allows us to see time as "a drama, a multiplicity of acts where the following act resolves the prior one" (*TI*, 284). The resolution, in other words, consists in one generation remembering the deeds of the earlier one and deciding on their reality—that is, deciding whether it will continue to enact them. This is the pardon it confers on the previous generation.

Levinas reminds us how different this account is from Heidegger's. He writes: "It is not the finitude of being that constitutes the essence of time, as Heidegger thinks, but its infinity" (*TI*, 284). The finitude of being referred to is that of our being-in-the-world. It is finite, for Heidegger, because we face death. Facing it, we grasp our life as a finite whole. Such finitude characterizes temporality itself insofar as Heidegger takes "temporality as the meaning of the being that we call Dasein" (*SZ*, 17). Thus, the future is the meaning of our being ahead of ourselves in our projects, the past is the meaning of our "having been," which includes our having acquired the resources for these projects, while the present is the meaning of our ongoing, present actualization of the possibilities such projects project forward as our goals. The finitude of our being-in-the-world is the finitude of these temporal dimensions. Correspondingly, it is the finitude of my disclosure and, hence, of being as disclosed by me. Such finitude means that I am limited to the possibilities available to my generation. It also means that in choosing to actualize one set of possibilities, I also implicitly choose not to actualize another set. As Heidegger expresses this, "in having a potentiality to be [*seinkönnen*], Dasein always stands in one possibility or another: it constantly is *not* other possibilities; it has forgone these in its existentiell projection" (*SZ*, 285). In other words, it projects one of its finite possibilities by choosing *not* to project the other possibilities that its finite situation affords.

While Heidegger positions death as denying the infinitude of being, Levinas takes such infinitude as demanding death. He writes: "The death sentence does not approach as an end of being . . . The constitution of the interval that liberates being from the limitation of fate calls for death" (*TI*, 284). The reason why death does not signify "an end of being" is because of natality. With each new birth, there is a beginning of being-in-the-world and, hence, of being as disclosed by Dasein. Death signifies, for Levinas, the discontinuity of time, a discontinuity that is matched by the recommencement of time through the birth of the child. What we have then is both an end and a beginning of the disclosure of being. In Levinas's words: "Resurrection constitutes the principal event of time. There is therefore no continuity in being." What bridges this discontinuity is the "fecundity . . . which constitutes time" (ibid.). Fecundity, in other words, bridges death by resurrecting the I of the parent in the child. Doing so, it resurrects disclosure. This is also the resurrection of being as disclosed. Its indefinite continuance is being's infinitude.

Heidegger, it should be noted, cannot avail himself of this argument. He takes death, not as paired with birth, but rather as fundamentally isolating, that is, as excluding every relation. On the one hand, this "non-relational character of death individualizes Dasein down to itself" (*SZ*, 263). It makes one confront the fact that no one can die your death for you since you are individually, uniquely responsible for your being and its continuance through your projects. Thus, death individualizes Dasein since it makes it realize that it "can be *authentically itself* only if it, itself, makes this possible." On the other hand, the uniqueness of our responsibility for our being is profoundly isolating. Thus, facing death, we realize that we are neither what we own, nor what we have accomplished, nor the relations to Others that we have established. If we were, then they would preserve us from death. The contrary, however, is the case. According to Heidegger, "all being alongside the things we are concerned with and all being-with-Others will fail us when our very ability to be is at stake" as it is in death. Death, in other words, "breaks one's being fixed in the existence one has accomplished" (*SZ*, 264).

For Levinas, by contrast, death does not announce the failure of our being-with-Others. It is inherent in the latter's notion. Our being with others includes their successive generations. Thus, the I of the parent includes that of the child; through the child, it also includes the successive I's of the following generations. Implicit in this succession is the eventual death of the members composing it. Death occurs successively and is successively bridged by the engenderment of the child. As Levinas puts this, as the work of fecundity, "being" (rather than being isolated), "is produced as multiple. It is society" (*TI*, 269). Similarly, rather than pointing to the finitude of being, death indicates its infinitude. Such finitude, for Heidegger, comes from the fact that in its finite lifetime, Dasein can realize some possibilities only by sacrificing others. It is, thus, always limited to a finite disclosure of being. Against this, Levinas asserts: "The fact and the justification of time consist in the recommencement it makes possible in the resurrection, across fecundity, of all the compossibles sacrificed in the present" (*TI*, 284). The resurrection of these compatible possibilities comes with the resurrection of the I in the child. I may, for example, have sacrificed my possibilities to become an artist by choosing to study medicine. But my child is not limited by my choice. He can choose what I had to forego, thus disclosing an aspect of being that I could not exhibit.

Levinas concludes by noting that the infinitude of ever recommencing time brings with it the possibility of making good the failures of previous generations to judge things correctly, to get at the truth of them, to ensure goodness. In Levinas's words: "Behind the failure of the goodness of today, time's infinite existing ensures the situation of judgment, [which is the] condition of truth. By fecundity I dispose of an infinite time, necessary for truth to be told, necessary for the particularism of the apology to be converted into efficacious goodness" (*TI*, 284, my translation). Of course, this is only a possibility. The same infinitude is also open to "the putting back into question of the truth it promises." The freedom of the child with regard to the past also comprehends the possibility of the child's misinterpreting it, of his refusing to make effective the goodness it contained. To guard against this, we require not just "an infinite time" with its infinite compensation for the finitude of each generation's disclosure. Truth also requires "a time it will be able to seal, a completed time" (ibid.). This completion of infinite time, Levinas asserts, "is not death, but messianic time where the perpetual [recommencement of human time] is converted into eternal" (*TI*, 285). Such eternal, messianic time is "pure triumph; it is secured against the revenge of evil whose return the infinite [discontinuous] time does not prohibit." What is the nature of this messianic time? How can we speak of "completed time" without falling into totalization? What is the alterity that would prevent this? Are we, in fact, still speaking of a "structure of time" or have we shifted our focus to "an extreme vigilance of the messianic consciousness"? The problem here is that of justice beyond history and, ultimately, that of the pardon of history. It is one that Levinas says "exceeds the bounds of this book" (ibid.).

Conclusions

Totality and Infinity, IV, Conclusions, §§1–12

Levinas's Analytic of Dasein

Levinas now presents the conclusions of his existential analytic. They are, first of all, conclusions about the nature and meaning of being. Their significance can best be seen by recalling the original, Heideggerian context for such an analytic. Heidegger writes: "With regard to the subject of our inquiry"—the being [*Sein*] of entities—"the question of being [*Seinsfrage*] requires that we acquire and secure in advance the right way of access to entities [*Seienden*]" (*SZ*, 6). This access is through Dasein, defined by Heidegger as "the entity that we ourselves are and that includes among its ontological possibilities that of inquiring" about being (*SZ*, 7). Dasein is not an origin of being; he is the entity that discloses the various senses of entities through his projects. Heidegger believes that if we can comprehend the structures of this disclosure, we can understand the meaning of being. This point can be put in terms of constitution, taken as the process by which we disclose the sense of things and, hence, the sense of the world for ourselves. Heidegger writes in a letter to Husserl, "What is the nature of the being of the entity in which the 'world' constitutes itself? This is the central problem of *Being and Time*, i.e., a fundamental ontology of *Dasein*. At issue is showing that human *Dasein*'s kind of being is totally distinct from all other entities and that it is precisely this [kind] that contains in itself the possibility of transcendental constitution."[1] For Heidegger, the constitution of the sense of entities occurs through our practical dealings with them. These dealings are guided by an underlying understanding of their being—one set by the particular epoch in which we find ourselves. The being of entities is thus to be understood in terms of this underlying understanding and the historical process that guides it through its changing standards for what counts as "real." Such standards inform our projects and, hence, our methods of disclosure.

For Husserl, by contrast, the disclosure of entities occurs perceptually rather than pragmatically. Their sense is set by the interpretation we place on the sensuous perceptual data we receive from them. Perceptual interpretation, he asserts, is what first yields their perceptual presence. In his words:

> It belongs to perception that something appears within it, but *interpretation* makes up what we term appearance—be it correct or not, anticipatory or overdrawn. The *house* appears to me through no other way but that I interpret in a certain fashion actually experienced contents of sensation. I hear a *barrel organ*—the sensed tones I take as *barrel organ tones*. Even so, I perceive via interpretation what mentally appears in me, the *penetrating joy, the heartfelt sorrow*, etc. They are termed "appearances" or, better, appearing contents precisely for the reason that they are contents of perceptive interpretation."[2]

The role that perceptual interpretation plays in the appearing of objects can be seen when we regard optical illusions. Such illusions are often constructed so as to support two different opposing figures—for ecample, that of a young girl and that of an old woman. As we gaze at the illusion, first one figure and then its alternate appears. The two, however, never appear simultaneously. For Husserl, the difference between the figures is not explained by the sense data we receive, which remains unchanged. It is a function of our shifting perceptual interpretation. We always try to make sense out of what we perceive by perceiving it *as something*. In Husserl's terminology, our action is that of sense-giving (*Sinngebung*). Husserl's answer to the question of "the nature of the being of the entity in which the 'world' constitutes itself" is, thus, the kind of being that is exemplified by perceptual consciousness. The being of entities is understood by him in terms of such consciousness. Dasein, for him, is, first of all, a perceiver. By contrast, disclosive Dasein for Heidegger is a practically engaged individual.

Levinas, who introduced both Husserl and Heidegger to the French public, is essentially engaged in asking the same question. As a phenomenologist, he is interested in the disclosure of entities and thus in the entity—Dasein—that engages in this disclosure. Like Heidegger, he investigates the nature of Dasein in order to understand how entities are disclosed. Similarly, it is in terms of such disclosure that he delineates the meaning of being (*être*). For Levinas, however, the nature of *Dasein* is given by what he calls the "social relation," the relation of the I to the Other. His claim is that this relation forces us to abandon the traditional logical categories of being. The social relation, he writes, consists of "the idea of infinity, [that is, the idea of] the presence in a container of a content exceeding its capacity" (*TI*, 289). If we take this as "the logical plot of being," that is, if we take the social relation ontologically, we must redo the traditional "plot" or storyline of being.

According to the traditional account, individuality arises through the "specification of a concept" (*TI*, 289). At the point where we add the "ultimate specific difference" (that of the here and the now), we get the "this." The "this here," the τόδε τί (*todei ti*), is correlate of the act of pointing to an individual. Hegel, as Levinas observes, undermines this view "since the act of pointing to a here and a now implies references to the situation, in which the finger's movement is identified from the outside" (ibid.). Thus, as Hegel notes, the "this here" involves both the "here" and the "now." The "here" changes as we point to different things and the now changes with the time of day. If, for example, we ask, "what is it now?" and answer, "it is night," this truth soon turns "stale." In a few hours it will be morning.[3] Such reflections show, as Levinas writes, that the "Hegelian dialectic is all powerful to reduce this individuality of the τόδε τί (*todei ti*) to the concept" (ibid.). They show that, rather than designating a concrete individual, the "this here," which can designate an indefinite multiplicity of objects pointed to, is, in fact, an abstract concept. According to Levinas, this failure to conceptually define an individual through an ultimate specific difference indicates that "the identity of the individual does not consist . . . in letting itself be identified from the outside by the finger that points to it; it consists . . . in identifying oneself from within" (ibid.). A thing internally identifies itself through its characteristics, that is, through the features that form the focus of Dasein's access to it. As for Dasein, it identifies itself through its self-presence in sensuous enjoyment and, then, in transcending this, through its responding to the Other.

For Levinas, then, Dasein's identity as an individual comes from its first-person self-presence, one that is expanded to include its second-person relation to the Other.

Given this, we have to break with the traditional logical categories of being. If we stay with them, then "relations such as the idea of infinity" appear absurd. At best, such categories prompt us to interpret these relations "in theological or psychological terms as a miracle or as an illusion" (*TI*, 289). But this is only because the traditional categories are those of the third person. Employing these, we specify relations from the outside. *Dasein* thus appears as a *he* or a *she*, never as an *I* and a *you*, as it does from within the social relation. In fact, this insistence on the third person misunderstands *Dasein* and, hence, our access to entities. For Levinas, the fact that the Dasein's type of being is that of the "social relation" means that this access must be understood in terms of the *I* and the *you*, that is, in terms of the face-to-face. Social relations are not posterior to the third-person relation. They "do not simply present us with a superior empirical matter to be treated in terms of the logic of genus and species." In fact, they "are the original deployment of the Relation that is no longer open to the gaze that would encompass its terms"—the Relation being the face-to-face (*TI*, 290). Levinas terms the all-encompassing gaze that claims to grasp the face-to-face the "panoramic." If this gaze characterizes Dasein's access to entities, then "being is produced as a panorama, a coexistence" and "the face-to-face would be a modality" of this. For Levinas, however, the opposite is the case. He writes: "This whole work opposes this conception. The face-to-face is not a modality of coexistence, nor even of the knowledge (itself panoramic) one term can have of another, but is the primordial production of being on which all the possible collocations of the terms are founded" (*TI*, 305). In other words, for Levinas, Dasein's nature is such that the I-you relation has priority over the third-person relation. In fact, "The revelation of the third party, ineluctable in the face, is produced only through the face" (ibid.). The I-you relation, understood as the face-to-face, founds the third-person relation. The latter relation claims to be objective. But such objectivity, as we saw, is founded on the social relation. Objectivity's quality of being-there-for-everyone presupposes language and, hence, the I in relation to its Others.

Given this, we have to transform the traditional view that "being is exteriority"—that is, that being is to be understood in terms of an exterior, all-encompassing, panoramic view. If being were really exteriority in this visual, spatial-temporal sense, then interiority would be nonexistent. Regardless of how we cut or divide an entity, it always shows an exterior view; we see only its parted surfaces. This point recalls a striking scene from a Latin American movie, where an inmate in an asylum is assisting in an autopsy. He takes the brain of the cadaver, begins to crumble it between his fingers, and remarks that within it lie all the person's memories, hopes, and desires—in short, the person himself.[4] In fact, however, he never gets "within" the person. As the movie suggests, to locate the self in this crumbling piece of matter is to join in the madness of the asylum. For Levinas, this insistence on the exterior view undermines itself since exteriority is paired to interiority, being defined as its opposite. Thus, were being exteriority in a spatial-temporal sense, "exteriority would then no longer mean anything since it would encompass the very interiority that justified this appellation [of exteriority]" (*TI*, 290). To avoid this, we have to redefine the opposition of exteriority to interiority. We must define exteriority as "alterity." What is exterior is the Other. What is interior is the I in its sensuous self-presence. The interiority of the I is transcended in the face-to-face relation—the relation that is inaccessible to the vision that terminates on the surface of things. With this, we have the redefinition of "being is exteriority." Its "truth," that is, the disclosure that it makes possible, is not limited to vision—that is, to the panoramic gaze. Rather "exteriority is true . . . in a face-to-face that is no longer entirely vision, but goes further than vision" (ibid.).

Truth

For Levinas, then, the meaning of being is "exteriority" in this redefined sense. Dasein exemplifies this in having the "social relation" as its kind of being. This redefinition of being brings about a corresponding re- definition of truth. As a point of comparison, we can take Heidegger's conception of truth. According to Heidegger, "Being true (truth) means being-uncovering" (*SZ*, 219).[5] The basic sense of truth is uncovering or disclosing; and the behavior (*Verhalten*) of Dasein that accomplishes this is called "true." Thus, what is "true" in the sense of being true (*Wahrsein*), is, in the first instance, Dasein, since Dasein is what uncovers. Heidegger thus writes, "being-true as being-uncovering is a way of being for Dasein. What makes this uncovering possible must be called 'true' in an even more primordial sense" (*SZ*, 220). The point follows because without Da- sein there is no disclosure and, hence, no truth. Levinas agrees with this, but sees such disclosure not in terms of projects that reveal the "what is it for" of objects, but rather in the face-to-face. For him, the being-true of Dasein involves the face. In his words, "The true essence of man is pre- sented in his face" (*TI*, 290). Corresponding to this, "the truth of being is not the image of being, the idea of its nature; it is the being situated in a subjective field which deforms vision, but precisely thus allows exteriority to state itself." The "subjective field" is that of the face-to-face. It is the field in which I cannot arbitrarily disclose the senses of the world, but must respond to the other who questions my behavior, my projects. Ac- cording to Levinas, "This curvature of the intersubjective space . . . does not falsify being, but makes its truth first possible" (*TI*, 291).

Chapter 4 describes how the face-to-face makes objective truth pos- sible. Instead of repeating its arguments, let us turn to the being-true of Dasein, which, according to Levinas, "is presented in his face." He writes in this regard, "Man as Other comes to us from the outside, [from] a separated—or holy—face. His exteriority, that is, his appeal to me, is his truth" (*TI*, 291). To understand this reference to the "holy," we have to recall the etymological sense of the word "sacred," which is that of being "inviolable" in the sense of "not to be touched." "Sacred" comes from the Latin *sacer*, which signifies "dedicated or consecrated to a divinity, holy, sacred." Its Greek root is *sáos*—σῶος," which means "safe." Thus, the sacred is safe in the sense of kept apart or reserved for the divinity.[6] As consecrated to the god, the sacred cannot be used by us. You cannot, for example, cut down and use the timber of a sacred grove. The trees forming the grove are inviolate. You should not, in fact, even enter the grove. Thus, as Sophocles has the stranger say to Oedipus who has strayed into a sacred place, "It is forbidden to walk on that ground . . . It is not to be touched."[7] A similar sense of the sacred is present in Moses's encounter with God.[8] In both cases, we have to do with the exceeding quality of the appearing of the divine. The presence of the divinity sets limits to my behavior and, hence, to the interpretative intentions that animate what I do and say. Facing the divine, my intentions are controlled by a context that I do not set. I am not master of the sacred. The sacred is first. I, in my intentions, am second. It calls to me. I have to respond.[9]

Levinas believes that this primitive sense of the sacred is present in the face. Speaking of "the metaphor of 'the curvature' of intersubjective space" that he uses to describe the face-to-face relation, he remarks: "This 'curvature of space' is, perhaps, the very presence of God" (*TI*, 291). In the presence of the face, I am second. Being put into question, I have to answer. That Dasein as the Other appeals to me, that he calls on me to respond is his "truth, his "unhiddenness" in Heidegger's terminology. For Heidegger, as cited earlier, "being-true as being-uncovering is a way of being for Dasein." He discloses or uncovers things through his projects. His own unhiddenness or truth is his role in this. For Levinas, by contrast, such unhiddenness or truth involves both inviolability and an appeal. The Other, he writes, "arrests and paralyzes my violence by his call" (*TI*, 291). He discloses himself as inviolable. But he also speaks to me and calls on me to answer. He is exterior and yet, in discourse, is in relation to me. The restraints on my arbitrary freedom that discourse involves are essential for our disclosure of the world. Responding to Others, I am prevented from treating the world simply as my use-value. Its sense involves more than the "what it is for" that I impose through my projects. Responding, I have to face the world as it objectively is both for me and my Others. My being-uncovering thus assumes a different form than that assumed by Heidegger. Inherent in it is the social relation.

Society, Separation, and Creation

According to Levinas, this social relation determines our access both to Others and to God. If the kind of being that characterizes our Dasein is that of the social relation, then for us "the face-to-face is a final and irreducible relation." By virtue of its exteriority, this relation "makes possible the pluralism of society" (*TI*, 291). This is because society presupposes alterity. It assumes that we cannot reduce the many to the one. The fundamental principle here is that of "exteriority, taken as the essence of being" (*TI*, 292). It demands that we conceive the finite's relation to the infinite (and hence to God) such that the finite is not absorbed in the infinite. An example of such an absorption would be the collapse of the "City of Man" into the "City of God," the latter being taken as a monarchy where all wills conform to God (the divine ruler) and thereby express a general will.[10] From a Levinasian perspective, this view assumes a false conception since "the production of infinity calls for separation." Functioning as the desire for the transcendent, it starts from "the absolute arbitrariness of the I" and its egotism (ibid.). Not that it remains with this. My goodness involves my transcending my egotism when I respond to the Other. Going beyond the egotism of my needs, I act for the sake of the Other. Such transcendence, however, does not signify a loss of my identity. For Levinas, the "austere happiness of goodness would invert its meaning and would be perverted if it confounded us with God" (ibid.). We do not act as a part of God in doing good for the other. His action does not absorb ours. We do, however respond to God in the face of the Other. But the God that is present in the face, in the appeal of the Other, does not compel us, does not absorb us. In Levinas's words, "the relation between the finite being and the infinite does not consist in the finite being absorbed in what faces him, but in remaining in his own being" (ibid.).

The key assumption here is "the idea of a separation resistant to synthesis" (*TI*, 293). It is that of plurality as resistant to conceptual unity. In Levinas's words: "The I's form no totality; there exists no privileged play where these I's could be grasped in their principle. There is an anarchy essential to multiplicity" (*TI*, 294). In Levinas's view, this idea of separation is implicit in the biblical notion of creation. In the traditional metaphysics, God cannot create since he cannot limit itself. As infinite, there can never be anything outside of him. Thus, to affirm an infinite God is to affirm an a priori community of everything from eternity. Everything is always already there in an infinite God, who, by definition, absorbs all finitude. This is why Levinas writes, "To affirm the origin from nothing by creation is to contest the prior community of all things within eternity. The absolute gap of separation that transcendence implies could not be better expressed than by the term creation" (*TI*, 293). Such creation is "neither a negation nor a limitation nor an emanation of the One" (*TI*, 292). All of these presuppose a prior unity between beings, one that must be negated or limited. But creation, when thought in terms of exteriority, is an acting beyond the ontological neediness that makes each entity dependent in its being on all the others. It transcends the unity that such neediness presupposes. Here, as Levinas writes, "Exteriority is not a negation, but a marvel" (ibid.).

The Surplus of Goodness over Being

Levinas expresses this marvel by speaking of the surplus of goodness over being. In his words: "The concept of a Good beyond Being and beyond the beatitude of the One announces a rigorous concept of creation" (*TI*, 292; see Plato's *Republic* 509b). This is because creation is acting beyond need. God does not need the created. His relation to the created has the same form as the actions of metaphysical desire—that is, those actions that respond, not to our needs, but rather to those of the Other: the Other's not having clothing, food, shelter, and so on. The form of such neediness is that of non-being—the Other's *not* being clothed, fed, sheltered, and so on. The *not* expresses the lack of some aspect of being necessary for the Other to be. Creation in the face of nothing, creation ex nihilo, is the ultimate expression of such action. It is the supreme exemplar of metaphysical desire.

Implicit here is a special notion of transcendence. The transcendence that characterizes the relation of creation is not one between two beings, the second transcending the first. The second—the being that is to be created—lacks being. Creation, thus, presents us with a transcendence that goes beyond being. This "beyond being" is beyond the ontological neediness that links one being to another. What is beyond being is the goodness inherent in acting beyond such neediness for the sake of the Other. Levinas puts this in terms of the fact that, objectively regarded, being consists of the totality of entities. The creative transcendence that exceeds this involves a relation to what is not a member of this totality. Here, "transcendence precisely refuses totality, does not lend itself to the view that would encompass it from the outside" (*TI*, 293). It is not something that can be externally described since its action goes beyond the totality that is the object of an exterior, third-person description. As such, its conception resists traditional categories of being. What is in play here is the surplus of goodness over being. In his words: "If the notions of totality and being are notions that cover one another, the notion of the transcendent places us beyond categories of being. We thus encounter, in our own way, the Platonic idea of the Good beyond Being" (ibid.). In Levinas's interpretation, this Good is the goodness of acting for the

Other, an action whose object is not what the Other has—such possession being part of his "substance" or being. The object is rather what he lacks. When we engage in such actions, we are, in fact, acting in continuity with God's creative action. Our action is our own, but it has the same form as the original act of creation.

Language

In "Language and Exteriority," Levinas continues to restate his conclusions in terms of the principle that "being is exteriority." Again, the implicit contrast is with Heidegger's existential analytic. This analytic takes language as a function of disclosure. For Heidegger, as I gain more and more skill in making my way in the world, the world itself becomes more practically meaningful. I "understand" it in the sense of knowing the purpose of its elements. "Interpretation," defined as the "considering . . . of something as something," articulates this understanding. It makes explicit the meanings of the objects I encounter by expressing "what one does" with them. Such interpretations form the core of a language. They constitute the significance of its expressions. As Heidegger writes in the *History of the Concept of Time*, "There is *verbal expression—language*—only insofar as there is considering, and such consideration of something as something is possible only insofar as there is interpreting; interpretation in turn exists only insofar as there is understanding, and understanding exists only insofar as *Dasein* has the structure-of-being of discoveredness, which means that *Dasein* itself is defined as being-in-the-world."[11] In other words, because Dasein's being-in-the-world is disclosive, Dasein understands the world by interpreting it. Language expresses these interpretations.

What is at work here, Levinas suggests, is "an ontology that is . . . equivalent to panoramic existence and its disclosure" (*TI*, 294). Panoramic existence refers to the possibility of things being available for disclosure—concretely, their being available for our projects. To call such existence "panoramic" is to assert the *totality* of such availability. Everything can be disclosed in terms of its "what is it for." It can be understood through knowing "what one does" with it to achieve one's goals. According to Levinas, "The Heideggerian thesis that every human attitude consists in 'bringing to light' [or disclosure] . . . rests on this primacy of the panoramic" (ibid.). Such primacy signifies not just the total availability of things for disclosure, but also that disclosure as such is definitive of mankind. Dasein is, in all his activities, inherently disclosive. Understood ontologically, this primacy also signifies that "panoramic existence and its disclosure are equivalent to the very production of being, since truth or disclosure is at the same time the work or the essential virtue of being, the *Sein* of the *Seiendes.*" There is here an implicit reference to Heidegger's position that being itself (*Sein*) determines disclosure by disclosing itself as a given standard for what-is. The standard expresses a particular epoch's understanding of the meaning of being, a meaning that sets the standards for the disclosive behavior that characterizes the epoch. Thus, in our modern, technological age, we take power to be the essence of reality. The technical procedures that increase our power, be this physical, political, or economic power, are understood as actually disclosive of reality. In this view, "modern technology," rather than being simply a source of modern conveniences, "itself would be but a mode of extracting things or producing them in the sense of 'fully bringing [them] to light'" (ibid.). Thus, if we accept Heidegger's account, "every human behavior that [the *Sein* of the *Seiendes*] would in the last analysis govern" is reduced to "disclosure" (ibid.). Correspondingly, every entity is capable of being disclosed according to the particular standards that govern our behavior.

It is interesting to observe that Husserl, in his own way, embraces the idea of panoramic existence. For him, it implies "that a correlation to perceivability (*Wahrgenommen-werden-können*), intuitability, meanability and knowability is inseparable from the sense of being in general."[12] Thus, while there are things that are not perceived, "there is nothing that *cannot* be perceived. This however, means that the actual performance of the actual acts . . . is in an ideal sense *possible.*"[13] Ideally, then, everything existent is open to perceptual disclosure. Correspondingly, our Dasein, understood as perceptual consciousness, is essentially disclosive. In Husserl's view, man is a perceiver and to see is to make sense out of what we perceive. Husserl's theory of language is based on this premise. Thus, he takes our considering something as something as based on our perceptual interpretations. The sense we make out of the visual data we receive is a result of our *Sinngebung*—literally, our "sense-giving." To make sense out of such data is not just to establish the visual presence of an object. It is also to imbue this presence with a sense—namely, that of the perceptual interpretation that informs our seeing. For Husserl, the senses of these interpretations form the core of our language. Another person can confirm what we report having seen by enacting the perceptual interpretations that are implied in this report. If the data support them, he will see what we see and confirm our report.[14]

Levinas's view of language differs from the above since it does not privilege vision; it does not assume that everything, in principle, is correlated to perceivability. Thus, Levinas's ontology "is not equivalent to panoramic existence" (*TI*, 294). In fact, its fundamental principle is that of "the exteriority of being" (*TI*, 295). What this signifies is given by the opening sentence of "Exteriority and Language": "We have begun with the resistance of beings to totalization, [we have begun] with an untotaled multiplicity they constitute, the impossibility of their conciliation in the same" (*TI*, 294). This, however, does not "mean that multiplicity is without relation." This relation "binds this multiplicity," even as it unbinds it. It "does not fill the abyss of separation; it confirms it" (*TI*, 295). This is because the relation in question is that of language. As enacted in the face-to-face, it shares in the face's exteriority. As Levinas defines this, the Other who speaks to me "does not give himself so that I could assume this manifestation, measure it to my own interiority, and receive it as coming from myself." Such assumption occurs when I perceive an object. Doing so, I "measure it" according to my interior perceptual interpretation. When this is successful, I receive it as coming from myself, that is, from the sense inherent in my perceptual interpretation. In Levinas's words, "Vision operates in this manner, totally impossible in discourse. For vision is essentially an adequation of exteriority with interiority: in it exteriority is reabsorbed in the contemplative soul and, as an adequate idea, revealed to be . . . the result of a *Sinngebung*" (ibid.). In Husserl's terms, the adequation, here, is that of the exterior sensuous data to the interior perceptual interpretation, an adequation that signifies the success of our sense-giving, that is, of our making sense of what we perceive. The Other who speaks to me, however, exceeds such interpretations. As a consequence, he exceeds perceptual disclosure. As Levinas expresses this conclusion: "The exteriority of discourse cannot be converted into interiority. The interlocutor can have no place in an inwardness; he is forever outside" (ibid.). This means that he is not part of panoramic existence, but continually exceeds this.[15]

The concrete expression of this excess is that of the surplus of the saying over the said that characterizes actual discourse. This surplus distinguishes discourse from disclosure. In Levinas's words, "In contradistinction to . . . disclosure, which manifests something as something . . . in expression . . . the manifested [the speaker] attends to its own manifestation [his words] and hence remains exterior to every image one would retain of" his manifestation. In actual discourse, then, "speech refuses vision, because the speaker does not deliver images of himself only, but is personally present in his speech, absolutely exterior to every image he would leave." Thus, rather than being enclosed by such images, he comments on what he says, he interprets it, adds to it, changes it, and so on. In other words, in actual discourse, language evinces infinity. As a saying, it is constantly surpassing the said taken as the sense that has been given through the interpretations of the auditors. In Levinas's words, "Whoever speaks attends his manifestation, is non-adequate to the meaning that the hearer would like to retain of it." As a result, his "presence in speech" is not "reducible to the *Sinngebung* of him who listens." In fact, "language is the incessant surpassing of the *Sinngebung* by the signification" of the ongoing saying (*TI*, 296).

As is obvious, while Heidegger's and Husserl's account of language privilege vision, Levinas's privileges hearing. In this, it forms a continuity with the five books of Moses, with their emphasis on hearing rather than sight. At the basis of this biblical preference are the prohibitions against idolatry. The God of the Israelites, as prior to the world, cannot be defined in its terms. Unlike the gods of the surrounding tribes, their God is not part of the world and, hence, cannot be visually represented in terms of the world's contents. The priority of language over the image appears each time the people are summoned to hear the "testimony" of the law that Moses has received. In the elaborate tabernacle that Moses constructs for God, such testimony replaces the image of the divinity (Exod. 40:20). Language, rather than some image, is thus taken as the way to present the exteriority of God, that is, his inability to be represented in worldly terms.

The Levinasian parallel to this is put in terms of the surpassing of the said by the saying. He describes this as the "overflowing of exteriority, non-adequate to the vision which still measures it" (*TI*, 296–97). Such overflowing, he adds, "precisely constitutes the dimension of height or the divinity of exteriority" (*TI*, 297). This reference to divinity of exteriority recalls the description of the face as "separated—or holy" (*TI*, 291). Once again, there is the sense of the holy as inviolable, that is, as not to be touched or reduced to a use value. In Levinas's words, "Divinity keeps its distances. Discourse is discourse with God and not with equals" (*TI*, 297). This does not mean that the Other I speak with is absorbed into God. It signifies, rather, "the moral dissymmetry of the I and the other" in discourse (ibid.). This dissymmetry follows from the fact that I cannot assume that the Other interprets the world as I do. Because her past is distinct from mine, the interpretations she draws from her experiences necessarily differ from my own. Similarly, the future she anticipates as she projects forward her previous experiences are beyond my own conceptions of what will be. Thus, rather than imposing my categories on her, I have to wait for her to speak. This waiting expresses the fact that my interpretative intentions are situated in a context that I do not control. The Other whom I wait upon is first. I, in my intentions, am second. I have to wait for her to speak in order to respond. This dissymmetry that marks every genuine conversation recalls the sacred and its priority. Discourse with the Other is like discourse with God insofar as both evince an irreducible exteriority.

Levinas sums up the ontology that underpins his view of language by writing, "we have thus the conviction of having broken with the philosophy of the Neuter: with the Heideggerian Being of the existent . . . [and] with Hegel's impersonal reason" (*TI*, 298). Both Hegel and Heidegger "exult the obedience that no face commands." For Hegel, the "exultation of the Neuter" presents itself "as the anteriority of the We with respect to the I." This occurs in Hegel's conception of Mind or Spirit (*Geist*), which Hegel defines as "this absolute substance, which in the perfect freedom and independence of its opposition, i.e., of the distinct, self-existing self-consciousnesses [composing it], is their unity, is the I that is we and the we that is I."[16] This identification of the "I" with the "we" occurs, politically, in my self-identification with the state. I assert, "I am a Canadian" or "a German" or "an American," thereby indicating my identity with my country's legal and social norms. Not only do I find nothing alien in them; they are, in fact, norms that I freely impose upon myself. The "impersonal reason" that lies behind such laws—for example, the Kantian arguments against theft or making false promises—is not something that is alien to me. It rather expresses the substance of my convictions.[17] The corresponding Heideggerian "exaltation of the Neuter" occurs in "the anteriority . . . of the situation with respect to the beings [who are] in situation" (*TI*, 298). This situation is the epoch into which I have been "thrown" by virtue of the circumstances of my birth. Its standards of being guide my disclosure. For Heidegger, the *Sein des Seienden* or "the being of the existent is a *Logos* that is the word of no one" (*TI*, 299). Like Hegel's "impersonal reason," it determines Dasein "unbeknown to it" (*TI*, 298).

Levinas opposes this "obedience that no face commands" by beginning with "the face as a source from which all meaning appears, the face in its absolute nudity, in its destitution as a head that does not find a place to lay itself" (*TI*, 299). Such a face has nothing to offer us. It cannot, in its destitution, fulfill our needs. To begin with it is, thus, not just "to affirm that being is enacted in the relation between men"—that is, in the discourse that guides disclosure. It is also to affirm "that Desire rather than need commands acts." This Desire, understood as "an aspiration that does not proceed from a lack . . . is the desire of a person." Thus, it is not my practical needs that guide my disclosure of the world as the early Heidegger asserts. It also is not the revelation of being, that is, of a standard of being, that does this as the later Heidegger claimed. What is active here is the desire for the Other (*TI*, 299). This involves both the generosity of my offering my view of the world to the other and the hospitality of accepting his and letting it call mine into question. Both characterize language as disclosive.

Freedom

We can conclude this commentary by noting how the conception of "being as exteriority" determines Levinas's concept of freedom. According to Levinas, "Freedom . . . maintains the relation with the exteriority that morally resists every appropriation and every totalization in being" (*TI*, 302). The contrast here is with the notion of freedom as autonomy. Given our essential interdependence, an insistence on autonomy inevitably leads to an appropriative relation with exteriority. As was earlier noted, we need Others to survive. Given this dependence, our autonomy demands, not simply that we join their forces to our own, but that we bring them under our control. It is only by ruling over them, that is, by assuming sovereignty, that we can be free, that is, genuinely independent. When we think of knowledge in these terms, its autonomy demands that it set its own standards, imposing them on the object.[18] For Levinas, this signifies that it becomes "the suppression of the other by the grasp, by the hold, or by the vision that grasps before the grasp" (*TI*, 302). The vision that grasps the object before the physical grasp is, for Heidegger, the vision that reduces the other to "its what is it for," that is, its use value. For Husserl, it is the vision that appropriates its sense to its own interpretative intentions. By contrast, the "metaphysics" that Levinas advances "has an entirely different meaning. If its movement leads to the transcendent as such, transcendence means not appropriation of what is, but its respect. Truth as a respect for being is the meaning of metaphysical truth" (ibid.). Such respect is respect for the "in-itself" of the other—the καθ'αὐτό (*kath'auto*)—of that which transcends us. It involves the attempt to transcend the categories, whether perceptual or pragmatic, that we impose on it. As such, it involves the attentiveness that is founded on restraint. This, as we saw, involves the restraint Others place upon our categories by calling them into question.

From Levinas's perspective, Heidegger's account of truth lacks such restraint. This is because he takes truth as unhiddenness (*aletheia*) and pairs it to Dasein's disclosive behavior. As we saw, this disclosure has no inherent limits. It would, if Dasein's behavior were itself inherently limited, that is, if it were set by Dasein's having a given essence or nature. Lacking this, however, Dasein is thrown back upon itself. Its actions depend upon its choices. Thus, Dasein chooses by projecting forward its possibilities, but such possibilities have no inherent limits. As we earlier cited Heidegger, "Not only is the projection . . . determined by the nothingness [*Nichtigkeit*] of the being of its basis [*Grundseins*], but also, as projection, [Dasein] is itself essentially null [*nichtig*] . . . the nothingness meant here belongs to Dasein's being-free for its existential possibilities" (*SZ*, 285). The nothingness referred to stems from the fact that Dasein is no thing. It cannot be captured by the categories used to describe things since it lacks any inherent essence. This very lack is inherent in its being free for its existential possibilities—that is, for the possibilities confronting it regarding its own being. Thus, when I confront myself as "care," that is, as the entity whose being is the result of my choices regarding these possibilities, I confront my freedom. Such freedom, however, is anguished given the openness of these choices. I cannot really base them on the disclosed world since what is disclosed is determined by how I act, which is, itself, determined by my free choices. As Heidegger expresses this, such "anxiety makes manifest in *Dasein* its Being towards its ownmost potentiality for being—that is, its *being-free* for . . . the freedom of choosing itself and taking hold of itself. Anxiety confronts *Dasein* with its being free for the authenticity of its being as the [open] possibility it always already is" (*SZ*, 188). In other words, I am anxious because I realize that it is all up to me. My choices decide who and what I am as the accomplisher of the actions I decide upon. They also determine the "world" that my behavior will disclose. Its "truth" or unhiddenness is my responsibility, a responsibility I face without any pregiven referents. For Heidegger, as we saw, this openness of freedom corresponds to the openness of reason. The question of reason—why this rather than that?—which asks for a ground or a reason for the way things are, can be applied to everything I encounter. This is because the way things appear—their disclosure—is ultimately up to Dasein's choice of projects. Confronting Dasein's freedom, I confront their contingency. I, thus, am open to investigating why they appear as they do. As we cited Heidegger in this regard, freedom is the "origin itself of 'ground.' Freedom is the ground of ground [*Grund des Grundes*]," that is, the origin of the question of grounding.[19] In fact, since nothing determines it, "freedom is the abyss [*Ab-grund*] of Dasein."[20]

As Levinas observes, "the founding of truth [or disclosure] on freedom would imply a freedom justified by itself" (*TI*, 303). There is, however, an inner contradiction between the groundlessness of freedom and its finitude. Such groundlessness implies freedom's infinitude. So regarded, it cannot be limited or determined. From this perspective, then, there would be "for freedom no greater scandal than to discover itself to be finite." Heidegger, however, insists on such finitude. The circumstances of our birth, the accidents of our upbringing—for example, the fact that we were born in this country, at this time, with these parents and siblings, were endowed with this specific gender, and were offered these opportunities and not others, and so on—all mark our "thrownness" or *Geworfenheit*. As Levinas observes, "The Heideggerian *Geworfenheit* marks a finite freedom" since all these circumstances necessarily limit the choices open to me. In Heidegger's system, however, this is not just a "scandal," but is "irrational." Circumstances, in their given content, can limit something else with a given content, the limitation being based on the incompatibility of such contents. But Dasein has no content since it has no essence. Heidegger, then, is in the position of asserting both the unlimited and limited nature of our freedom, making it both groundless and grounded by the circumstances it encounters. This, however, is both to deny and to affirm that Dasein has a given nature.

For Levinas, the arbitrariness of freedom points, not to its groundless quality, but to its inherent lack of self-subsistence. Were it self-subsistent, it would not require something outside of itself to give it a distinct quality. It would by itself have those features that allow it to be identified as itself. Its arbitrariness, the fact that it has no inherent limits, does not, then, point to its infinity, but rather to its insufficiency when we try to grasp it in terms of itself. Levinas thus writes: "The irrational in freedom is not due to its limits, but to the infinity of its arbitrariness. Freedom must justify itself; reduced to itself it is accomplished not in sovereignty but in arbitrariness" (*TI*, 303). Descartes attempted to combat such arbitrariness by having the will be determined by a "clear and distinct conception." In his words, "whenever I restrict my volition within the bounds of my knowledge, whenever my volition makes no judgment except upon matters clearly and distinctly reported to it by the understanding, it cannot happen that I err."[21] Here, as Levinas remarks, "the free adherence to truth, an activity of knowledge, the free will which, according to Descartes, in certitude, adheres to a clear idea, seeks a reason which does . . . coincide with the radiance of this clear and distinct idea itself" (*TI*, 303–4). The problem with this solution, according to Levinas, is that it does not call into question my standards of clarity and distinctness. In his words, "A clear idea which imposes itself by its clarity calls for a strictly personal work of a freedom, a solitary freedom that does not put itself in question, but can at most suffer a failure" as when I am mistaken about what is "clear and distinct" (*TI*, 304). What is required for solitary freedom to be called into question is the face of the Other. In Levinas's words: "To approach the Other is to put into question my freedom, my spontaneity as a living being, my emprise over the things, this freedom of a 'moving force,' this impetuosity of the current to which everything is permitted, even murder" (*TI*, 303). The face, in other words, shows the need of my freedom for a ground. It convicts it of arbitrariness, that is, of needing something beyond itself to give it its specific quality as human freedom. The same holds for the reason, whose question freedom founds. What confronts us with the contingency of the world we disclose is not the "abyss" of our freedom, but rather the Other with his different standards for disclosure, his different interpretations of the purposes and senses of things.[22]

For Levinas, then, "in morality alone is [freedom] called into question. Morality, thus, presides over the work of truth" (*TI*, 304). It does so since, as determining our choices, it determines the disclosure that allows things to appear. As such it presides over truth as unhiddenness. With this, we return to the fundamental claim of *Totality and Infinity*: "Morality is not a branch of philosophy, but first philosophy" in Aristotle's sense (ibid.). It is the science of being qua being since it determines the disclosure that allows beings to appear. When we ignore it, we do not just fall into moral error, we fundamentally misunderstand the way things are. We fail to grasp the very meaning of their being.

Notes

Introduction

1. This occurs in the *Mishnah*, Sanhedrin 4:5.

2. *The Babylonian Talmud*, ed. Rabbi I. Epstein (London: Soncino, 1935), Sedar Nezikin, 233.

3. Ibid., 234. Some versions do not have "of Israel," which may be a later addition.

4. Ibid.

5. Emmanuel Levinas, *Totality and Infinity: An Essay on Exteriority*, trans. Alphonso Lingis (Pittsburgh: Duquesne University Press, 1969). This commentary will use this translation, which will be referred to hereafter as TI. The pagination of this and later reprints of the text by the publisher is unchanged.

6. Leopold von Ranke's account of these factors has often been criticized for putting ethnic, political, and spiritual influences on the same plane. It is, nonetheless useful for understanding the totalitarian attitude. See Albert Mirgeler's excellent study, *Mutations of Western Christianity*, trans. Edward Quinn (Montreal: Palm, 1964), 6–11. It was originally published as *Rückblick auf das abendländische Christentum* (Mainz: Matthias Grünewald Verlag, 1961).

7. See Christopher Dawson, *Understanding Europe* (New York: Doubleday, 1960), 26–27.

8. Emmanuel Levinas, *Ethics and Infinity*, trans. Richard Cohen (Pittsburgh: Duquesne University Press, 1985), 37–38, hereafter cited as *EI*. Levinas valued *Being and Time* much more highly than Heidegger's later work. In his words, "the later work of Heidegger . . . does not produce in me a comparable impression . . . it is much less convincing" (41).

9. Ibid.

10. Emmanuel Levinas, *Nine Talmudic Readings*, trans. Annette Aronowicz (Bloomington: Indiana University Press, 1994), 25. Despite this, the admiration for Heidegger remains. As Levinas writes in a lecture delivered in March 1987 at the Collège International de Philosophie: "Dispite all the horror that eventually came to be associated with Heidegger's name—and which will never be dissipated—nothing has been able to destroy in my mind the conviction that the *Sein und Zeit* of 1927 cannot be annulled, no more than can the few other eternal books in the history of philosophy—however much they may disagree" (*Levinas, Entre Nous: Thinking of the Other*, trans. Michael Smith and Barbara Harshaw [New York: Columbia University Press, 1998], 208).

11. Martin Heidegger, *Sein und Zeit* (Tübingen: Max Niemeyer, 1968), 17. All translations of this text are my own.

12. Jean François Courtine agrees with J. Taminiaux that Levinas's work can be considered a "'reply' . . . to *Being and Time* and its fundamental ontology. He adds, however, "À condition de préciser aussi qu'il s'agit moins, dans cette Auseinander-setzung, de réplique point par point, que d'une réponse globale, d'une tentative de prise ou de reprise renversante" (Courtine, "L'ontologie fondamentale d'Emmanuel Levinas," in *Emmanuel Levinas et les territoires de la pensée*, ed. Danielle Cohen-Levinas and Bruno Clément [Paris: Presses Universitaires de France, 2007], 105–6). See J. Taminiaux, "La première réplique à l'ontologie fondamentale," *Cahiers de l'heure: Levinas* (Paris, 1991), 275–84. This global response involves Levinas's emphasis on Dasein's embodiment.

13. This focus on embodiment is what Courtine, as a Heideggerian, most objects to. Commenting on Levinas's remark, "Dasein is never hungry," he writes that the person who is hungry or cold is not Dasein: "L'homme qui a faim et froid, pas plus que l'homme replet et rassasié, pour avoir exploité ou non le travail d'autrui, ne sont le Dasein, même si le Dasein est en l'homme": "'Plus originel que l'homme est la finitude du Dasein en lui,' indiquait Heidegger dans le Kantbuch de 1929. Dire que le Dasein chez Heidegger n'a jamais faim (c'est peut-être un bon mot . . . !), mais cela ne constitue en rien une objection à l'analytique qui n'est pas une anthropologie, pas plus que l'élaboration lévinassienne du processus de subjectivation n'est une anthropologie" (Courtine, "L'ontologie fondamentale d'Emmanuel Levinas," 115). At issue is whether the analytic of Dasein includes its animality. For Courtine, it does not. Such animality is the "subhuman in man." See ibid., 113.

14. As Alexander Schnell remarks in this regard: "La phénoménologie lévinassienne est une apologie de la vie. Si Levinas a toujours été extrêmement attentif aux critiques que Heidegger a adressées à l'encontre de l'approche husserlienne d'une phénoménologie de la 'conscience,' censée être 'privée de monde,' il formule à son tour une critique virulente de la conception d'un Dasein incorporel, asexué, utilitariste—donc dépourvu de vie. Une pénétration de la subjectivité se doit d'abord de cerner ce que le Dasein (bien compris) a d'irréductiblement *vivant*" (Schnell, *Levinas et la question de la subjectivité* [Paris: Vrin, 2010], 51).

15. Aristotle, *Metaphysics*, bk. IV, 1, 1003a, 20–33.

Chapter 1

1. As Heidegger writes to Husserl, "What kind of being [*Seinsart*] is the being in which the 'world' constitutes itself? This is the central problem of *Being and Time*, i.e., a fundamental ontology of Dasein. At issue is showing that human Dasein's kind of being is totally distinct from all other beings and that it is precisely this [kind] that contains in itself the possibility of transcendental constitution" (Heidegger, *Phänomenologische Psychologie*, ed. W. Biemel [The Hague: Mar-

tinus Nijhoff, 1962], 601). The entire letter appears in the textual critical notes to *Phänomenologische Psychologie*, 600–602.

2. Here Heidegger implicitly adopts William James's pragmatic conception of disclosure. For James, the cardinal fact is: "My thinking is first and last and always for the sake of my doing, and I can only do one thing at a time" (James, *Psychology, Briefer Course* [Cleveland, Ohio: World, 1948], 355). What I actually do determines my thinking about what a particular object is. It determines what I take its essence to be (356). In James's words, "The essence of a thing is that one of its properties which is so important for my interests that in comparison with it I may neglect the rest" (357). The essence, according to James, is the thing's instrumental character; it is its function as a means for the accomplishment of our projects. The same holds for all the particular properties of the object. They only appear as correlates of the projects that reveal them. Thus, depending on my project, the same paper can be disclosed as "a combustible, a writing surface, a thin thing, a hydrocarbonaceous thing, a thing eight inches one way and ten another, a thing just one furlong east of a certain stone in my neighbor's field, an American thing, etc., etc." (355). *Per se*, "every reality has an infinity of aspects or properties" (354). It is simply undifferentiated before my purposes inform it. Once they do, however, the properties which are of interest to me, that is, which can serve as the means or instruments for my purpose, immediately stand out. This "teleological" determination of its disclosed properties by my "interests," James claims, is ever present (ibid., 357).

3. Martin Heidegger, *History of the Concept of Time*, trans. Theodore Kisiel (Bloomington: Indiana University Press, 1985), 261.

4. In Heidegger's words, "There exists no comportment to beings that would not understand being" (*The Basic Problems of Phenomenology*, trans. Albert Hofstadter [Bloomington: Indiana University Press, 1988], 327). Since being is disclosed through this comportment, Heidegger can assert: "Certainly only so long as Dasein exists—that is, as long as the ontological possibility of an understanding of being exists—'is there' being. If Dasein didn't exist, then neither do the 'independence' nor 'in-itself' [of being] exist" (*Sein und Zeit*, 212). The point is that there is being only as correlated to Dasein's disclosive conduct. This is what gives it its meaning as the "what-for" (*Wozu*) and the "in-order-to" (*Worumwillen*).

5. Jean-Paul Sartre, *Being and Nothingness*, trans. Hazel Barnes (New York: Washington Square, 1966), 112.

6. As the word "marathon" indicates, this tradition stretches back to ancient Greece.

7. Heidegger expresses this in terms of the "resoluteness" that characterizes us when we genuinely confront the possibilities inherent in our situation. He writes: "Coming back to itself futurally [that is, closing the gap between the future and the present], resoluteness brings itself into the situation [of Dasein's having been] by making present. Having been [*Gewesenheit*] arises from the future in such a way that the future that has been (or rather the future that is in the process of having been) releases the present from itself" (*SZ*, 326). This is a rather complicated way of saying that the present is released from the future as

we realize the latter—that is, accomplish our goals. Doing so, we bring *ourselves* into our situation since the past *that we are* has been augmented.

8. "Standing out" is the Greek etymological sense of "ecstasies."

9. These are the categories of *Zuhandensein* and *Vorhandensein*. We are neither *available* for a project nor *simply there* as a mere thing is.

10. Sartre makes the same point in his discussion of bad faith. Bad faith is possible only because "human reality" or Dasein "must be what it is not and not [be] what it is" (Sartre, *Being and Nothingness*, 112). Given that its being is essentially projective, Dasein is, in its future possibilities, what it presently is not. As such possibilities, it is not what it presently is. To accept this, we must assert with Heidegger: "the projection is the way in which I *am* the possibility; it is the way in which I exist freely" (*The Basic Problems of Phenomenology*, 277).

11. As Levinas puts this, "Si l'existence est un comportement à l'égard de la possibilité de l'existence, et si elle est totale dans son existence à l'égard de la possibilité, elle ne peut être que pour-la-mort . . . . (si l'être-pour-la-mort est supprimé, du même coup est supprimé le au-devant-de-soi, et le Dasein n'est plus une totalité)" (Levinas, *Dieu: La mort et le temps*, ed. Jacques Rolland [Paris: Bernard Grasset, 1993], 64).

12. For Heidegger, such responsibility involves our freeing them for their own choices. Rather than caring for them in the sense of looking after their needs, it involves letting others "'be' in their innermost potentiality for being" by allowing them to "resolutely" face the choices that are available to them (*Sein und Zeit*, 298).

13. In his words, for Heidegger, "la crainte d'être assassin n'arrive pas à dépasser la crainte de mourir" (Levinas, *Dieu: La mort et le temps*, 108).

Chapter 2

1. Fr. 22, DK 22B80, *The First Philosophers: The Presocratics and the Sophists*, trans. Robin Waterfield (Oxford: Oxford University Press, 2000), 40.

2. Fr. 23, DK 22B53, 40.

3. Fr. 4, DK 28B3, my own translation.

4. "Autrui" is translated as "Other," and "autre" is translated as "other" in Lingis's translation.

5. Jacques Derrida, *The Gift of Death*, trans. David Wills (Chicago: University of Chicago Press, 1995), 68.

6. See ibid.

7. Here, we cannot agree with Edith Wyschogrod when she writes, "The Other is opposed to us . . . through the absolute unpredictability of his responses" (Wyschogrod, *Emmanuel Levinas: The Problem of an Ethical Metaphysics* [New York: Fordham University Press, 2000], 94). A certain amount of predictability is necessary for us to communicate at all. It is also required, as Husserl shows, to recognize the Other as a subject like myself. That he is *like* myself does not mean that he is myself, that he is not other, that he does not continually exceed the intentions I have of him.

Chapter 3

1. In Heidegger's words, "metaphysical thinking rests on the distinction between what truly is and what, measured against this, constitutes all that is not truly in being" (Heidegger, "Who Is Nietzsche's Zarathustra?" in *Nietzsche*, 4 vols., trans. D. F. Krell [San Francisco: Harper Collins, 1987], 2:230).

2. The irony implied by the word "alibi" may well refer to Nietzsche's account of "How the 'True World' Ultimately Became a Fable." The account begins with Plato for whom the "true world" is "attainable by the sage, the pious man and the man of virtue." This man is the philosopher who leaves the cave of the sensuously appearing world to enter the world of the ideas. Doing so, "he lives in it." Christianity substitutes the believer for the philosopher. The distinction between the apparent and the real world is translated into one between this world and the next (the world of the afterlife). The latter is "the true world, which is unattainable for the moment," but "promised to the sage, to the pious man and to the man of virtue ('to the sinner who repents')." With Kant, the distinction takes the form of the division between the noumenal and the phenomenal—the nonappearing and the appearing worlds. Here, the nonappearing true world exists for us as "an obligation, a command"—that is, as the categorical imperative that is our sole positive contact with the world "in itself." This is the "intelligible world" where the obligations I recognize through my reason hold universally. As Nietzsche remarks, what we confront in Kant is "the idea [of the "true world"] become sublime, pale, northern, Königsbergian." As non-appearing, it is "unattainable, it cannot be proved." The next stage in Nietzsche's history appears when we realize that, as noumenal and, hence, unknowable in itself, the "true world" cannot be obligatory. As Nietzsche asks, "what could something unknown constrain us to?" At this point "the true world" becomes "a useless idea that has become quite superfluous, consequently an exploded idea." Thus, the cry of the next stage is "let us abolish it!" The final stage occurs when we realize that "in abolishing the true world we have also abolished the world of appearance!" (Nietzsche, *Twilight of the Idols*, trans. Anthony Ludovic [New York: Russell and Russell, 1964], 24–25). The twentieth century's drive to overcome metaphysics with its separation of the apparent from the real world is based on this realization.

3. As Husserl puts this in the second volume of the *Ideen*, "I thus see here *an essential lawfulness of the pure ego*. As the one identical, numerically singular ego, it belongs to 'its' stream of experiences, which is constituted as a unity in unending, immanent time. The one pure ego is constituted as a unity with reference to this stream-unity; this means that it can find itself as identical in its course" (Husserl, *Ideen zu einer reinen Phänomenologie und phänomenologischen Philosophie, Zweites Buch*, ed. W. Biemel [The Hague: Martinus Nijhoff, 1952], 112).

4. Descartes's words, "it is one and the same mind which as a complete unit wills, perceives, and understands." Since I cannot say I am a different mind when I will or understand or sense, as I often perform these activities simultaneously, these activities do not, for Descartes, point to different "parts" of myself (Descartes, *Meditations on First Philosophy*, VI, trans. L. LaFleur [New York: Macmillan, 1990], 81).

5. In Kant's words, "The 'I think' must accompany all my representations, for otherwise something would be represented in me which could not be thought; in other words, the representation would either be impossible, or at least be, in relation to me, nothing" (Kant, *Kritik der reinen Vernunft*, A123 [Hamburg: Felix Meiner Verlag, 1998], 227). All references to the *Kritik* will be to this edition. All translations from the *Kritik* will be my own.

6. In French, "L'absolument Autre, c'est Autrui."

7. As Kant expresses this, "everything which belongs to inner determinations is represented in relations of time." But only the "inner sense, by means of which the mind intuits itself or its inner state," grasps such relations (Kant, *Kritik der reinen Vernunft*, B37, p. 97). Similarly, time does not appear in my outer sense: "Time cannot be outwardly intuited, any more than space can be intuited as something in us," the point being that it is always "now" in the world out there (ibid.). The point holds even for astronomical observations since what we see is the light that reaches us now.

8. Emmanuel Levinas,"Time and the Other," in *Time and the Other, and Additional Essays*, trans. Richard Cohen (Pittsburgh: Duquesne University Press, 1994), 77. For Husserl, by contrast, it is the primal impression that bears the new. As he describes it: "It is what is primally produced—the 'new,' that which has come into being as alien to consciousness, that which has been received, as opposed to what has been produced through consciousness's own spontaneity" (Husserl, *Zur Phänomenologie des inneren Zeitbewusstseins* [The Hague: Martinus Nijhoff, 1966], 100). The question that arises here is which is prior: the newness of the impression or that of the other. As present within me, the impression (along with the retention that retains it as a past impression) is, for Husserl, the root of my self-alterity. For Levinas, this root is the alterity of the other. As Rudolf Bernet poses the issue: "it has not seemed possible to purely and simply reduce the experience of temporal self-alterity to the encounter with the alterity of the other . . . Nor have we been able to settle the question of the nature of the link which makes the experience of temporality and the experience of alterity depend on each other: is *time* the initial horizon that presides over any appearance of alterity, or on the contrary is it the advent of an *alterity* or an alteration that allows time to appear?" (Bernet, "Levinas's Critique of Husserl," in *The Cambridge Companion to Levinas*, ed. Simon Critchley and Robert Bernasconi [New York: Cambridge Univerisity Press, 2003], 96–97). For Bernet, as for most Husserlians, time is the initial horizon. For Levinas, it is the alterity of the Other, a position demanded by his positioning ethics as first philosophy.

9. This is the answer to Waldenfels's comment: "we wonder why animals and plants should be omitted. The Cartesian dualism seems to throw its shadow on this philosophy of the face." The question, here, is "if Levinas is right to restrict the 'face' to the human face, neglecting the appeal of things, the call of other living beings" (Bernhard Waldenfels, "Levinas and the Face of the Other," in *The Cambrdge Companion to Levinas*, ed. Simon Critchley and Robert Bernasconi [New York: Cambridge University Press, 2003], 68, 77). For Levinas, what makes the face a face is its infinity, but this is manifested in the speaking face. Todd May, among many others, also misses this point. See note 10 on next page.

10. In Todd May's words, "Being a bat is infinitely other in the precise sense Levinas articulates. . . . But that the experience of the bat transcends my own experience does not imply that there is some responsibility I have towards bats" (May, *Reconsidering Difference* [University Park: Pennsylvania State University Press, 1997], 143).

11. Immanuel Kant,"Grundlegung zur Metaphysik der Sitten" in *Kants gesammelte Schriften*, ed. Königlich Preussische Akademie der Wissenschaften, 23 vols. (Berlin: Georg Reiner, 1955), 4:429.

12. Emmanuel Levinas,"Ethics as First Philosophy," in *The Levinas Reader*, ed. Seán Hand (Oxford: Blackwell, 1989), 76.

13. Here, "knowledge is re-presentation, a return to presence, and nothing may remain *other* to it" (Levinas, "Ethics as First Philosophy," 77). Correspondingly, what is beyond knowledge is beyond such immanent presence. This is the Other in his or her alterity.

14. Ibid., 77–78.

15. As Joseph Cohen points out, this ignores the fact that for Heidegger, being in its distinction from beings cannot be reduced to a concept or a category. In his words, "l'être demeure toujours—parce qu'il pré-cède la présence concrète de *l'ens*, parce qu'il ne saurait se réduire à un prédicat, à un concept ou à une catégorie, et parce qu'il est fondamentalement *retrait* de l'étant et de la pré-sence de l'étantité—la possibilité même de la différence. L'être est déjà *transcendens* et donc demeure réfractaire à la catégorie, à la prédication, à la conceptualisation, à la présence" (Cohen, *Alternances de la métaphysique: Essais sur Emmanuel Levinas* [Paris: Éditions Galilée, 2009], 147).

16. With this, we have what for Cohen is the genuine difference between Levinas and Heidegger. Both want to overcome the limitation of thinking to the individually present entity. Both want to surpass this by opening thinking "à une différence "qui ne fusionne pas en unité." For Heidegger, this opening occurs through being in its distinction from beings. Being exceeds beings. It has, with regard to them an "ex-cendance." In Cohen's words: "Or, pour Heidegger, cette ex-cendance ou cette incesance est nommée par l'être en son altérité, altérité qui, sans jamais se confondre avec l'étant, conditionne toujours, dans son retrait et par sa rétraction, la présentification de l'étant" (Cohen, *Alternances de la métaphysique*, 147). For Levinas, this excess comes from the Other, from his withdrawal from presence (148).

17. René Descartes, *Meditations on First Philosophy*, III, 43.

18. See ibid., 44.

19. The conception that God necessarily exceeds our conception, that the reality (ideatum) of God exceeds the idea, is, of course, very old. Anselm with his conception of God as "that than which nothing greater can be conceived" admits that this very conception forces us to it. In his words, "Therefore, Lord, not only are you that than which nothing greater can be thought, but you are also something greater than can be thought (*quiddam maius quam cognitari possit*). For since it is possible to think that there is such a one, then, if you are not this same being, something greater than you could be thought—which cannot be" (*St. Anselm's Proslogion*, trans. M. J. Charlesworth [Oxford: Clarendon, 1965],

137). As Francis Guibal points out, this excess signifies for Levinas that we leave onto-theology behind. At issue is not the *theos*, but the *logos* of onto-theo-logy. In Guibal's words, "Si le théo-logique se trouve refusé, ce n'est certes pas pour le *theos* dont il témoigne, mais pour le *logos* qui s'en empare: 'Avec la théologie, qui a partie liée avec l'ontologie, Dieu se fixe en concept'" (*Autrement qu'être ou au-delà de l'essence* [La Haye: M. Nijhoff, 1974], 191, n. 21). What replaces the *logos* in testifying to God is the ethical action: "Pour Levinas, il n'est que l'attestation du Dire éthique pour signifier justement un 'autrement que savoir' seul suscep-tible de renvoyer les énoncés doxiques des théologies à une inspiration scriptur-aire dont la hauteur même appelle le risque d'une traduction dégrisée de tout 'enthousiasme' sacralisant" (*Emmanuel Levinas: Le sens de la transcendance, autre-ment* [Paris: Presses Universitaires de France, 2009], 46).

20. This "testifying" even goes to the point of taking responsibility for the other person's responsibility. As Levinas expresses this: "Positively, we will say that since the Other looks at me, I am responsible for him, without even having *taken* responsibilities in his regard; his responsibility is *incumbent on me*. It is a respon-sibility that goes beyond what I do. Usually, one is responsible for what one does oneself." Here, however, "I am responsible for his very responsibility" (*EI*, 96). Thus, normally my responsibilities are limited to my actions. If I harm others, I am responsible for undoing evil, making good the loss. In testifying, I also take on the responsibility for combating the harm others have done. It is their re-sponsibility to do so, but I do not wait for this. I act on my own. Such witnessing was evinced, for example, by aid workers in Darfur trying to alleviate the misery caused by others. It is, in fact, evinced by all kinds of war and social relief.

21. Emmanuel Levinas, "God and Philosophy," in *Of God Who Comes to Mind*, trans. Bettina Bergo (Stanford, Calif.: Stanford University Press, 1998), 68.

22. Ibid., 69.

23. For a list of the philosophical expressions of such standards, see Martin Heidegger's "The Onto-theo-logical Constitution of Metaphysics," in *Identity and Difference*, trans. Joan Stambaugh (New York: Harper and Row, 1969), 66. Hei-degger's "Vom Wesen der Wahrheit," in *Wegmarken* (Frankfurt am Main: Vittorio Klostermann, 1967), 79–80 describes the notion of a *Bezugsbereich*.

24. The result of this move, as Joseph Cohen notes, is to break the tie between sense and being. In his words, the result is a "scission du sens *et* de l'être qui s'entendra comme une suspension du mouvement de conditionnalité et de présentification signifié par le sens de l'être. Comme si cette scis-sion infligeait une interruption non ontologique à même la pos-sibilité de l'ontologie" (Cohen, *Alternances de la métaphysique*, 148). This is a "scission dans la modalité même du sens de l'être et donc dans la co-appartenance du sens et de l'être. Une scis-sion d'où s'éveillerait une subjectivité inédite et irréductible. Or éveiller une subjectivité *avant* l'ordre et l'ordination du sens de l'être, avant cela même qui implique tous-jours que l'étant (et l'étant privilégié qu'est le *Dasein*) apparaisse là où se tient la possibilité même de sa compréhension signifiée par l'être" (149).

25. Such remarks are behind Derrida's critique of Levinas's treatment of history. Derrida writes that Levinas describes "history as a blinding to the other and as a laborious procession of the same. One may wonder whether history

can be history, *if there is history*, when negativity is enclosed with the circle of the same" (Jacques Derrida, "Violence and Metaphysics," in *Writing and Difference*, trans. Alan Bass [Chicago: University of Chicago Press, 1978], 94). Remarking that "Being is history" for Heidegger, he adds, "The anhistoricity of meaning at its origin is what profoundly separates Levinas from Heidegger" (148). Robert Bernasconi responds to this by writing: "Levinas's strategy is to question totality and history so as to show that they themselves refer to the beyond, although not as the transcendental conditions of their possibility" (Bernasconi, "Levinas and Derrida: The Question of the Closure of Metaphysics," in *Face to Face with Levinas*, ed. Richard Cohen [Albany: State University of New York Press, 1986], 194). The Levinasian alternative to Heidegger's history of being as well as Derrida's history of writing is, in Bernasconi's words, "a 'history of the face.'" He writes, "this phrase does not mean that the face has a history but that the face ruptures history from within just as, in the history of being, being ruptures the history of philosophy as an excess that at the same time conditions that history. The phrase *history of the face* is disruptive" (195).

Chapter 4

1. According to Levinas, death is agony because it ends this projecting forward from our past. We have no more future to breathe in. In Levinas's words, "Dying is agony because in dying a being does not come to an end [in his projecting forward] while coming to an end; he has no more time, that is, he . . . suffocates" (*TI*, 56).

2. In Heidegger's words, Dasein "is ontically distinguished by the fact that, in its very Being, Being is an issue for it" (*Sein und Zeit*, 32).

3. See Plato, *Phaedo*, 79d.

4. "And I must not imagine that I do not conceive infinity as a real idea, but only through the negation of what is finite in the manner that I comprehend rest and darkness as the negation of movement and light" (Descartes, *Meditations on First Philosophy*, 43–44).

5. There is a secondary reference to ourselves insofar as the more excellent sciences, as not driven by need, are appropriate to free inquirers.

6. Simone Weil, *Waiting on God*, trans. Emma Craufurd (London: Fontana Books, 1965), 72.

7. Ibid., 75.

8. Thus, behind the "potius quam," the why this "rather than" that of the question of reason, lies our finite freedom. In Heidegger's words, "Das Widerschein dieses Ursprungs des Wesens von Grund im Gründen der endlichen Freiheit zeigt sich in 'potius quam' der Formeln des Satzes vom Grund" (Heidegger, "Vom Wesen des Grundes" in *Wegmarken*, 69–70).

9. Ibid., 69.

10. "Als dieser Grund aber ist die Freiheit der Ab-grund des Daseins" (ibid.).

11. As Merold Westphal notes, with this emphasis on the καθ' αὐτό (*kath'-auto*), Levinas distinguishes himself from not just Heidegger but from contem-

porary French philosophy, which asserts that all knowing is horizonal, that is, it "occurs against a background or in a context to which it is relative" (Westphal, "Levinas and the Immediacy of the Face," *Faith and Philosophy* 10, no. 4 [October 1993], 497). For Heidegger, this context is set by the project (*TI*, 64). For others, the context is that of history, language, culture, and so on. In every case, the knowledge shaped by this horizonal context is mediated by it. As Westphal writes, "The . . . claim . . . that nothing is immediate and that everything is mediated, was, in 1961, when Levinas wrote this, and has been ever since, the Shibboleth of continental philosophy from existential phenomenology, hermeneutics, and critical theory through structuralism to the varieties of poststructuralism. Especially in France, to be radical has meant to give unquestioning allegiance to this orthodoxy" (Westphal, "Levinas and the Immediacy of the Face," 494). For Levinas, by contrast, "The immediate is the face to face" (*TI*, 52). As other, it escapes the relativization of the contexts that we impose upon it. It possesses "an infinity that surpasses all attempts to relativize it by representing it" in terms of some context (Westphal, 492).

12. Aristotle, *Nichomachean Ethics*, trans. Martin Ostwald (New York: Macmillan, 1962), 112.

13. See ibid., 117ff.

14. Kant, *Kritik der reinen Vernunft*, B75, p. 130.

Chapter 5

1. Rene Descartes, *Meditations on First Philosophy*, trans. L. LaFleur (New York: Macmillan, 1990), III, 34.

2. Ibid., V, 62.

3. Kant, *Kritik der reinen Vernunft*, Bxvi, p. 21.

4. Edmund Husserl, *Logische Untersuchungen*, ed. Ursula Panzer, in *Edmund Husserl, Gesammelte Schriften* (Hamburg: Felix Meiner Verlag), 2:226.

5. According to Mill, the "principle" of utilitarianism is that "equal amounts of happiness are equally desirable, whether felt by the same or by different persons." Its "premise" is that "the truths of arithmetic are applicable to the valuation of happiness, as of all other measurable quantities" (John Stuart Mill, *Utilitarianism* [Indianapolis, Ind.: Hackett, 1979], 61).

6. The implicit reference here is to Kant, who writes: "A constitution of the greatest possible human freedom according to laws, by which the liberty of every individual can consist with the liberty of every other . . . is . . . a necessary idea, which must be placed at the foundation not only of the first plan of the constitution of a state, but of all its laws" (Kant, *Kritik der reinen Vernunft*, B373, p. 423, my translation).

7. In Kant's words, "Our knowledge springs from two fundamental sources of the mind; the first is the capacity of receiving representations (receptivity for impressions), the second is the power of knowing an object through these representations (spontaneity [in the production] of concepts). . . . If the *receptivity* of our mind, its power of receiving representations in so far as it is in any wise affected, is to be entitled sensibility, then the mind's power of producing repre-

sentations from itself, the *spontaneity* of knowledge, should be called the under-standing" (Kant, *Kritik der reinen Vernunft*, B74, p. 129).

8. Sartre, *Being and Nothingness*, 60.

9. In a later text, Levinas speaks of the Other as "in" me, that is, as inher-ent in my selfhood. Yet, as Levinas writes, I have to think "the *in* differently than a presence." He adds, "the other is not another same. The *in* does not signify an assimilation" (Levinas, *Dieu: La mort et le temps*, 133). He is not something "in" me that I could assimilate in the sense of synthesize into something present. Rather, he is within me as an absence. This absence gives me the self-separation, the self-alterity that makes me a for-itself. The result of confronting it is, in Levinas's words, "the awakening of the for-itself . . . by the inabsorbable alterity of the Other" (32). It is also, in terms of Sartre's citation of Descartes, the awakening of the basis of our freedom.

10. Jean-Michel Salanskis sees here two opposing ways: A Jewish one privi-leging ethics, a Western one privileging freedom. He writes: "la voie de l'Occident est celle du droit de la liberté, cependant que la voie juive est celle du droit de l'obligation." (On the Jewish side, the organizing principle of the social world is obligation, on the Western side, the principle is that of liberty.) "Dans l'optique juive l'excellence éthique et une socialité vibrant à sa mesure ne peuvent venir que parmi des hommes 'éduqués' par *l'avodah*. Le droit organise donc un monde social traversé par l'obligation. Dans l'optique 'occidentale' on espère que la pas-sibilité à autrui, l'ouverture vers lui, et la disponibilité à le secourir émergeront et coloreront le monde *à partir de la liberté* et de la reconnaissance de la liberté. Le droit encadre donc une socialité conçue comme expression de la liberté" (Salanskis, *L'émotion éthique: Levinas vivant I* (Clamecy: Klincksieck, 2011). If Levi-nas's analyses are correct, however, these are not just two opposed and mutually balancing points of view. If liberty is not to become license, then it presupposes ethical obligation to the Other.

This linking of freedom to the Other may be contrasted with Sartre's posi-tion. As Sartre argues in his section, "The Look" in his *Being and Nothingness*, the presence of the Other undermines my freedom. For Levinas, on the contrary, it awakens it. Their resulting views on ethics are correspondingly different. See, in this regard, Christina Howells, "Sartre and Levinas," in *The Provocation of Levinas: Rethinking the Other*, ed. Robert Bernasconi and David Wood (New York: Rout-ledge, 1988), 91–99; Joanne Pier, "Sartre/Levinas: An Is/Ought Gap of Ethics?" *Dialogue* 31 (1989): 52–57; David Jopling, "Levinas, Sartre and Understanding the Other," *Journal of the British Society for Phenomenology* 24, no. 3 (October 1993): 214–31; Arne Vetlesen, "Relations with Others in Sartre and Levinas: Assessing Some Implications for an Ethics of Proximity," *Constellations: An International Journal of Critical and Democratic Theory* 1, no. 3 (January 1995): 358–82; Stéphane Habib, *La responsabilité chez Sartre et Levinas* (Paris: L'Harmattan, 1998); Maria Schafstedde, "Begegnung statt Konstitution: Zur Frage nach dem Anderen bei Jean-Paul Sartre und Emmanuel Levinas," in *Kritik und Praxis* (Luneburg: zu Klampen, 1998), 450–57; Holger Zaborowski, "On Freedom and Responsibil-ity: Remarks on Sartre, Levinas, and Derrida," *Heythrop Journal* 41, no. 1 (2000): 47–65.

11. This holds even when in an act of reflection it intends itself.

Chapter 6

1. *The Pre-Socratic Philosophers: A Critical History with a Selection of Texts* (Cambridge, Eng.: Cambridge University Press, 1966), 269.

2. There cannot be two gods, whose essence is to be since being per se, being apart from essence, is not diverse. Thus, the two gods would collapse into one.

3. Levinas, "God and Philosophy," 69.

4. Levinas, *Ethics and Infinity,* 89. This does not mean that one cannot kill the other; it means, rather, that one cannot overcome his inherent alterity. As Robert Bernasconi puts this: "*You shall not commit murder* is the primordial expression because it is my introduction to the alterity of the other, my introduction to a realm that exceeds my control" (Bernasconi, "Levinas and Derrida: The Question of the Closure of Metaphysics," 189). This realm, as Edith Wyschogrod points out, is that of the ethical. She writes: "As a purely ethical possibility murder is impossible, for if the resistance to murder were not ethical but 'real,' we would be able to perceive it [in the face], and perception would then restore the Other to the realm of the totalizing self. The face would be brought again into the world of objects" (Wyschogrod, *Emmanuel Levinas: The Problem of an Ethical Metaphysics,* 95).

5. Levinas, *Ethics and Infinity,* 89. Waldenfels asks: "What does Levinas have in mind when he proclaims the command: 'Thou shalt not murder' as the 'first word'? Reckoning with the worst when speaking of human affairs is one thing, relying on it is something other. Even the worst may differ from one culture, epoch or age to the other" (Waldenfels, "Levinas and the Face of the Other," 72). This misses Levinas's point, which is that the "first word" combines two opposites, the command and the vulnerability and exposure from which it issues. It is this very ability to see the big in the little, authority in vulnerability that marks the ethical consciousness.

6. Levinas, *Ethics and Infinity,* 92.

Chapter 7

1. The sense of "living" here is that of the German *erleben*, which means to "live through" and, hence, "experience."

2. In Greek, *ex* (ἐξ) and *istemi* (ἴστμι). The idea is that only what can stand out from its background can be said to exist. Thus, in the dark room when you bump into something, you know that it exists.

3. Courtine strongly objects to the use of enjoyment (*jouissance*) to analyze our existence. He writes: "Ce moi de la jouissance est, me semble-t-il, un artefact, sans aucune nécessité descriptive ou phénoménologique." His objection is that to define man in its terms is to focus on our animality: "Pourquoi définir ainsi l'humain (je rappelle la formule déjà citée : l'étant par l'excellence, c'est l'homme)—et non pas plutôt l'infra-humain, l'animalité en l'homme?" In other words, to define man in terms of enjoyment is to define him in terms of

"the sub-human, the animal within him" (Courtine, "L'ontologie fondamentale d'Emmanuel Levinas," 113).

4. Aristotle, *Nicomachean Ethics*, 1170a26, p. 266.

5. Ibid., 1170b1, p. 266.

6. Ibid., 1170b4–5, p. 266.

7. Ibid., 1097b1, p. 15

8. Ibid., 1097aa23, p. 14.

9. Kant, *Kritik der reinen Vernunft*, A5, p. 52.

10. Husserl, *Logische Untersuchungen*, III, 405.

11. Ibid., III, 360–61.

12. Ibid., III, 396.

13. Ibid., IV, 762. The second edition of the *Logical Investigations* (1913) changes "interpretation" to "apperception" and interpret to "apperceive."

14. Ibid., III, 12. We here follow the first edition.

15. Ibid., III, 358. We here follow the first edition.

16. Edmund Husserl, *Cartesianische Meditationen*, ed. Strasser (The Hague, 1963), 80.

17. According to François-David Sebbah, from a Levinasian perspective, Husserl's conception of intentionality is insufficiently radical. If all consciousness is consciousness of something, then consciousness itself is simply self-transcendence. In his words, "la conscience . . . est le pur dynamisme d'une visée, le pur acte de se jeter vers, pure flèche, qui, tout entière dans l'acte de sortir de soi, rien que cette pure sortie de soi, coïncide intégralement avec elle-même dans le mouvement de s'échapper, en raison précisément de la radicalité de cette 'sortie de soi' avec laquelle elle coïncide absolument. Elle est tout entière pure auto-transgression d'elle-même" (Sebbah, *Lévinas: Ambiguïtés de l'altérité* [Paris: Les Belles Lettres, 2003], 102–3). As such self-transcendence, it is not a substance (102). This means that intentionality, when thought through is a de-substantialization of the subject, a placing it outside or otherwise than being: "l'intentionnalité husserlienne . . . c'est un pur mouvement de dé-substantialisation: l'intentionnalité est le pressentiment . . . de l'autrement qu'être qu'il reviendra à Lévinas de désigner enfin radicalement" (104–5).

18. When we come to discuss Husserl's theory of the instincts, however, another side to his doctrine will become apparent.

19. Edmund Husserl, *Ideen zu einer reinen Phänomenologie und phänomenologischen Philosophie, Erstes Buch*, ed. R. Schuhmann (The Hague: Martinus Nijhoff, 1976), 107. In *the Cartesian Meditations*, which Levinas helped translate, Husserl calls such transcendencies "constituted products" of subjectivity. In his words, "Genuine epistemology is, accordingly, only possible [*sinnvoll*] as transcendental-phenomenological epistemology which, instead of dealing with contradictory inferences which lead from a supposed immanence to a supposed transcendence—that of some undetermined "thing-in-itself" which is allegedly unknowable in principle—has to do exclusively with the systematic explanation of the accomplishment of knowing, an explanation in which this becomes thoroughly understandable as an intentional accomplishment. Precisely thereby, every sort of being itself [*Seiendes selbst*], be it real or ideal, becomes understand-

able as a constituted *product* [*Gebilde*] of transcendental subjectivity, a product that is constituted in just such an accomplishment [of knowing]. This sort of understanding is the highest form of rationality" (*Cartesian Meditations*, ed. Strasser, 118).

20. *Cartesian Meditations*, 120.

21. As Aristotle observed, the particular as the particular can be sensed, but cannot be represented in a language we share with our others (*Metaphysics* VII, x, 1036a 2–7). Such sharing involves common meanings, which express the common features of objects. My body as mine, however, cannot be common. It is the flesh that incarnates me, making me this particular person and not anybody else. Given that the meanings we use always apply to more than one object, this bodily particularity that we sense and daily live is always inexpressible.

22. Maurice Merleau-Ponty, *The Visible and the Invisible*, trans. A. Lingis (Evanston, Ill.: Northwestern University Press, 1968), 8.

23. Aristotle, *Nicomachean Ethics*, 1094a20, p. 4.

24. James Edie, "The Question of the Transcendental Ego: Sartre's Critique of Husserl," in *Husserl in His Contemporary Radiance: Proceedings of the 24th Annual Meeting of the Husserl Circle* (Waterloo, Ontario, 1992), 271–72.

25. Hans Jonas, *Mortality and Morality: A Search for the Good after Auschwitz*, ed. Lawrence Vogel (Evanston, Ill.: Northwestern University Press, 1996), 86.

26. Ibid.

27. In Jonas's words, "organisms are entities whose being is their own doing . . . the being that they earn from this doing is not a possession they then own in separation from the activity by which it was generated, but is the continuation of that very activity itself" (Jonas, *Mortality and Morality*, 86).

28. Edmund Husserl, Ms. C 16 IV, p. 36b, in *Späte Texte Über Zeitkonstitution (1929–1934) Die C-Manuscripte*, ed. Dieter Lohmar (Dordrecht: Springer Verlag, 2006), 326.

29. "Das Streben ist aber instinktives und instinktiv, also zunächst unenthüllt 'gerichtet' auf die sich 'künftig' erst enthüllt konstituierenden weltlichen Einheiten" (Husserl, Ms. A VI 34, p. 34b).

30. Husserl came to see such striving as the basis of our intentionality. Animated by the affective force of impressions, it is what gives intentionality its future-directed character. It is responsible for its directedness towards what we intend to see as we focus our eyes and move forward to get a better look. As Husserl writes in his *Analyses of Passive Synthesis*, "*Ceteris paribus*, the primal impressional occurring in the living present has a stronger affective tendency than what has already been retained. Precisely because of this, with regard to the direction of propagation, affection possesses a unitary tendency towards the future. Intentionality is primarily directed to the future" (*Analysen zur passiven Synthesis*, ed. M. Fleischer [The Hague: Martinus Nijhoff, 1966], 156). Husserl here is basing himself on the basic sense of *intentio*, the Latin word signifying a "stretching out" or "straining" towards something. As Didier Franck observes, Levinas in *Autrement qu'être ou au-dela de l'essence* also comes to see intentionality as rooted in the affective quality of sensation. Franck writes: "Il y a là un désir en dehors de la simple conscience de . . . Intention encore, certes, mais dans un

sens radicalement différent de la visée théorique, quelle que soit la pratique propre que la théorie comporte. Intention comme Désir, de sorte que l'intention, placée entre déception et Erfullung, réduit déjà l''acte objectivant' à la spécification de la Tendance, plutôt qu'elle ne fait de la faim un cas particulier de la 'conscience de . . .'" (Franck, *L'un-pour-l'autre: Levinas et la signification* [Paris: Presses Universitaires de France, 2008], p. 62). Unfortunately, Franck does not know Husserl's later position and hence draws too strong a contrast between Levinas and Husserl. He writes, for example, "En prêtant ainsi attention à l'acception pré-philosophique du mot avec et par lequel Husserl caractérise la relation de l'intuition à l'intention de signification ou au concept, Levinas distingue, dans l'ordre de la connaissance, ce qui tranche sur cet ordre même. En effet, la sensation gustative n'est pas le remplissement d'un sens visé par une donnée incarnée qui s'y identifie, n'a pas la distance d'un savoir ou de l'intentionalité qui ne va pas sans l'écart de la rétention, elle est rassasiement d'une faim, satisfaction dont 'la concrétude . . . est jouissance'" (ibid.).

31. Hannah Arendt, *The Human Condition* (Chicago: University of Chicago Press, 1958), 234.

Chapter 8

1. The I-Thou relation for Buber can include the nonverbal relations to a tree or a work of art. See Martin Buber, *I and Thou*, trans. W. Kaufmann (New York: Simon and Schuster, 1996), 57–58, 60–61.

2. John Locke, "Second Treatise on Government," §27, in *John Locke: Political Writings* (Indianapolis, Ind.: Hackett, 2003), 274.

3. Such a view of public space is, of course, inadequate. For a more positive conception see James Mensch, "Public Space," *Continental Philosophy Review* 40, no. 1 (March 2007): 31–47.

4. See Aristotle, *Physics*, bk. II, ch. 1, 192b, 8–22.

5. See Liddell and Scott, *An Intermediate Greek-English Lexicon* (London: Oxford University Press, 1961), 579.

6. Other animals, of course also do this, which means that they also have this open temporal structure.

7. Immanuel Kant, *Groundwork of the Metaphysics of Morals*, trans. H. J. Paton (New York: Harper and Row, 1964), 125.

8. Ibid., 91.

9. Levinas, *Ethics and Infinity*, 89.

10. Levinas, *Dieu: La mort et le temps*, 108

11. Heidegger, *Sein und Zeit*, 285.

12. Descartes, *Meditations on First Philosophy*, III, 36.

13. Edmund Husserl, "Nachwort," in *Ideen zu einer reinen Phänomenologie und phänomenologischen Philosophie, Drittes Buch*, ed. M. Biemel (The Hague: Martinus Nijhoff, 1971), 145.

14. Husserl, *Ideen I*, 105.

15. See page 81.

16. For an extended account of Levinas's relation to Hegel, see Silvia Benso, "Gestures of Work: Levinas and Hegel," *Continental Philosophy Review* 40 (2007): 307–30.

17. G. W. F. Hegel, *Phänomenologie des Geistes* (Hamburg: Felix Meiner Verlag, 2006), 121–22.

18. Ibid., 133.

19. Heidegger, *Sein und Zeit*, 45.

20. Ibid., 42.

21. This objectifying self-description includes our taking ourselves as a subject. According to Heidegger, "if we posit an 'I' or subject as that which is proximally given we shall completely miss the phenomenal content of Dasein." This is because, "ontologically, every idea of a 'subject' still posits a subjectum ('ὑποκείμενον) along with it" (ibid., 47). The notion is taken over from that of a thing as something which underlies its properties.

22. There is a striking contrast here with Sartre's position. For Sartre, the encounter with the Other also involves a decentering of my consciousness. Such decentering, however, does not move me from the phenomenal to the noumenal. Rather, it results in my objectification. In fact, my experience of the Other is primarily the experience of my being reduced to an object relative to the centering of the world around *his* consciousness. In Sartre's words, "He is the subject who is revealed to me in that flight of myself toward objectification" (*Being and Nothingness*, 345). Thus, while for Levinas, my responding to the Other brings me to my "final reality . . . as a thing-in-itself," for Sartre, the encounter with the Other reduces me to a thing for the Other. In Sartre's words, the decentering signifies that "I have my foundation outside myself. I am for myself only as I am a pure reference to the Other" (349).

Chapter 9

1. Emmanuel Levinas, "Diachrony and Representation," in *Time and the Other, and Additional Essays*, trans. Richard Cohen (Pittsburgh: Duquesne University Press, 1994), 107.

2. Ibid.

3. "Die ontisch bildliche Rede vom lumen naturale im Menschen meint nichts anderes als die existenzial-ontologische Struktur dieses Seienden, daß es ist in der Weise, sein Da zu sein. Es ist 'erleuchtet,' besagt: an ihm selbst als In-der-Welt-sein gelichtet, nicht durch ein anderes Seiendes, sondern so, daß es selbst die Lichtung ist" (Heidegger, *Sein und Zeit*, 171).

4. Descartes in the *Meditations* constantly uses it in this sense.

5. See Plato, *Republic*, 514a–517c.

6. Heidegger, *Sein und Zeit*, 171.

7. The relation between the clearing provided by our temporal structure and our understanding of being is that such structure serves "as the horizon for all understanding of being and for any way of interpreting it" (Heidegger, *Sein*

und Zeit, 17). This means that this understanding is always expressed in terms of standards of disclosure and, hence, of care.

8. See page 40.

9. Husserl, *Logische Untersuchungen*, III, 762.

10. As Aristotle remarks with regard to the need of external goods for happiness, "the man who is very ugly in appearance . . . is not very likely to be happy" (*Nicomachean Ethics*, 1099b3).

11. Mill, *Utilitarianism*, 60.

12. Ibid., 61n. Mill adds: "If there is any anterior principle implied, it can be no other than this, that the truths of arithmetic are applicable to the valuation of happiness, as of all other measurable quantities" (ibid.).

13. Emmanuel Levinas, *Existence and Existents*, trans. Alphonso Linguis (Dordrecht: Kleuwer Academic, 1995). This originally appeared as *De l'existence à l'existant* (Paris: Vrin, 1947).

14. Levinas, *Ethics and Infinity*, 48–49.

15. See Descartes, *Meditations*, 45.

16. The "Introduction" to George Berkeley's *A Treatise concerning the Principles of Human Knowledge* presents this view, which Hume also adopts.

17. Husserl's *Investigations III* and *IV* examine the unifiability of contents into complex wholes. The two fundamental notions in this logic are those of foundation and whole. Non-independent "moments" or contents of objects are called by Husserl "founded contents" (*fundierte Inhalte*). A content is founded or dependent on another if it needs the other in order to be. More precisely, as Husserl says, "A content of type A is founded in the content of type B, if A, by its essence (i.e., lawfully, on the basis of its specific character) cannot exist without B also existing" (*Logische Untersuchungen* III, 281–82). This determines the notion of a whole which, according to Husserl, is "a sum of contents covered by a unitary foundation without the help of any further contents" (282).

18. The nature of this abstraction in the *Logical Investigations* is apparent when Husserl writes: "There is certainly a good sense in speaking of the unifiability of contents whose factual union has always remained and always will remain excluded" in individual consciousnesses (*Logische Untersuchungen*, IV, 635; see also III, 109–10). This follows since Husserl agrees with Frege that conception of a species as a pure possibility does not include the conception of its factual instances. We can thus speak of the union of the contents of the species without referring to these instances.

19. Heidegger, "Vom Wesendes Grundes" in *Wegmarken*, 69.

20. Aristotle describes this in the *Nichomachean Ethics*, bk. V, sec. 2.

21. Paul Ricoeur, *Oneself as Another*, trans. Kathleen Blamey (Chicago: University of Chicago Press, 1992), 189.

22. Ibid., 339.

23. Ibid., 337.

24. Ibid., 339.

25. Adriaan Peperzak provides an extensive commentary on Levinas's derivation of social justice from the face-to-face encounter. He sees here three

different arguments. The first is that the face of the Other reveals to me "'the third,' that is, any other human being." It does so because my responsibility to you "stems from you being a miserable other, not from any specific or particular feature" (Peperzak, *To the Other: An Introduction to the Philosophy of Emmanuel Levinas* [West Lafayette, Ind.: Purdue University Press, 1993], 167). This means that "the other is at the same time unique—and thus incomparable—and nothing special—and therefore in a very special sense 'universal' . . . Insofar as any other other ('the third') is present 'under the species' of your face, all others are equal" (ibid.). Seeing your face as just one of many other equally commanding faces, I am thus moved from a one-to-one assymetrical relationship to that embracing social justice. As Peperzak notes, this first argument is framed so as to avoid deriving the equality of all others from "a universal concept of all human others" (168). The second argument, according to Peperzak, begins by asserting that the Other who obligates me is also obligated by his Others. Thus, I and every other ego are constituted as equals in the obligations imposed on us. In Peperzak's words, "you are completely equal to me not identical—because we are both constituted as unique egos by the infinite claim of a unique, yet equal other" (170). This equality moves us to the level of social justice. As Peperzak notes, this argument comes close to the assertion of the identity of all egos since all are constituted in the same manner. Can we, however, speak of the identity of unique individuals (171)? The third argument is that of the other commanding me to command. As Peperzak analyzes it, it is an extension of the second argument. He writes: "You, who are the demanding presence of the other, you command me to be your servant, but since you yourself are a servant, you order me to assist you in your serving the third. Thus your commanding me specifies only your associating me to yourself, which was stated in the second argument" (172–73). The difficulty here is that of destroying "the asymmetry of the orginary relation" since it implies that we are all equally obligated to "respect everyone else" (173). We could save the asymmetry by assuming the height of the Other we encounter. But this "seems to lead to the contradictory conclusion that all people are simultaneously 'higher' than all people" (174). Our own analysis of this part of Levinas's argument is different since our focus is on the realization of the justice implicit in language, while Peperzak does not mention language in his account.

26. *The Babylonian Talmud*, 234.

27. Kant, *Groundwork of the Metaphysics of Morals*, 100–101.

28. Ibid., 108.

29. Adriaan Peperzak does see a hidden connection between Levinas and Kant. For both, what a person is in himself is unknowable and, hence, other. Thus, Kant, he reminds us, "'saved' the dimension of metaphysics through morality. The spatiotemporal order of phenomena permits us to wrest knowledge of the phenomena, but we do not know what and how things and persons in themselves are. We enter, however, into the dimension of 'being-in-itself' through respect for human autonomy as it reveals itself in the existence of others, as well as in our own existence." The difference between the two philosophers is that the alterity of the other is, for Kant, mediated by the use of reason. For Kant, he writes, "a 'fact of reason' corresponds to the epiphany of the other's face

and speech . . . Kant stresses the universality and fundamental equality of being human manifested in that 'fact.'" Thus, our use of reason, whose laws are not those of natural causality, shows that we are outside of the spatiotemporal order of phenomena. By revealing the moral law, it is what makes us moral agents worthy of respect. Doing so, it obligates us to treat the Other as an end in himself. For both, then, "the ethical 'experience,' the ego of I think discovers itself as an I am obliged." Yet, according to Peperzak, "Kant translated and betrayed the discovery of this submission, or 'subjection,' by formulating it in terms borrowed from the structure of theoretical reasoning. He described it as a universal law, to which the individual must submit his/her particular inclinations, thus preparing Hegel's synthesis in which morality is only an intermediate moment of the concept of Sittlichkeit." In spite of this, there is a connection between Levinas and Kant. In Peperzak's words, "But behind this betrayal, the structure of a receptive subject is still legible: I must obey and follow an orientation not chosen by me, but 'choosing' me as a reasonable, that is, human being; my being human is the command to respect humanity as an end in itself; my life is being-for-this-end from which I cannot escape—morally relevant behavior on the basis of radical passivity" (Adriaan Peperzak, "Some "Remarks on Hegel, Kant and Levinas," in *Face to Face with Levinas*, ed. Richard Cohen [Albany: State University of New York Press, 1986], 211).

Chapter 10

1. The common measure or unit is that by virtue of which each is to count as one. If, for example, it is an apple, then I can count apples, if it is fruit, then I can count fruit, and so on according to increasing levels of generality.

2. The unending nature of conversation reflects itself in the nature of teaching. As Jean-François Rey points out, education in the Jewish tradition is distinct from that of the Greek model, which was essentially political and had as its goal the politically engaged citizen. The Jewish model is that of Talmudic studies, which have no finite end. In Rey's words, "Mais, bien entendu, ici, le terme essentiel est l'étude infinie : lecture et commentaire. La base en est l'oral, là aussi, mais la parole s'adosse au livre, et l'on a vu en quoi le rapport aux livres distingue les deux traditions . . . On peut imaginer un terme à la formation de l'homme grec, celle-ci dût-elle durer toute une vie. On ne peut fixer un terme à l'étude de la Torah quels que soient les malheurs et les catastrophes de l'histoire" (Rey, *La mesure de l'homme: L'idée d'humanité dans la philosophie d'Emmanuel Levinas* [Paris: Editions Michalon, 2001], 181). In other words, the endless study of the Torah mirrors the non-finite character of genuine dialogue with the Other.

3. Such a place can, of course, assume various forms. These can range from the newspaper, to public forums, to Facebook and the other forms of social media on the Web.

4. Molière, *Le médecin malgré lui*, act 1, scene 5, in *Molière oeuvres complètes* (Paris: George Lang, 1962), 352.

5. Heidegger, *Sein und Zeit*, 250.

6. Jacques Derrida, *Aporias*, trans. Thomas Dutroit (Stanford, Calif.: Stanford University Press, 1993), 76. In fact, given that the notions of "authentic" and "inauthentic" existence involve the ways we face death, the unknowability of death undermines this crucial Heideggerian distinction. See ibid., 77.

7. In projecting ourselves forward, as Husserl writes, "the style of the past becomes projected into the future" (*Die Bernauer Manuskripte über das Zeitbewusstsein (1917/18)*, ed. R. Bernet and D. Lohmar [Dordrecht: Kluwer Academic, 2001], 38). Thus, experiencing, we constantly anticipate "the continuance of the sequence [of our experiences] in the same style" as the past (13). Doing so, we expect that fresh experience, in continuing "the style of the past," will confirm what we have already experienced. When fresh experience does meet our expectations, the protentional consciousness, which "grows" from the retained, "fulfills itself" (20).

8. For an extended account of the relation Husserl draws between intentionality and futurity, see James Mensch, "Husserl's Concept of the Future," *Husserl Studies* 16, no. 1 (1999): 41–64.

9. For an extended account of this see James Mensch, "The Temporality of Merleau-Ponty's 'Intertwining,'" *Continental Philosophy Review* 42, no. 14: 449–63.

10. What links the Other and the future is their sheer alterity. Levinas writes in *Time and the Other*, "the future is what is in no way grasped . . . the future is . . . what befalls and lays hold of us. The Other is the future. The very relationship with the other is the relationship with the future" (76–77). In *Totality and Infinity*, this futurity is manifest in the Other's behavior. It is present in the excess this behavior manifests beyond what we intend.

11. This is why Levinas says that "in the access to the face there is also an access to the idea of God" (*Ethics and Infinity*, 92).

12. Ibid., 99.

Chapter 11

1. A parallel question, according to Bettina Bergo, is that of its ethical import. For Levinas, she writes: "paternity, filiality, and fraternity . . . arise out of biological relations but also point beyond their origin to illustrate aspects of the face-to-face encounter" (Bergo, *Levinas between Ethics & Politics: For the Beauty That Adorns the Earth* [Duquesne: Duquesne University Press, 2003], 107–8). Given this, she asks "whether this section of *TI* can effectively hold phenomenological description and its interpretation at the biological level?" (107). For Bergo, it cannot "without great cost to his logic" (130). Thus, in the section "Beyond the Face," she notes, "the theme of maternity is massively overshadowed by that of paternity." While one might argue that Levinas privileges paternity "because he remains faithful to the analysis of his own experiences of intentionality," this leaves him open to "the charge of psychologism, which refuses to universalize this experience of responsibility" by remaining within the male perspective (113–14). "Levinas," she admits, "might justify this discussion by reminding us that a phenomenology that would account for the pre-reflective bases of experi-

ence cannot avoid being hermeneutic" (113). But, for Bergo, "there is here an acute problem of levels of description and deduction . . . And we must at the very least recognize that even hermeneutic phenomenology must be careful when it speaks of what is beyond being while having recourse to factical structures such as those adumbrated here. The impasse appears insurmountable" (126). This biologism along with the problems of grounding sociality on fraternity, according to Bergo, "led Levinas to abandon the dialectic of eros and fecundity in *OBBE*"—*Otherwise Than Being, or Beyond Essence* (107). The position of this commentary is much less critical. In our view, the focus of this section is not so much the face-to-face but an analytic of embodied Dasein. While Levinas's account of the feminine is, to say the least, one-sided, this does not vitiate his point that the erotic relationship is fundamentally different from the ethical. His interest in this section is not on the ethical per se, but on the origin of sociality as an existentiel of embodied Dasein.

2. Jacques Derrida, "Differance," in *Speech and Phenomena and Other Essays*, trans. David Allison (Evanston, Ill.: Northwestern University Press, 1973), 88.

3. Ibid., 68.

4. The one exception is humankind. Humans are not called good since they can be tempted by the serpent. The possibility of temptation implies that they are capable of both good and evil.

5. Derrida, "Circumfession: Fifty-Nine Periods and Periphrases," in *Jacques Derrida*, by Geoffrey Bennington and Jacques Derrida (Chicago: University of Chicago Press, 1993), 155.

6. Kant, *Groundwork of the Metaphysics of Morals*, 108.

7. Ibid., 101.

8. Jeffrey Bloechl criticizes this ambiguity, attempting to separate love from sexual desire. See his "How Best to Keep a Secret? On Love and Respect in Levinas's 'Phenomenology of Eros,'" *Man and World: An International Philosophical Review* 29, no. 1 (January 1996): 1–17. This article also contains an interesting comparison of Levinas's and Sartre's accounts of the erotic.

9. Gérard Benussan argues that what separates the Levinasian from the Husserlian conception of temporality is precisely the fact that for Levinas the body is sexed. For both the access through the world is through the body. This access determines our temporalization. For Husserl, however, "there is no sexual difference" is his account of the body and its role in temporalization. As Benussan writes: "La phénoménologie husserlienne dégage une signification temporelle du corps selon une ligne temps-monde-corps tenue avec rigueur par Husserl et d'ailleurs partagée ou reprise par Levinas sous bien des aspects. Le perçu accède en effet à la conscience sous le mode du corporel comme remplissement originaire. L'expérience mondaine en laquelle vivent tous les hommes se soutient d'une référence partagée dont notre existence corporelle est le lieu premier d'expérience. Mais la « signification corporelle du temps » décentre le propos husserlien et en bouleverse les articulations. Ce lien temps-monde-corps, Levinas le reçoit, le désintrique et le retresse autour et à partir d'eros-amour-sexe . . . il faut noter, et c'est ici décisif, qu'il n'y a pas chez Husserl de différence sexuelle" (Benussan, "Fécondité d'Eros: Équivoque et dualité," in *Lire*

Totalité et Infini d'Emmanuel Levinas: Études et interprétations, ed. Danielle Cohen-Levinas [Paris: Hermann, 2011], 100). According to Benussan, the sexual difference introduces the diachronicity, the non-synchronicity of intersubjective time. Thus, Benussan defines this diachronicity as "l'interruption pré-originaire du temps par l'autre, sa déstabilisation antérieure à toute substantialité, rassemblement, communauté, dit synchronisé" (92). This destabilization, he affirms, is occasioned by the erotic, which always, in fact, exceeds what we normally understand as the erotic (106).

10. Such remarks make the feminist reaction to Levinas particularly fraught. On the one hand, the feminine face rules over the dwelling and provides the first welcome. On the other, Levinas's remarks seem to undercut its status as providing a model for our obligation to the Other. The question that has driven the feminist interpretations of Levinas has been to what extent, if any, Levinas can provide a theoretical resource for the concerns of feminist theory. This is a subject that far exceeds the limited aims of this commentary. We can only note here some of the major figures in this controversy and point the reader to some of the sources that inform this debate.

In some sense, the debate is as old as feminist theory. Simone de Beauvoir, in her seminal text, *The Second Sex*, sets the tone for a number of authors. Commenting on Levinas's treatment of the feminine in his *Time and the Other*, she writes: "it is striking that he deliberately takes a man's point of view, disregarding the reciprocity of subject and object. When he writes that woman is mystery, he implies that she is mystery for man. Thus his description, which is intended to be objective, is in fact an assertion of masculine privilege" (de Beauvoir, *The Second Sex*, trans. and ed. H. M. Parshley [London: Jonathan Cape, 1956], 16, n. 1). Derrida echoes this sentiment when he notes "that *Totality and Infinity* pushes the respect for dissymmetry so far that it seems to us impossible, essentially impossible, that it could have been written by a woman. Its philosophical subject is man (vir). (Cf., for example, the Phenomenology of Eros, which occupies such an important place in the book's economy.) Is not this principled impossibility for a book to have been written by a woman unique in the history of metaphysical writing? (Derrida, "Violence and Metaphysics," in *Writing and Difference*, trans. Alan Bass [Chicago: University of Chicago Press, 1978], 320, n. 92). This critique is taken up and extended by Luce Irigaray in a number of essays, most notably: "Questions to Emmanuel Levinas," trans. Margaret Whitford, in *The Irigaray Reader*, ed. Margaret Whitford (Oxford: Blackwell, 1991) and "The Fecundity of the Caress: A Reading of Levinas, *Totality and Infinity*, 'Phenomenology of Eros,'" in *An Ethics of Sexual Difference* (Ithaca, N.Y.: Cornell University Press, 1993). This essay first appeared in French in *Exercices de la patience* 5 (Spring 1983): 119–37. An excellent study of Irigaray's reading of Levinas is provided by Kate Ince in her "Questions to Luce Irigaray," *Hypatia* 11, no. 2 (Spring 1996): 122–40. A principal source for the feminist reaction to Levinas is provided by Tina Chanter's edited collection, *Feminist Interpretations of Emmanuel Levinas* (University Park: Pennsylvania State University Press, 2001). Chanter has, herself, written extensively on this subject. See, for example, her essays "Feminism and the Other," in *The Provocation of Levinas: Rethinking the Other*, ed. Robert Bernasconi and David Wood

(New York: Routledge, 1988) and "The Alterity and Immodesty of Time: Death as Future and Eros as Feminine in Levinas," in *Writing the Future*, ed. David Wood (New York: Routledge, 1990).

While Chanter, despite reservations, tends to see Levinas as a theoretical resource for feminist theory, Stella Sandford takes a more negative view. She writes that those who do make use of Levinas "do not . . . succeed in explaining, beyond the mere coincidence of words (which is not even a coincidence of terminology), (1) how Levinas's invocation of the feminine is not irremediably compromised by the details of its conventionally patriarchal characterization, its identification with sexual difference as secondary to the human, and its exclusion from the ethical; and (2) how any thinking of the feminine which excludes all of the above is in any sense Levinasian or otherwise indebted to Levinas . . . If, therefore, one were to ask whether the thinking of the feminine in Levinas's philosophy could provide resources for feminism, I think the answer would have to be 'no'" (Stella Sandford, "Levinas, Feminism and the Feminine," in *Cambridge Companion to Levinas*, ed. Simon Critchley and Robert Bernasconi [New York: Cambridge University Press, 2002], 156–57). A much more positive view of Levinas is provided by Claire Katz in her book *Levinas, Judaism, and the Feminine: The Silent Footsteps of Rebecca* (Bloomington: Indiana University Press, 2003). While acknowledging Irigaray's critique of Levinas, she brings fresh insight into the question by focusing on the connection between Levinas's characterization of women and the women of the Hebrew Bible. For Bettina Bergo's position, see the first endnote for chapter 11 as well as the following endnote.

11. There is also the further objection, which Bettina Bergo raises, namely, that the face per se has an ethical import. In her words, "Already the gaze of the other signifies as pure exteriority. The self-presentation of the face halts the 'I' in its tracks. It short-circuits the I's inclination to suppress alterity . . . Here the distinction fades between the face of the other and the feminine face" (*Levinas between Ethics & Politics*, 119). Etienne Akamatsu and Alexander Schnell both attempt a kind of defense of Levinas by emphasizing the fact that, as a phenomenologist, Levinas proceeds from a male perspective, this being immediately (phenomenologically) available to him. For Schnell, there is the additional point that Levinas, in adopting the male perspective, is attempting to counter "the philosophy of the neuter." In Schnell's words, "Si l'on rencontre parfois, chez Levinas, des phrases qui peuvent paraître troublantes pour peu qu'on les isole de leur contexte, il faut bien voir que la position prise délibérément par Levinas vis-à-vis de la question du genre—savoir la décision de s'exprimer 'contre la philosophie du Neutre,' 'le seul genre que la logique formelle connaisse'— exige et implique—compte tenu du fait que, d'une part, il assume pleinement une philosophie de la subjectivité qui le lie à son propre genre, et que, d'autre part, la féminité se soustrait par essence à la généralité (propre au Même)—une forme d'écriture qui est forcément tributaire de sa propre constitution (masculine)" (Schnell, *Levinas et la question de la subjectivité*, 77–78). Akamatsu also points out that the adoption of a male perspective, which allows "the feminine to appear as a special difference among all the possible ones that constituted the sense of human relations," does not involve "any subordination of one [perspec-

tive] to the other" (Akamatsu, *Comprendre Levinas* [Paris: Armand Colin, 2011], 186). In defense of this, he quotes Levinas's Talmudic lectures: "'Qu'est-ce que l'humain? Le fait pour un être d'être deux tout en étant un,' ou encore 'le partage en féminin et masculin—la dichotomie—à partir de l'humain' (Levinas, *De sacré au saint: Cinqu nouvelles telmudiques* [Paris: Minuit, 1997], 128 et 132)" (ibid.). In our view, these defenses of Levinas's position still do not explain the value-laden description of the feminine.

12. As Husserl observes, no other sense can substitute for touch in establishing the identity of our embodied consciousness. While I can feel myself being touched, I cannot see myself being seen, hear myself being overheard, smell myself being smelt, and so on. What about the case of looking at myself in the mirror? Don't I then see myself seeing and, hence, see myself being seen? Husserl objects, "I do not see the seeing eye as seeing. The eye I regard is like the eye of another. I have to employ empathy to indirectly judge that it is identical with my eye" (Husserl, *Ideen zu einer reinen Phänomenologie und phänomenologischen Philosophie, Zweites Buch*, ed. W. Biemel [The Hague: Martinus Nijhoff, 1952], 155, n. 1). The eye that regards me from the mirror is, in other words, experienced as an object. My seeing it does not give me a first-person experience of *its* seeing. To have this I would have to *directly* experience its seeing as my seeing. Touch does this since the hand that is touched also feels. By contrast, the eye that I regard in the mirror is like the inanimate objects that I touch. I feel their properties, but I do not feel them feeling me. They do not return my awareness to me.

13. As Bernasconi remarks, Levinas's references to Parmenides are meant to refer to Heidegger and Husserl as well: "In this context, Parmenides represents for Levinas the philosophy of the unity of being that suppresses the beyond; both Husserl and Heidegger are to be counted among its representatives (Bernasconi, "Levinas and Derrida: The Question of the Closure of Metaphysics," 185).

14. Parmenides, "Proem," in *The Pre-Socratic Philosophers: A Critical History with a Selection of Texts* (Cambridge, Eng.: Cambridge University Press, 1966), 269–73. The translations are my own.

15. As Rudolf Bernet observes, "Levinas's new conception of the alterity of the future and of the past no longer owes anything to Husserl or to Heidegger, but is rather reminiscent of certain pages in Hannah Arendt" (Bernet, "Levinas's Critique of Husserl," 89). For Arendt, the genuinely new is made possible by natality. In her words: "It is in the nature of beginning that something new is started which cannot be expected from whatever may have happened before." This newness "is possible only because each man is unique so that with each birth something uniquely new comes into the world" (Arendt, *The Human Condition*, 177–78).

16. The distinction is equally striking with Husserl's account of temporalization, where retention, which preserves the self's past as *its* past, opens up its self-alterity (between its past and its present), even while giving it an extended unity over time. As Bernet notes, regarding "the Husserlian conception of temporality": "Its limits have to do essentially with the fact that it envisages temporal alterity within the framework of a phenomenology of consciousness. Though this consciousness is sensible and non-objectifying, originally divided and thus

separated from itself, it will always seek to re-unite with itself in order to preserve its identity" ("Levinas's Critique of Husserl," 93).

17. See the section "Lordship and Bondage" in Hegel's *Phenomenology of Spirit*, in particular, para. 186.

18. Teste thus denies all impersonal forces controlling the "I." He asserts: "Je sens infiniment le pouvoir, le vouloir, parce que je sens infiniment l'informe et le hasard qui les baigne, les tolère, et tend à reprendre sa fatale liberté, sa figure indifférente, son niveau d'égale chance" (Paul Valéry, "Monsieur Teste," *Oeuvres* II [Paris: Éditions Gallimard, 1960], 41). This chance and indifference liberates the "I" to be a first principle. As Teste advises himself in a poem written in the "language of Self": "Tu te fais souvenir non d'autres, mais de toi, Et tu deviens toujours plus semblable à nul autre. Plus autrement le même, et plus même que moi. O Mien—mais qui n'es pas encore tout à fait Moi!" (43).

19. *The Babylonian Talmud*, Sedar Nezikin, 233.

20. Ibid.

21. See Martin Heidegger, "Vom Wesen der Wahrheit" in *Wegmarken*, 91–94.

22. Bettina Bergo sees such equality as an idealization. In her words, "The relation of elected brothers, as a paradigm for the same-other relation, excludes anything like a paradigm of the enemy brothers. Here the fraternal relation is idealized into a 'we,' in which the 'I' serves the others. Why should one who is unique and equal to the others suddenly be said to serve them?" (128). This leads her to the question, "Is there not, contemporaneous with the 'we' of fraternity, a certain refusal of the brother? What, after all, is the meaning of Cain' s response to God, 'Am I my brother' s keeper?'" (Bergo, *Levinas between Ethics & Politics*, 129). Such questions point to the flaw of attempting to base the social on the biological. As she puts this: "The biological and meta-biological relation of fraternity makes sociality possible by placing the 'I' in an environment composed of elected third parties and elected others. The 'I' serves all of them. But together with them the 'I' becomes a 'We.' The ethical structure thus encompasses the biological structure which gave it its origin. If this were not so, then what good is the extensive thought devoted to the meaning, or the *meta-meaning*, of the biological? Could not Levinas have stopped his analyses with the face-to-face relationship? His expositions of paternity and fraternity have provided us insight into the chiasmus of individual responsibility and social existence. However, the illustration is drawn at a great cost to his logic" (129–30). This, given Levinas's project of providing an analytic of embodied Dasein, seems an excessively harsh judgment. Levinas would probably respond by saying that the demands of the face-to-face do not eliminate the possibility of the refusal of such demands— even in the case of siblings. As for Levinas stopping with the face-to-face relationship, this would be, in his eyes, to ignore the fact that this is an embodied relation with all this entails with regard to sexuality, human generation, and the family.

23. Arendt, *The Human Condition*, 237.

24. Ibid., 246.

25. Ibid., 8.

26. Ibid., 247.

Chapter 12

1. This letter appears in the textual critical notes to Husserl's *Phänomenologische Psychologie*, 600–602. The passage quoted is on p. 601.

2. Husserl, *Logische Untersuchungen*, 4:762.

3. G. W. F. Hegel, *Phänomenologie des Geistes* (Hamburg: Felix Meiner Verlag, 2006), 71.

4. *Man Facing Southeast*, director, Eliseo Subielo, 1986.

5. In German: "Wahrsein (Wahrheit) besagt entdeckend-sein."

6. *A Latin Dictionary*, ed. Lewis and Short (London: Oxford University Press, 1966), 1610.

7. Sophocles, *Oedipus at Colonus*, in *Sophocles I*, trans. Robert Fitzgerald (Chicago: University of Chicago Press, 1954), lines 36ff, p. 81.

8. As the Bible relates their initial encounter, "God called to him out of the [burning] bush: 'Moses! Moses!' He answered, 'Here I am.' And He said, 'Do not come closer. Remove your sandals from your feet, for the place on which you stand is holy ground'. . . . And Moses hid his face, for he was afraid to look at God" (Exod. 3:4–6, in *The Torah: The Five Books of Moses*, 2nd ed. [Philadelphia: Jewish Publication Society of America, 1962], 102).

9. Thus, when God appears to Job, he says: "It is my turn to ask questions and yours to inform me" (Job, 38:3, in *Jerusalem Bible* (Garden City: Doubleday, 1966), 772.

10. Augustine, *City of God*, bk. 14, §28 presents a variant of this.

11. Martin Heidegger, *History of the Concept of Time*, trans. Theodore Kisiel (Bloomington: Indiana University Press, 1985), 261.

12. Husserl, *Logische Untersuchungen*, 4:730.

13. Ibid., 4:717.

14. For an extended description of Husserl's conception of language, see James Mensch, *Postfoundational Phenomenology: Husserlian Reflections on Presence and Embodiment* (University Park: Pennsylvania State University Press, 2001), 119–84.

15. As Sebbah notes, the golden rule of phenomenology is the correlation of being with appearing: "la règle d'or de la phénoménologie est 'autant d'apparaître, autant d'être'" (Sebbah, *Lévenas: Ambiguïtés de l'altérité*, 107). This implies that the Other, who does not appear, is otherwise or outside of being (108). The reverse implication also holds given that intentionality is "a pure movement of the de-substantialization" of the conscious subject (see note 17, chap. 7). Not being a substance (or a being), the subject, according to the golden rule, cannot appear. The upshot is that Levinas can claim to be faithful to phenomenology since he assumes its basic premise with regard to the correlation of being and appearing (99–100).

16. Hegel, *Phänomenologie des Geistes*, §177, p. 127.

17. This is the assertion of Hegel's *Philosophy of History*, trans. J. Sibree (New York: Dover, 1956), 38–39.

18. This is the point of Kant's famous Copernican turn. As Kant writes in the "Preface to the Second Edition" of his *Critique of Pure Reason*, "Hitherto it has

been assumed that all our knowledge must conform to objects. But all attempts to extend our knowledge of objects by establishing something in regard to them a priori, by means of concepts, have, on this assumption, ended in failure. We must therefore make trial whether we may not have more success in the tasks of metaphysics, if we suppose that objects must conform to our knowledge" (*Kritik der reinen Vernunft*, B xvi, p. 21).

19. Heidegger, "Vom Wesendes Grundes" in *Wegmarken*, 69.

20. "Als dieser Grund aber ist die Freiheit der Ab-grund des Daseins" (ibid.).

21. Descartes, *Meditations on First Philosophy*, IV, 59.

22. Such a view, Levinas remarks, is very different from Sartre's. He writes: "The encounter with the Other in Sartre threatens my freedom, and is equivalent to the fall of my freedom under the gaze of another freedom" (*TI*, 303). Levinas is referring to Sartre's claim that when I am seen by the Other, "I am conscious of myself as escaping myself" (*Being and Nothingness*, 349). No longer am I the center of the universe. Under the gaze of the Other, "there is a regrouping of all the objects which people my universe" (343). They have an alternate center, that provided by the gaze of the Other. The same holds for myself. Under his gaze, I become an object for the Other. As such, "I have my foundation outside myself. I am for myself only as I am a pure reference to the Other" (349). This experience, according to Sartre, is fundamental to my grasp of the Other as other. It is not just that "my fundamental connection with the Other-as-subject must be able to be referred back to my permanent possibility of *being seen* by the Other" (344); the point is that "'being seen by the Other' is the *truth* of 'seeing the Other'" (345). "Truth" here is taken in Heidegger's sense of unhiddenness or disclosure. For Sartre, the decentering of my experience and my accompanying objectification *reveal* the Other as other. In Sartre's words, "He is the subject who is revealed to me in that flight of myself toward objectification" (ibid.). Such a flight, for Sartre, is a loss of my freedom. For Levinas, on the contrary, the decentering of myself occasioned by the Other is what makes my freedom non-arbitrary. In forcing me to look at the world from another perspective, it opens up the possibility of an objective, non-relative knowledge.

Bibliography

Akamatsu, Etienne. (2011). *Comprendre Levinas*. Paris: Armand Colin.

Anselm. (1965). *St. Anselm's Proslogion*, trans. M. J. Charlesworth. Oxford: Clarendon.

Arendt, Hannah. (1958). *The Human Condition*. Chicago: University of Chicago Press.

Aristotle. (1962). *Nichomachean Ethics*, trans. Martin Ostwald. New York: Macmillan.

———. (1996). *The Physics, Books I–IV*, trans. Philip Wicksteed and Francis Cornford. Cambridge, Mass.: Harvard University Press.

Beauvoir, Simone de. (1956). *The Second Sex*, trans. and ed. H. M. Parshley. London: Jonathan Cape.

Benso, Silvia. (2007). "Gestures of Work: Levinas and Hegel." *Continental Philosophy Review* 40: 307–40.

Bensussan, Gérard. (2011)."Fécondité d'Eros, Équivoque et dualité." In *Lire Totalité et Infini d'Emmanuel Levinas: Études et interprétations*, ed. Danielle Cohen-Levinas, 91–106. Paris: Hermann.

Bergo, Bettina. (2003). *Levinas between Ethics & Politics: For the Beauty That Adorns the Earth*. Duquesne: Duquesne University Press.

Berkeley, George. (1963). *A Treatise concerning the Principles of Human Knowledge*. La Salle, Ill.: Open Court.

Bernasconi, Robert. (1986). "Levinas and Derrida: The Question of the Closure of Metaphysics." In *Face to Face with Levinas*, ed. Richard Cohen. Albany: State University of New York Press.

Bernet, Rudolf. (2003). "Levinas's Critique of Husserl." In *The Cambrdge Companion to Levinas*, ed. Simon Critchley and Robert Bernasconi. New York: Cambridge University Press.

Bloechl, Jeffrey. (1996). "How Best to Keep a Secret? On Love and Respect in Levinas's 'Phenomenology or Eros.'" *Man and World: An International Philosophical Review* 29, no. 1 (January): 1–17.

Buber, Martin. (1996). *I and Thou*, trans. W. Kaufmann. New York: Simon and Schuster.

Chanter, Tina. (1988). "Feminism and the Other." In *The Provocation of Levinas: Rethinking the Other*, ed. Robert Bernasconi and David Wood. New York: Routledge.

———. (1990). "The Alterity and Immodesty of Time: Death as Future and Eros as Feminine in Levinas." In *Writing the Future*, ed. David Wood. New York: Routledge.

————, ed. (2001). *Feminist Interpretations of Emmanuel Levinas.* University Park: Pennsylvania State University Press, 2001.

Cohen, Joseph. (2009). *Alternances de la métaphysique: Essais sur Emmanuel Levinas.* Paris: Éditions Galilée.

Courtine, Jean François. (2007). "L'ontologie fondamentale d'Emmanuel Levinas." In *Emmanuel Levinas et les territoires de la pensée,* ed. Danielle Cohen-Levinas and Bruno Clément. Paris: Presses Universitaires de France.

Dawson, Christopher. (1960). *Understanding Europe.* New York: Doubleday.

Derrida, Jacques. (1973). "Differance." In *Speech and Phenomena and Other Essays,* trans. David Allison. Evanston, Ill.: Northwestern University Press.

————. (1978). "Violence and Metaphysics." In *Writing and Difference,* trans. Alan Bass. Chicago: University of Chicago Press.

————. (1993a). "Circumfession: Fifty-Nine Periods and Periphrases." In *Geoffrey Bennington and Jacques Derrida,* trans. Geoffrey Bennington. Chicago: University of Chicago Press.

————. (1993b). *Aporias,* trans. Thomas Dutroit. Stanford, Calif.: Stanford University Press.

————. (1995). *The Gift of Death,* trans. David Wills. Chicago: University of Chicago Press.

Descartes, Rene. (1990). *Meditations on First Philosophy,* VI, trans. L. LaFleur. New York: Macmillan.

Edie, James. (1992). "The Question of the Transcendental Ego: Sartre's Critique of Husserl." In *Husserl in His Contemporary Radiance: Proceedings of the 24th Annual Meeting of the Husserl Circle,* Waterloo.

Franck, Didier. (2008). *L'un-pour-l'autre: Levinas et la signification.* Paris: Presses Universitaires de France.

Habib, Stéphane. (1988). *La responsabilité chez Sartre et Levinas.* Paris: L'Harmattan.

Hegel, G. W. F. (1956). *Philosophy of History,* trans. J. Sibree. New York: Dover.

————. (2006). *Phänomenologie des Geistes.* Hamburg: Felix Meiner Verlag.

Heidegger, Martin. (1962). Letter to Husserl, in *Phänomenologische Psychologie,* ed. W. Biemel, 600–602. The Hague: Martinus Nijhoff.

————. (1967). "Von Wesen der Wahrheit." In *Wegmarken.* Frankfurt am Main: Vittorio Klostermann.

————. (1968). *Sein und Zeit.* Tübingen: Max Niemeyer.

————. (1969). "The Onto-theo-logical Constitution of Metaphysics." In *Identity and Difference,* trans. Joan Stambaugh. New York: Harper and Row.

————. (1985). *History of the Concept of Time,* trans. Theodore Kisiel. Bloomington: Indiana University Press.

————. (1987). "Who Is Nietzsche's Zarathustra?" In *Nietzsche,* 4 vols., trans. D. F. Krell. San Francisco: Harper Collins.

————. (1988). *The Basic Problems of Phenomenology,* trans. Albert Hofstadter. Bloomington: Indiana University Press.

Heraclites. (2000). Fr. 22 in *The First Philosophers: The Presocratics and the Sophists,* trans. Robin Waterfield. Oxford: Oxford University Press.

Howells, Christina. (1988). "Sartre and Levinas." In *The Provocation of Levinas: Rethinking the Other*, ed. Robert Bernasconi and David Wood, 91–99. New York: Routledge.

Husserl, Edmund. (1952). *Ideen zu einer reinen Phänomenologie und phänomenologischen Philosophie, Zweites Buch*, ed. W. Biemel. The Hague: Martinus Nijhoff.

———. (1962). *Phänomenologische Psychologie*, ed. W. Biemel. The Hague: Martinus Nijhoff.

———. (1963). *Cartesianische Meditationen*, ed. S. Strasser. The Hague: Martinus Nijhoff.

———. (1966a). *Zur Phänomenologie des inneren Zeitbewusstseins*. The Hague: Martinus Nijhoff.

———. (1966b). *Analysen zur passiven Synthesis*, ed. M. Fleischer. The Hague: Martinus Nijhoff.

———. (1971). "Nachwort." In *Ideen zu einer reinen Phänomenologie und phänomenologischen Philosophie, Drittes Buch*, ed. M. Biemel. The Hague: Martinus Nijhoff.

———. (1976). *Ideen zu einer reinen Phänomenologie und phänomenologischen Philosophie, Erstes Buch*, ed. R. Schuhmann. The Hague: Martinus Nijhoff.

———. (1992). *Logische Untersuchungen*, ed. Ursula Panzer. In *Edmund Husserl, Gesammelte Schriften*. Hamburg: Felix Meiner Verlag.

———. (2001). *Die Bernauer Manuskripte über das Zeitbewusstsein, 1917/18*, ed. R. Bernet and D. Lohmar. Dordrecht: Kluwer Academic.

———. (2006). *Späte Texte Über Zeitkonstitution: 1929–1934 Die C-Manuscripte*, ed. Dieter Lohmar. Dordrecht: Springer Verlag.

Ince, Kate. (1996). "Questions to Luce Irgaray." *Hypatia* 11, no. 2 (Spring): 122–40.

Irigaray, Luce. (1991). "Questions to Emmanuel Levinas," trans. Margaret Whitford. In *The Irigaray Reader*, ed. Margaret Whitford. Oxford: Blackwell.

———. (1993). "The Fecundity of the Caress: A Reading of Levinas, *Totality and Infinity*, 'Phenomenology of Eros.'" In *An Ethics of Sexual Difference*. Ithaca, N.Y.: Cornell University Press.

James, William. (1948). *Psychology, Briefer Course*. New York: World.

Jerusalem Bible. (1966). Garden City, N.Y.: Doubleday.

Jonas, Hans. (1996). *Mortality and Morality: A Search for the Good after Auschwitz*, ed. Lawrence Vogel. Evanston, Ill.: Northwestern University Press.

Jopling, David. (1993). "Levinas, Sartre and Understanding the Other." *Journal of the British Society for Phenomenology* 24, no. 3 (October): 214–31.

Kant, Immanuel. (1955). "Grundlegung zur Metaphysik der Sitten." In *Kants gesammelte Schriften*, ed. Königlich Preussische Akademie der Wissenschaften. Berlin: Georg Reiner.

———. (1964). *Groundwork of the Metaphysics of Morals*, trans. H. J. Paton. New York: Harper and Row.

———. (1998). *Kritik der reinen Vernunft*. Hamburg: Felix Meiner Verlag.

Katz, Claire. (2003). *Levinas, Judaism, and the Feminine: The Silent Footsteps of Rebecca*. Bloomington: Indiana University Press.

Levinas, Emmanuel. (1969). *Totality and Infinity: An Essay on Exteriority*, trans. Alphonso Lingis. Pittsburgh: Duquesne University Press.

———. (1985). *Ethics and Infinity*, trans. Richard Cohen. Pittsburgh: Duquesne University Press.

———. (1989). "Ethics as First Philosophy." In *The Levinas Reader*, ed. Seán Hand. Oxford: Blackwell.

———. (1993). *Dieu: La mort et le temps*, ed. Jacques Rolland. Paris: Bernard Grasset.

———. (1994a). "Time and the Other." In *Time and the Other, and Additional Essays*, trans. Richard Cohen. Pittsburgh: Duquesne University Press.

———. (1994b). "Diachrony and Representation." In *Time and the Other, and Additional Essays*, trans. Richard Cohen. Pittsburgh: Duquesne University Press.

———. (1994c). *Nine Talmudic Readings*, trans. Annette Aronowicz. Bloomington: Indiana University Press.

———. (1995). *Existence and Existents*, trans. Alphonso Linguis. Dordrecht: Kluwer Academic.

———. (1997). *De sacré au saint: Cinqu nouvelles telmudiques*. Paris: Minuit.

———. (1998a). *Entre Nous: Thinking of the Other*, trans. Michael Smith and Barbara Harshaw. New York: Columbia University Press.

———. (1998b). "God and Philosophy." In *Of God Who Comes to Mind*, trans. Bettina Bergo. Stanford, Calif.: Stanford University Press.

Lewis and Short, eds. (1966). *A Latin Dictionary*. London: Oxford University Press.

Liddell and Scott, eds. (1961). *An Intermediate Greek-English Lexicon*. London: Oxford University Press.

Locke, John. (2003). "Second Treatise on Government." In *John Locke, Political Writings*. Indianapolis, Ind.: Hackett.

May, Todd. (1997). *Reconsidering Difference*. University Park: Pennsylvania State University Press.

Mensch, James. (1999). "Husserl's Concept of the Future." *Husserl Studies* 16, no. 1: 41–64.

———. (2001). *Postfoundational Phenomenology: Husserlian Reflections on Presence and Embodiment*. University Park: Pennsylvania State University Press.

———. (2007). "Public Space." *Continental Philosophy Review* 40, no. 1: 31–47.

———. (2013). "The Temporality of Merleau-Ponty's 'Intertwining.'" *Continental Philosophy Review* 42, no. 14: 449–63.

Mirgeler, Albert. (1964). *Mutations of Western Christianity*, trans. Edward Quinn. Montreal: Palm.

Merleau-Ponty, Maurice. (1968). *The Visible and the Invisible*, trans. A. Lingis. Evanston, Ill.: Northwestern University Press.

Mill, John Stuart. (1979). *Utilitarianism*. Indianapolis, Ind.: Hackett.

Moliere. (1962). *Le médecin malgré lui*. In *Molière oeuvres complètes*. Paris: George Lang.

Nietzsche, Friedrich. (1964). *Twilight of the Idols*, trans. Anthony Ludovic. New York: Russell and Russell.

Parmenides. (1966). "Proem." In *The Pre-Socratic Philosophers: A Critical History with a Selection of Texts*. Cambridge, Eng.: Cambridge University Press.

BIBLIOGRAPHY

Peperzak, Adriaan. (1986). "Some Remarks on Hegel, Kant and Levinas." In *Face to Face with Levinas*, ed. Richard Cohen. Albany: State University of New York Press.

———. (1993). *To the Other: An Introduction to the Philosophy of Emmanuel Levinas*. West Lafayette, Ind.: Purdue University Press.

Pier, Joanne. (1989). "Sartre/Levinas: An Is/Ought Gap of Ethics?" *Dialogue* 31: 52–57.

Plato. (1961). "Republic," trans. Paul Shorey. In *The Collected Dialogues of Plato including the Letters*, ed. Edith Hamilton and Huntington Cairns. Princeton, N.J.: Princeton University Press.

———. (1977). "Phaedo." In *Plato I: Euthryphro, Apology, Crito, Phaedo, Phaedrus*, trans. Harold Fowler. Cambridge, Mass.: Harvard University Press.

Rey, Jean-François. (2001). *La mesure de l'homme: L'idée d'humanité dans la philosophie d'Emmanuel Levinas*. Paris: Editions Michalon.

Ricoeur, Paul. (1992). *Oneself as Another*, trans. Kathleen Blamey. Chicago: University of Chicago Press.

Sandford, Stella. (2002). "Levinas, Feminism and the Feminine." In *Cambridge Companion to Levinas*, ed. Simon Critchley and Robert Bernasconi. New York: Cambridge University Press.

Sartre, Jean-Paul. (1966). *Being and Nothingness*, trans. Hazel Barnes. New York: Washington Square.

Schafstedde, Maria. (1998). "Begegnung statt Konstitution: Zur Frage nach dem Anderen bei Jean-Paul Sartre und Emmanuel Levinas." In *Kritik und Praxis*, 450–57. Luneburg: zu Klampen.

Schnell, Alexander. (2010). *Levinas et la question de la subjectivité*. Paris: Vrin.

Sebbah, François-David. (2003). *Lévinas: Ambiguïtés de l'altérité*. Paris: Les Belles Lettres.

Sophocles. (1954). *Oedipus at Colonus*. In *Sophocles I*, trans. Robert Fitzgerald. Chicago: University of Chicago Press.

Subielo, Eliseo. (1986). Director, *Man Facing Southeast*.

Taminiaux, Jacques. (1991). "La première réplique à l'ontologie fondamentale." In *Emmanuel Lévinas*, ed. Chalier and M. Abensour. Cahiers de l'herne: Paris, 275–84.

The Babylonian Talmud. (1935). Ed. I. Epstein. London: Soncino.

The Torah: The Five Books of Moses. (1962). 2nd ed. Philadelphia: Jewish Publication Society of America.

Valéry, Paul. (1960). "Monsieur Teste." In *Oeuvres II*. Paris: Éditions Gallimard.

Vetlesen, Arne. (1995). "Relations with Others in Sartre and Levinas: Assessing Some Implications for an Ethics of Proximity." *Constellations: An International Journal of Critical and Democratic Theory* 1, no. 3 (January): 358–82.

Waldenfels, Bernhard. (2003). "Levinas and the Face of the Other." In *The Cambridge Companion to Levinas*, ed. Simon Critchley and Robert Bernasconi. New York: Cambridge University Press.

Weil, Simone. (1965). *Waiting on God*, trans. Emma Craufurd. London: Fontana Books.

BIBLIOGRAPHY

Westphal, Merold. (1993). "Levinas and the Immediacy of the Face." *Faith and Philosophy* 10, no. 4 (October).
Wyschogrod, Edith. (2000). *Emmanuel Levinas: The Problem of an Ethical Metaphysics.* New York: Fordham University Press.
Zaborowski, Holger. (2000). "On Freedom and Responsibility: Remarks on Sartre, Levinas, and Derrida." *Heythrop Journal* 41, no. 1: 47–65.

Index

Akamatsu, Etienne, 215n11
alterity, 28–29; of the child, 158, 166–67; of death, 16, 138; of the desired, 28; and embodiment, 8–9; of the face, 134; feminine, 96, 152–56; of God, 58, 145; and language, 122–26; of the mother, 93; and newness, 55, 212n9, 216n15; of the Other, 27, 30–31, 67, 136, 198n13, 204n4, 210n29; presupposed by society, 181; prior to identity, 148–49; self, 16–17, 198n8, 203n9, 216n16; and sexuality, 165
Anselm, 199n19
Arendt, Hannah, 91, 158, 168–170, 216n15
Aristotle, 9, 24, 47, 52–53, 75–76, 86, 98, 116, 117, 191, 206n21, 209n10

being, 6, 10–12, 41–42, 69–70, 128, 157–58, 169, 178; human, 5–9 (*see also* Dasein); in-the-world, 12–14, 18, 44, 46, 74, 83, 94, 115, 137, 171, 183
Benso, Silvia, 208n16
Bergo, Bettina, 212n1, 215n11, 217n22
Berkeley, George, 209n16
Bernasconi, Robert, 200n25, 204n4, 216n13
Bernet, Rudolf, 198n8, 216nn15–16
Bloechl, Jeffrey, 213n8
Buber, Martin, 96, 207n1

care (*Sorge*), 11–16, 66, 75–76, 83–84, 86, 103–7, 189, 208n7
caress, 153–54, 160
Chanter, Tina, 214n10
child, 93–94, 96–97, 156–63, 165–73
Cohen, Joseph, 199nn15–16, 200n24
conscience, call of, 15–18, 103

consciousness, 30, 66–67, 79–83, 95, 100–102, 107, 123–25, 139–42, 176, 184; self-, 110–11, 121, 205n17, 208n22, 216n16
constitution, 79–83, 161, 175, 194
corporeity, 122, 133–34
Courtine, Jean François, 194nn12–13, 204n3
creation, 45, 57–58, 70–72, 78, 96, 128, 166–68, 181–83

Dasein, 7–9, 11, 29, 42–46, 74–75, 92–94, 100–101, 103–4, 112, 114–15, 126, 132, 137, 139, 148, 159, 161, 163–64, 172–73, 175–80, 183–84, 188–90, 194nn13–14, 194n1 (ch. 1), 195n4, 196nn10–11, 201n2, 201n10, 208n21
Dawson, Christopher, 5
de Beauvoir, Simone, 214n10
death, 7, 16–18, 78, 103, 133–34, 137–39, 145, 166, 171–74, 201n1, 212n6
Derrida, Jacques, 21, 139, 149, 200n25, 212n6, 214n10
Descartes, Rene, 3, 28–29, 37, 46, 60, 64, 104–5, 117, 120, 158, 190, 197n4
desire, 75, 86, 104, 129, 151–52; erotic, 152–56, 159, 161, 213n8; Hegelian, 110–11, 160; metaphysical, 27–29, 32, 38, 47–48, 71–72, 74, 93, 159, 182, 187
discourse, 9, 50–55, 65–68, 73, 113, 118–19, 122, 124, 127, 135, 151, 180, 185–87

economy, 58–59, 72, 98–99, 109–13
Edie, James, 87–88
ego, 28–29, 34, 87–88, 94–95, 197n3
egotism, 29, 32, 34, 45, 74, 77, 85–86, 143, 145, 181